DEAR BLACKSMITH

Beverley Ward lives in Sheffield with her two children. She has been writing for over twenty years and has spent most of her career supporting other writers through facilitating writing workshops and literature projects.

She regularly writes about grief for *The Huffington Post* and has been present at policy-making discussions at the House of Commons as a thought leader in the world of bereavement. Find her on Twitter @BeverleyWard.

Dear Blacksmith

BEVERLEY WARD

Valley Press

First published in 2020 by Valley Press
Woodend, The Crescent, Scarborough, YO11 2PW
www.valleypressuk.com

First edition, first printing (January 2020)

ISBN 978-1-912436-37-8
Cat. no. VP0157

A CIP record for this book is available from the British Library.

Cover photograph by Paul Harding.
Cover and text design by Jamie McGarry.

Printed and bound in Great Britain by
TJ International Ltd, Padstow, Cornwall.

Contents

SUMMER

AUTUMN

SPRING

for Paul

Dear Blacksmith Paul,

If you look at the photos, you might wonder why they seem dark and smudged, even though it's spring. It's a new kind of filter on the lens. Called grief. It's a bit like looking through the rain all the time, or maybe that's the tears. Hard to tell sometimes.

You'll notice though the buds on the trees. It's April now and the magnolia tree outside my window is flowering. I don't think you ever saw it flower. My daughter doesn't want to leave the magnolia tree and move house but I can't live here anymore. Too many things have happened here. I need a fresh start.

Don't worry, I will take you with me. I'm collecting things slowly that remind me of you, to incorporate into this new life that I have been catapulted into. The one where all our hopes and dreams have been silenced and I am left with fragments of memories. I will find a space where I can put the half-finished lamp that you were making. Someone will know how to wire it, I'm sure. The new place will have a log-burning stove – your family said maybe I can have yours. I know, you told me about the regulations, I'll work it out, make sure it's safe. I will prod the embers at night with the poker we made and look at the book of photos and words that I will make just like we planned.

I'll find someone else to take down your beautiful hooks and find a new wall to fix them onto. I'll bring some things from my mother's house too, find a way to make them scenery to some kind of new life that I can't envisage. Her house is on the market now, you know. I would take you there one more time and show you around properly. You could help me pack things away. You would like to see the family albums. I've seen yours now; your mum and I sit and look at them. You were cute. But I'm not surprised.

I'll bring the clock too. The one my father gave me. You took the mechanism to fix so it has no hands at the moment but that suits me fine. There is no time anymore, or too much time.

I would take you to the park but I see you there anyway. And I would take you back to the house at Redmires where we first walked. But maybe it won't be the same without the heather. I know it won't be the same without you.

I miss you and love you,
Beverley Writer

Introduction

I T I S T W O years, eight months and four days since my love, Blacksmith Paul, died. A strange day to note you may think, but it has been logged on my calendar for two years, four months and eight days. On that day I was sitting sobbing again in the pale blue room of the hospice, the one just down the corridor from where my mother had also recently died, the one marked 'Counselling, Do not Disturb'. I was asking when it would end, when I could hope to feel some semblance of normality return. My bereavement counsellor paused, recognising perhaps that I might not like her answer and told me that, statistically-speaking, two years, eight months and four days is the average time it takes to recover from a major bereavement. I broke off from crying to snort with laughter. It was clearly ridiculous. The date seemed to be impossibly far away. It seemed impossible that I could survive for that long. It was also impossible to think that it could ever be over. I put it in my phone, maybe as a date to work towards, maybe as a black joke or ironic statement. 13th November 2018: Grief Ends.

As a writer, I am fascinated by endings and beginnings, by story and narrative. When Paul died just eight months into a beautiful love affair, I couldn't make sense of it at all. 'The end just happened in the middle,' I wrote. It was how I felt. Unexpectedly and completely without warning, his story was over and the story I had been writing in my head (you know the one: unconventional hero rescues unlikely heroine, happy ever after ensues) was over too. The narrative was fractured and the writer (me) was broken. It wasn't the story I wanted to live. It wasn't a story I wanted to write. But it was the life I was left with and somehow, it seemed that writing was the only thing I still wanted to do. I didn't set out to write a memoir. I didn't even set out to write a blog. I just put words on the page, one after the other, the way other people put one foot in front of the other and I wrote. I wrote to capture my memories and I wrote as a student of my own grief. Mostly, I wrote in order to survive.

It is hard when constructing a memoir to know where to begin and where to stop. I search for a place to start and think of Paul. If this is Paul's story then it begins back in 1963 with a baby at a mother's breast. It begins at Hunters Bar, Sheffield, in the rented terraced house on Penrhyn Road, the one over the hedge from my old back garden, the one we could see from my bedroom window as we lay in each other's arms years later. It begins even earlier than that, with an antique-dealing father and the mother who hoarded treasures like she already knew love would be scarce. It begins with a youthful romance that gave birth to a baby boy. But I am not qualified to write that narrative without Paul here to guide me, not when the mother who nurtured him followed him swiftly out of reach. No, this cannot be Paul's story.

So perhaps this is *our* story, his and mine, the story of our love. But when does that story begin? Does it begin back in 1992 when he slept and worked in the blacksmith's forge on Garden Street, across the yard from the office of Swamp Circus where my I served an apprenticeship in the arts? Does it begin as the sound of hammer on iron rings out across the cobbled yard to the unheated garret where I shiver, attempting to make peace with the taste of soy milk in tea? Or does it start circa 1997 when, as a young divorcee, I was introduced to Paul in The Lescar by our mutual friend, Ed? Does it begin with his thwarted attempts to play Cupid? Or does it start almost twenty years later in 2014, when, at forty-five and fifty-three years of age, Ed reunited us again and we finally fell in love? Perhaps.

But, though this story is our love story, it is also the story of the year following Paul's death – and though Paul's presence echoes through those days like the ring of hammer on iron, for most of the story, he is absent. So what's left is my story, of love, loss and grief – and where does *that* begin? Does it begin with love or with loss, and how can I separate the two? In order for you to understand the precious love we shared, do I need to write about the other loves who came and went: the one who broke my heart six months before we met, the children's father who left the year before, my first true love whom I divorced at twenty-six? Do I need to write about the other losses too? The mother whose long dance with cancer ended twelve weeks before Paul's death, the son whose babyhood was lost to sickness and stress, his older sibling who died on the day of the twelve week scan? Does it go back to the father who died of brain tumours when I was thirty-one, to the inheritance I lost to his second wife? No, I cannot cover it all in one book. My story of love and loss is long.

Still, if I can't tell you when the story began, I can at least tell you when I began to write it. It was Easter 2015 and I was in the little tutor's bedroom at the Ty Newydd Writing Centre on the Llyn Peninsula in Wales. It is a place I go to every year, a place where I can be alone but among writers, a space in which I can focus on myself and on my craft. It was only a few weeks after Paul's mysterious death. The post-mortem took time, his body was still in the mortuary. But the retreat was already arranged, the children's father already booked to have them. It seemed as good a place to be as any.

That year, I didn't do much writing. I only wrote one poem. But I also wrote the eulogy for Paul's funeral and an email to a young widow who had only recently asked me for advice about publishing a book. I remembered that she'd found the act of writing helpful in her grief, and as she was the only person of my generation that I knew who had lost a partner, I reached out to her across the web. She suggested that I sign up to Megan Devine's Writing Your Grief programme. I needed no encouragement; I knew already that writing would be my handrail in the darkness and the only way I could survive.

I followed Megan's prompts for thirty days, often writing late at night in snatched moments when the children were asleep, onto a blog that I initially just called 'griefwriting'. I shared the results with other members of the online writing group and then, one day, I decided to share something with friends on Facebook. They wanted to hear more and so, gradually, I started sharing more of my writing and soon I was creating my own posts. As I watched the numbers of hits on my blog rising from tens, to hundreds and then to thousands, I realised that my writing was resonating far beyond my immediate circle and I changed its title to 'Swimming through Clouds'. The motif of clouds kept recurring and swimming was one of the activities that kept me sane. When I swim, the world and my cares recede – and when I swim outdoors, suspended between water and sky, I feel part of something bigger. My mind is as still as the water's surface and I feel at peace. Even in the early days of grief, when I was swimming, I could stop crying. When I was swimming I felt okay. 'Swimming through Clouds' seemed to capture something both literal and metaphorical about the way I journeyed through grief.

At first I wrote daily, then weekly, then monthly. Eventually the memories were all recorded (there were only eight months of them, after all) and I'd used up every metaphor for agony that I could think of. Slowly synapses began to reconnect and a new life started to emerge. When I returned to Ty Newydd a year later, it was with a potential new romance in mind. The year after that, my annual retreat signalled the end of that relationship. Having new love in my life had eased my loneliness but it hadn't been the saviour I might have expected after all. In fact, falling in love again had unleashed whole new layers of grief and tipped me into something close to a breakdown. If I spent the first year of grief wallowing in a pit of despair, I spent the second year grappling to climb out of it, trying to navigate my way in a new world with no faith in my map or my compass and no hope that some guardian angel was working for my greater good. In the second year I battled with anxiety, depression and what I eventually realised was post-traumatic stress. It was a very hard journey. It was hard to trust again. It was hard to love again. And it was very hard to lose love again. In fact, all of it was hard.

I said it was difficult to know where the story began, but it was even harder to know where to end it. As a writer it is always a challenge to know when something is finished. There are always sentences that can be rearranged, paragraphs that can be cut, loose ends that can be tied up or left hanging. There are a multitude of ways in which a story can be told. A writer can change the viewpoint, alter the tense, start at the end, flash back to the beginning. Words, sentences and paragraphs rearrange the meaning, the reader's experience dependent, to some extent, on the narrative that the author chooses to present. But this story is true and there is only so much I can do to it without losing its authenticity.

When I sat this April in my room at the centre by the sea thinking about how to construct my writing as memoir, I wondered at first whether I should begin the story from scratch and write a memoir with the benefit of hindsight. I could have chosen to write it from my vantage point two years on, looking down like a seagull on the turbulent waves of grief. But I chose not to. I chose not to because there is something visceral about the way I recorded my grief, moment by moment, and I didn't want to smooth over those edges or wash away the pain. Though I know it makes for difficult reading, I also know that it is in seeing their anguish reflected that the grieving can feel companioned. And it is in reading about my resurrection that the grieving can find hope. (Rest assured, reader, the resurrection did happen.) In fact, it is mainly because of that resurrection that I chose not to start the story again. Because this is fact and not fiction, my *life*, not just my story, and though the writer in me may, given time, be able to find a better way to write the narrative, the human in me cannot live with this material any longer. The human is tired of looking backwards and of picking over carcasses. The human's eyes are on fresh horizons.

So, where does the story end? Does a love story finish just because the hero dies? Or do the threads that bind two lives together continue beyond the grave, beyond the last page? Does grief really end two years, eight months and four days after a traumatic loss? Or does sadness echo through the days that follow, seeping like wet ink onto the blank pages of the future? Of course it does. In fact, though it gets easier to live with, grief shifts and changes like clouds in the sky and goes on, in some form, forever. This book focuses solely on the first year of loss because I want to keep the focus on my precious relationship with Paul and not because I want to give the illusion that grief is resolved after a year. Grief, like love, goes on for eternity. I realise now that I wouldn't have it any other way.

A day with Beverley Ward – Wednesday 26th August 2015 (from Paul's diary)

After a brief meeting with Ed and co, I met B after an interval of some years. The last time I met her was at a Free Radicals gig … small world! Anyway, we spoke, chatted, she offered to give me a lift to my house (we were in Baslow at the time). It was dark, she dropped me off. I said perhaps you would like to come and have a go at something. A date was arranged.

Fast forward, she arrives. I am strangely smitten with this intelligent, proudly beautiful woman who has undergone many emotional trials – bad husbands, poorly son, difficult father. We have a fun day. We make a poker. We talk a lot. We have much to say. She has brought some homemade flapjack – very healthy and delicious.

The day draws to an end but there is a brief moment, I think a possibility of something more. It passes. Nothing has happened.

Later we embrace. I am restrained in my hug. I am not fully open. She leaves.

Afterwards I ponder on the feelings I have and recall what was said, her behaviour and begin to analyse it all. Perhaps a mistake! My first thoughts are how I yearn for her completely, physically and emotionally but as my assessment of the situation becomes ever more forensic I realise she is out of my league and I am seized with a deadening emotion. I feel paralysed, weakened by the realisation IT CAN NEVER BE.

Next day is work. I am out of sorts. I realise I must turn the situation around and just think of it all as one lovely day with a lovely woman.

SPRING

(APRIL – MAY 2016)

if grief had a voice

I will write this story because it is all I can do.
If I were a painter I would splash my grief across the
pavement.
If I were a singer, I would sing my love into the
midnight sky.
But I am a writer. And so I write.

I will write because the focus on the words gives my
mind something to do,
save for digging around in dark tunnels where there
are no lights,
staring at clouds where there is no hint of silver.

I will write this story because I loved you and I want
the world to know
that, at the end of life, there was love,
that at the end of life, love is all there is.

I will write this story because I want it recorded for all
eternity
that once there was a man like you
and that he loved a woman like me
and that it was beautiful.

I will write this story because I want to preserve
every precious moment that we shared.

I will write this story because it is my story, and your
story and our story.
In this story we can stay together, which is how you
wanted it.
As a writer, I am all-powerful: your wish is my
command.

I will write this story because it is a good story and a
  sad story
and a big story and a true story.

And I am a writer and I know a story when I see one
even when it is handed to me in the most abominable
  way.

I will write this story so that people who didn't know
  you
can understand how special you were.
I will write this story so that people who *did* know you
might see a side of you that they missed.
I will write this story so that people might understand
why I am so very sad.
I will write this story so that people might know that
  sometimes,
sadness is what is. And that's okay.

At times I thought by writing this story I could make
  sense of these events.
But I am wrong. I am not all-powerful after all.
Sometimes there is no sense to be made of things
and searching for meaning is what drives us mad.

Sometimes I will write because, in the writing,
I can forget for a moment that this isn't a story.
That this was your life and my life.
That you are gone.
And that it ended, sometime in the first act.

But mostly I will write to remember.

Once upon a time the man I loved died

THEY SAY THAT a story should throw us into the centre of the action and start with a bang. And so I start with a body, the body of the man I loved – your dead body. Without that appalling scene, this story wouldn't exist. And so here I am, standing in my pyjamas and dressing gown on your doorstep, staring at the dead body on your bed. It might seem surprising to some that I can see your bed from the doorstep, but those people don't know yet that you are a surprising hero, a blacksmith who lives in a tiny shack in a field. Also a little odd that I am out here in my pyjamas with two male friends of yours whose acquaintance I have barely made. They've just bashed the door of this shack in with a fire extinguisher as if we are in some kind of crime drama and a voice is saying the words, 'there's Paul'.

Before they've had time to stop me, I am pushing past them into the darkness of the room where you sleep and there is a breath in time where I think you might actually be asleep now, in which I feel guilty for dragging your friends out here in the dark. But as soon as I am near enough to see your body properly, I know that you are dead. Either that or you have been abducted and someone has left another deformed body on your bed. Part of me wants to run to you and hold you but a larger part recoils in horror and I stay in the doorway, wanting to leave but unable to move. I stay just long enough to take a picture in my mind, a picture that I will never be able to erase.

Your head is black and purple in hue and swollen so that your features are distorted. You look like the elephant man, completely unrecognisable aside from your clothes, clothes from which you are bursting, your body inflated and leaking. Your hands are clenched, there is blood on the bed and the stench makes me want to retch. One thing I know for sure – this is a body but it is not you. You are gone.

Your friend calls an ambulance. Someone on the end of the line asks routine questions, trying to ascertain whether there is any hope of resuscitation. We all know there is not but they force him to touch your skin anyway and check for signs of life even though he is saying repeatedly, 'he is definitely dead.' And I just stand there listening to the word: dead. How can you be dead?

Afterwards, I stand on the veranda shaking until someone ushers me into a car where I sit, still shuddering, and stare into space. I don't know how long I am there. At some point I see blue flashing lights moving up the long drive to the shack where you live (where you are dead), and sometime after that a policeman slides into the driver's seat of the car and asks me questions that make me feel like a terrible girlfriend. You have been out of touch for three days and judging by the state you are in, you have been dead for all of them. I wonder with him how it can have taken me three days to raise the alarm. Was it just yesterday that I was out on a day trip with a friend? What was I thinking going out for the day when you were lying dead on your bed? If this is a crime drama then I assume that I am a suspect. So I try to justify myself, explaining that you don't always answer your phone, that we don't live together, that we don't see each other every day because of my children. I tell him that I have been sending messages and calling for days but that you haven't answered. I don't tell him that I worried that you might be about to dump me, but I tell him about the notes that I left last night on your door and your van. I tell him that the lights were on but that I couldn't get in. I don't tell him that I was frightened and crying, banging on your door and shouting your name, pleading with you to talk to me.

He asks me what your mum's name is and I feel even worse. I don't know. I can tell him roughly where she lives because you once drove me past her house but I haven't met your mum yet. We've only been seeing each other for eight months and we just haven't found the time. I can tell him the first name of your sister but that is all I know. I don't know where she lives. I could tell him so many things about you if he asked: your favourite songs, what kind of tree you would be if you were a tree, how you have changed my life, but I can't tell him anything that he wants to know.

The policeman takes my number and eventually says that I am free to go. I wait for your friends and find myself browsing Facebook as if it is just a normal night except for the fact that I am sitting in a stranger's car in my pyjamas at one in the morning having just seen your dead body. I see that a friend is up and I message her to tell her that you are dead. How can you be dead? She phones and I try to explain through my tears. She says that she will catch a train in the morning to be there.

Your friends drop me back at home and I stand in the kitchen wondering what to do now that you are dead. I go upstairs and climb into bed with my daughter because I need to be next to someone whose heart is beating. I hold her hand and lie awake for hours. I think about the last time that I saw her, standing at the top of the stairs as I told her that I needed to go out to look for a missing friend, that I was leaving her with a stranger, that I would be back soon. I am wondering how I will tell her in the morning that I found you but that you were dead. It is only three months since I told her that my mum, her Grandma, was dead. It is only a week since she met you for the first time and gave me her approval. It is too much.

I am thinking about the last time that I saw you with her, sending messages on paper lanterns to Hephaestus the blacksmith god and the last time that I saw you later that evening. How we hugged in the hall of my house as we always did. How I didn't know that it would be the last time. How I told you that I loved you. How you said you loved me too.

I am wondering how on earth I am going to get up and get the children to school. I am thinking about you and every snapshot of our beautiful time together, time that is now over, snapshots that I will record later. I am remembering our last messages to each other, the new poem that I'd sent you and your last words to me, carried like lanterns to my phone: *I love your poem, I love clouds and I love you.* I am thinking that I couldn't make this story up. I am wondering where your body has gone and thinking that I never even turned back to say goodbye. I am wondering if they have found your mum or your sister and what happens next. But mostly I am just lying there thinking that you are dead. How can you be dead?

I am wondering how it can all be over now. This is not the way the story should end. It is not the way the story should begin. But it is the way it happened.

Clouds

I collect raindrops like tears

store them up for years
in a muffling grey blanket
protection from the searing
rays of the sun.

And it has begun.
We break through, nose first
hold tight as stomachs lurch
and then the bright blue glide.

Glad to be alive
all below is candyfloss and cotton wool
and we long to be released
to bounce on tiptoe,
light as fairies or feathers
in a pillow fight

a delight of primary colours.
But we land in gloom
and the earth's a dirty smudge
beneath a grey-white ceiling.

There is no meaning
no shapes, nor symbols, nor metaphors.
So bleak we cannot even see the clouds
for the sky.

Time passes by.
Rain falls, the ceiling breaks apart
shafts of sunlight warm the skin

illuminating everything.
Wind blows, clouds scud
like surf across the blue.

If only we knew
that it was there all along.
Clouds forming, moving, breaking

gone.

I am not the person that I used to be

I USED TO be a daughter, a partner. Within three months, I have lost two of my names. Now I am just a mother and a friend. I feel peripheral. Loved, no doubt, but not essential to anyone, aside from the children. I cling onto them. For them I must keep living.

'You are everything to me,' he said. I was his world, on his mind when he woke up and on his mind when he went to sleep. Even though we weren't together every day, I mattered to him more than anyone else in the world. He wasn't always on the end of my phone but he was the person I said goodnight to, the person I talked to about everything. He was my future.

Now I am on people's minds, I know. I get through each day with a rota of friends who keep a check on me, who come round and let me talk, who offer their hugs and let me cry. But none of them can hold me like he did and they go back to their own families, hug their own partners and leave me alone in this wilderness.

I want to call my mum. She wouldn't know what to say. She was never any good with emotions. But she would be there, an anchor to the past. I was an essential part of her world.

Now, I float above the world like an untethered balloon longing to dissolve into the clouds to be with him. I look down and wonder what they are doing, all these people who are still living their trivial little lives.

I do have one name left. He called me Beverley Writer. And so I write.

What they don't know

WHAT THEY DON'T know is that, for me, it doesn't go away. That grief doesn't just surface when someone mentions his name, or when I see something that reminds me of him. Grief is with me constantly. I am clothed in grief, I wear it inside out.

They say it hits you in waves and they are right, but I am swimming in grief all day long and the waves pound over me in relentless succession. Sometimes they actually knock me out. Yesterday morning I stumbled and fell as I tried to perform the routine task of depositing my son at school.

When they try to speak to me and I do not reply, it is not because I am rude. It is because I cannot see their faces through the spray of those waves. Everything is blurred.

Or maybe I am rude too. Because I don't give a damn. I don't want to speak to anyone unless they are saying his name. I don't want to know anything that isn't him. I would rather turn around and swim back out to sea, treading water and battered by waves that keep me close to his memory.

The times we missed

I want to remember the first time that we met.
I want it to be etched onto my brain,
hammered in with a chisel,
imprinted by the giant machine that you hated to clean.
I want it to be part of me, like the years of grime,
silted into the grooved landscape of your hands.
I want it welded to my neurons.
But it isn't there.

I remember you though, and the time,
spoke of you to my friend who encouraged me then
as she encouraged me later.
She knew what I was yet to learn,
that your iron was worth more than all the words
of the other suitors, the poets and tutors.
But I was enjoying my freedom, living my dream,
didn't want to choose, afraid to lose.
There was no rush.

I must have been doing my MA.
Maybe I spoke of it to you.
Maybe that's why you told me you were 'impressed' by
    me,
too impressed to get close.
Maybe you were recently out of that relationship,
the one your mum clearly had hopes for
though you told a different story.
She didn't want children,
was too much for you.

Maybe you saw that potential in me too
when you took me in over the wooden table in Ed's
    dining room.
Too clever.
Too much.
No rush.

Only once were we alone.
You came round to my home,
the one with the terracotta walls.
You put up iron coat hooks reclaimed from a station
    cloakroom.
You'd picked out the numbers in neat, white paint,
fine work for such big hands.
You charged other people but you gave me mine for
    free.
I can picture you standing at the top of my cellar steps,
wedged in with one leg a few stairs down,
grounded, anchored as you were,
drilling into my wall while I watched,
not quite seeing what was in front of me.
It wasn't the best place for the hooks
but I didn't have anywhere else to put them.
You were probably wondering why you were giving
    them for free
to someone who would shove them in a cupboard,
who didn't even make you a cup of tea,
who barely made conversation though she had so
    much to say.
It was wham, bam, thank you man and you had gone.
The first moment that we missed.

Or maybe I was already with Chris.
Because, the next time, that's what I remember,
sitting at Ed's table with Chris by my side and you
    opposite.
You were talking about your work and I was enthralled,
said 'it must be therapeutic',
probably imagining myself banging out my own
    incessant worries:
to stay or leave, that was the question going round and
    round my head.
(I should have left, of course, I know that now,
but we all know about hindsight and that's not how
    the story went.)
You said you'd show me how to make a poker one day,
planted a seed that would grow years too late.
You took Chris down a tunnel on a job.
I stayed at home when I should have come
but I was always too scared of being trapped.
'Lovely guy,' he said and we carried on
like a broken record until it snapped
and stuttered and could play no more.
And I was alone.

The next time is certainly carved in stone,
or stained in my mind's indelible ink.
Surrey Street on a summer's day.
We were going the same way,
me on foot, you on a bike.
You were smarter than I'd ever seen you,
under some female influence,
wearing beige shorts, a blue and white checked shirt,
it was even ironed.
You pulled into the kerb and stopped to chat.

I told you about the break-up.
You told me that you hadn't seen Ed for a while.
He was with someone new. And so were you.
You didn't have time for a coffee just then
or perhaps you thought you'd better not.
Things were going well maybe, with the new one,
not the time to rock the boat.
We didn't realise that we were barely afloat
and that this was it and one life is all we have.
Sometimes there isn't time to catch up later.
Keep in touch, I said. But you never did.
And you cycled off to look
like a stranger in photos of remembrance,
that I only see now

when you are gone.

On souls and soulmates

I MEET YOUR family for the first time a few days after I discover your body. It is surreal to say the least. With all of us in shock, we skip the small talk and set about the important business of discussing coffins and writing notices to go into the local press.

'How do you want to refer to Paul?' your mum asks, trying to get the wording right for the newspaper. 'Partner, boyfriend?'

She's looking at me over her spectacles, fragments of paper scattered on nearby sofas and coffee tables. She is trying to make order from chaos by ticking things off on the handy 'to do' list that the funeral director has delivered. She is waiting for my answer, the silence punctuated only by the pulse of the oxygen pumping through the tubes that I tiptoed around as I entered, the tubes that are keeping her alive even though I know that she must want more than anything to die. It seems like a simple question but I don't know the answer. I want someone to confer with. Actually, I want to confer with you but you are not here and it seems odd to ask if I can phone a friend. Anyway, which friend would I phone? No one really knew us together. Partner seems presumptuous when we weren't even living together and boyfriend seems ridiculous; you were fifty-three and a giant of a man. It just doesn't seem right. And suddenly I find myself speaking, before I have had time to censor myself.

'Soulmate?' I offer. 'Does that sound silly?'

And your mum, bless her, says no she thinks soulmate is just fine. I already like your mum.

Every once or twice in a lifetime, two people come together and something magical happens. Biologists might try to explain it with talk of pheromones and procreative urges and psychologists might tell us that we are drawn to each other in order to replay some familial drama but, for most of us, at the point of falling in love, all rational thought goes out of the window. In fact, we feel so far from science, that we might actually have slipped through that window, or perhaps have gone even further and broken through some space-time continuum into a different dimension. Suddenly we exist in a new galaxy where we and the object of our affection are the only living things. We are twin stars on a collision course that has been predetermined by some unfathomable force. (As I said, science is irrelevant. This is how it feels.) Where once we thought we were the arbiters of our own fortunes, we are now inexplicably tossed on the waves of destiny, pawns on a cosmic chessboard, out of control. We don't care if we mix our metaphors, we just know that there is a rightness to this connection and that we are meant to be together, even though we have no idea who meant it to happen or why. Things that were blurred come into focus. We see our best selves reflected in the other's eyes. We have met our soulmate. This is how it was for us, even though we had no idea how we could make it work. We were discussing it right until the day you died.

In the aftermath of your death a few of your friends have taken the opportunity to tell me that they aren't sure we could have made it in the long run. I want to punch those people. 'You could never have lived with him,' said one. 'He was a slob,' said another. I think they were trying to make me feel better. At least now that you have died, I can be spared the disappointment of finding that you squeeze the toothpaste from the wrong end. In fact, your erratic teeth-cleaning habits had already been a subject of negotiation. You had lived alone in a shack in a field for years and unconventional was too conventional a word for the way you lived. But both of us went into the relationship with our eyes wide open and what other people couldn't see was the focus and recognition of those eyes. What we had was unique. It was special. It was beautiful. It was not of this world.

It was, though, a paradox. We were deeply in love and, for both of us, nothing had ever felt more right and yet logic told us it couldn't make sense. I had two children who got me out of bed at seven in the morning and, left to your own devices, you would go to bed at two and get up in the afternoon. I'm hardly known for being house proud, but your messiness was on a scale unlike anything I had ever seen. Caring for a sick child had turned my life into a military operation, where you were disorganised and carefree. And yet, somehow it worked. And it didn't just work, it worked beautifully. When we were together, it was simple and magical and irrefutably right. But when we went back to our respective lives, sometimes, especially at the beginning, doubt would set in. Two or three times you sent me panicky messages saying that you couldn't envision yourself in my life, that our circumstances were too different, that it was doomed to fail. And then, one day, something changed. I wrote you a letter saying that I thought we had something special but that I needed to be able to trust you.

You wrote me a letter back saying that actually, now, you couldn't imagine me not being in your life. You wrote:

'After much soul searching, many tears, and wandering up and down the road talking to myself, sometimes, quite sternly, I know what I want beyond all doubt. I want you more than anything in the world.'

When something feels so right why shouldn't it work? It might not be logical, but since when did logic have anything to do with love? I will never know now whether we could have made it in the long run but I know we were soulmates and I know we had a chance.

The scent of you

IT HAS BEEN a month and I still haven't changed the sheets. If I shuffle over onto your side of the bed, lay my head where yours rested and pull the duvet tight around my mouth, there's a tiny patch where I can still smell you, where you had your armpit. I was never sure I liked your smell and it used to annoy me that I had to change the sheets so often. Now I bury my nose into that spot and inhale deeply, as though I can keep some part of you in my nostrils for all eternity.

I am still sleeping with your fleeces. The brown-checked one that you bought on eBay recently, that neither of us really liked and the big, thick blue one I saw you in just the other week. You were coming from a job to meet me in the park, galloping round the path to meet me. A giant bear of a man, running with his arms open wide, with no care for who was watching. We were so excited to see each other that walking wasn't fast enough. Turns out we should have run faster. I launched myself into your arms and you held me tight.

Now I hold tight to your memory in those fleeces. I pull them towards me and curl around them like I used to curl around you and sob into the fabric where I used to sob into your chest. 'I've got you,' you used to say. Not anymore. The smell in your house after you died was too strong and I had to wash them in an effort to erase the pungent scent of death, a smell that I will never forget. Beneath the scent of washing detergent, a hint of it remains, and beneath that stench, still a slight smell of you. I wish I could bottle it and wear it like perfume. But it's just a memory now. One day I will have to wash the sheets. But not today. Not yet.

The alignment of stars

I GUESS EVERYONE'S love story begins this way, with the 'what ifs'. If I hadn't gone out that night, if I hadn't broken up with that girl, if I hadn't been late for the tube… Looking back it seems like magic was at work, or chance or fate or luck. Whatever it is, it feels good and we weave it into the narrative that it was all meant to be and, sometimes, if we're lucky, it is mythologized in a wedding speech and, if we're even more blessed, we get to the end of our lives and it is validated by the fifty years of happy marriage that we shared. It was written in the stars. If we're unlucky, we end up as 'star-cross'd lovers' sacrificed for the greater good at the end of the play. Hey ho. Destiny is a tricky customer.

But still, if he hadn't left me broken-hearted that April, I wouldn't even have been single that summer. I never thought there would be a silver-lining to that cloud. But there was. If I hadn't seen you outside the gig two years previously, I wouldn't have known that Ed was divorced. If Ed hadn't got together with his new partner, he wouldn't have been taking kids to school with my friends' kids and she wouldn't have mentioned him. And maybe I wouldn't have gone searching for him on Facebook after 12 years.

If Ed hadn't been working round the corner from my house that day. If I hadn't bought my Bongo campervan. If he didn't have a Bongo too. If I hadn't rudely abandoned my friend in a cafe and rushed home for a cup of tea with him. If you hadn't phoned while he was there. If Ed and his gang hadn't been going for a walk near your house that evening. If the kids hadn't been at their dad's that night. If I hadn't decided at the last minute to drive at 90 miles an hour to join them, at least partly in the hope that you would be there. If you hadn't decided to meet us for a drink at the pub later. Maybe it would still have happened another way. But this is the way it happened. And the way it might just as easily never have happened.

It was a lovely walk. I nervously chatted to people I didn't know about questions of life and love but I was mostly focused on the main question of whether you would come to the pub or not. It was touch and go until the last minute. The pub near your house was shut and we had to go to Baslow instead. You probably wouldn't have bothered to walk that far just for a drink. You didn't even like drinking and liked your own company more. I could hear you on the phone to Ed, could hear you wavering. I almost said what he said, that I'd come and fetch you, but that seemed ridiculously keen. But he fetched you and you came.

'Blacksmith Paul!' I said.

'Beverley Ward!' you said.

We hugged with the warmth of old friends reunited after fifteen years.

'You look good,' you said. 'You've lost weight.'

Cue the same old story about the sick child and the allergies and how if you cut out dairy, gluten, eggs and

44

sugar from your diet, you will lose weight as a side effect. You had lost weight too but I had no idea how much. It is only when I look at old photos now that I realise what had happened to you in those intervening years. Later, you would tell me that you had sat alone on a hillside at New Year wondering if there was any point in going on. If you hadn't picked yourself up and lost all that weight, would we still have got together?

I made sure we sat side by side and we joined in the general chat. I wished everyone else would go away so that we could have a proper conversation. We had a little one, about my imminent camping trip to Matlock and the raft races you used to do there. You asked me to see if I could find you some gold. We bantered about Fool's Gold and crocks at the end of the rainbow. We were already on another planet. I asked you how the blacksmithing was going, reminded you that you once said you would teach me to make a poker. You said you would.

As we were leaving the pub, Ed could see what was happening. He'd tried once before to get us together. He tried again now.

'Are you giving Paul a lift home, Beverley?'

'Would you like a ride in my Bongo, Blacksmith Paul?' I asked.

'You don't get an offer like that every day,' Ed said.

"I know! I'm taking it!' you said and raced off in the direction of my new campervan.

You directed me in the blackness to the driveway up to your place, the driveway I have driven up more since you died than I did when you were alive. There was an air of anticipation, a feeling of hope. It was good to be alone together. I thought you might invite me in but you didn't, though clearly you were thinking about it.

'It's not suitable for ladies,' you said.

Instead, we exchanged numbers and said that we would meet up soon for poker making. My fingers were clumsy as I typed your name into my phone. Blacksmith Paul.

'I want an interesting name,' I said.

'Bongo Bev,' you said, smiling.

I laughed. We said goodnight. And I went off to Matlock in search of the gold at the end of the rainbow.

Grief is the thing with teeth

I come like a black cloud on a sunny day.
But I'm a cloud with teeth, big teeth –
all the better to eat you with, my dear.
I chew you up, grind your memories between molars,
hold you tight in my grip.
I tumble you on my tongue,
churn up all the what-ifs of your broken world
until you don't know truth from lies,
up from down.

Sometimes, at night, I take my teeth out and
then I swallow you whole into the damp cavity of my
   blackness.
You like it then, you know you do.
It is safe there where pain is the truth,
the whole truth and nothing but the truth.
There you feel alive.

Just when you're comfortable, settling in,
I spit you back out, still wet, to stumble blindly into
   sunlight.
I leave you numb with no compass in a foreign land,
frozen in the glare of another day.
Don't worry. I will come again soon.
When you least expect me.
When you don't want me.
I like to keep you on your toes.

The weight of grief

THERE IS AN image doing the rounds. It is of a sculpture of a body, a wire cage of stones, brought to its knees. And sometimes grief does feel like this. Heavy, like it could floor me right there in the middle of whatever I'm doing. Like my whole body is made of rocks that rub painfully together if I try to walk. The weight is too much and movement becomes impossible.

But mostly, it comes in waves, invisible waves that seem to bypass everyone else and target only me, knocking me over with their force, until I can't breathe and all I can see is blackness. If there are stones, they are being hurled at my head.

If I were to make my own sculpture it would be of a broken pier falling into the sea. When I look back to the beach, that is where I see my parents and my past. They waved me off to make my own way in the world. In the distance there are the people who walked alongside me for a while but they took a different turning. They preferred to walk on the cliff path or stayed safely on the promenade. But you were walking alongside me and walking with me into the future and suddenly you are gone. And the walkway stops abruptly at the edge of an unforgiving sea and I am left screaming into the darkness. There is nothing to hold onto out there. There is no desert island to swim to. There is no boat to rescue me and the walkway behind me has crumbled. There is nowhere left to go. I feel completely lost and alone, unanchored with nothing in the distance to reach for.

Frantically, I search for something to build a future from, weaving sticks and seaweed together, hoping to make a raft. But it is futile because sticks remind me of you and seaweed reminds me of you and you have the string.

I need someone to hold onto, someone who can hold me through this pain and torment, someone who can make this bearable. But that person is gone. There is no harbour in your arms anymore. All is sea and darkness and yes, sometimes, the weight of rocks.

You are elemental now

I see you in rainbows.
I see you in clouds.
I see you in big skies and bright stars.
I see you in shafts of light and pouring rain.
You are elemental now.
You always were elemental.

Red. For the blood. That is all.

Yellow like the daffodils in the poem I wrote on our last weekend away together. The hopefulness in that poem is like a smack in the face now. It feels like some malevolent force was listening to all my talk of spring and newness and rebirth and decided to come with a cleaver and chop down all the daffodils and take you with them. Not for me, the optimism of yellow. The hope of spring.

Pink, like the fleece I wore in the photos you took. The one where I am all woodland sprite on an autumn walk, climbing down from a tree with that beaming smile that only you seemed to capture, that only you gave rise to. We went looking for a highwayman's cave. Never found it but didn't care. Instead we found a patch of grass on a hillside and called it home. We lay down and watched the sun slowly slip out of the sky. A priceless moment, bathed in the pink light of dusk, perched on the edge of love.

There was so much green. Green fields around your house on the day we first sat together on your porch. Green grass in the park as we walked the dog. Green trees on woodland walks. Even though we mostly loved in winter, we lived in green on those magical days. Now I am green. Sick with horror, and green with envy for the people who loved you for longer than I did and the people who hold their loved ones close at night. Green is sprouting out all over now, like a reminder of a love that was just beginning to truly blossom. A love that will never ever see the summer.

Purple for the heather on that first September walk we took together. The joy of boundless discovery, rampaging across the moors, conversation never faltering, being completely present and yet aware that there was just the faintest purple tinge of forever in the air. There has never been a more perfect day. I'm so glad I spent it with you. I'm so sad that we will never do it again.

Orange for a man of fire. The flames of the bonfire you built for me on New Year's Eve. You carried the wood and an axe up the hill, breathed life into sticks just as you breathed life in to me. Sitting between your legs, feeling my shins burning, watching fireworks exploding over the city that was home to both of us for our whole lives, lives which were spent at less than half a degree of separation until last year. Flames of passion burning bright. Snuffed out, without warning, overnight.

It was always going to be blue. The colour for you. The blue of your eyes meeting mine in disbelief. 'Your eyes look sad,' you said, the first time that we kissed. I said I was terrified of risking my heart again. That malevolent force was watching then too, urging me on, telling me to take a chance. What could go wrong? Everything, as it happens. Blue for the shirt you wore every time we went out. I know you still think it was black, but I'm telling you it was dark blue. I bought you a new one at Christmas, light blue this time. It goes with your eyes, your mum said. The blue of the sea at Flamborough and the blue of skies. I see you in skies now. And in clouds. Love for us was fleeting and rare as the rainbows you leave as messages now you're gone. You are elemental now. You always were elemental.

Signs

YOUR MUM IS asking if I've had any signs that you are around. I don't believe in signs but when she asks me if I've felt anything, like movement in my hair perhaps, I remember the night in the early days when I felt something ruffle like a breeze through my hair as I was lying in bed crying. I remember the shivery sensation that I felt in my body and the immediate knowledge that it was you, followed swiftly by the equally clear knowledge that I was deluded and that it must be nits or the wind, though the skylight in my room was shut and neither of the kids have lice.

She tells me that friends of hers have felt this sensation and so I tell her that I have too, hoping that it will bring her some comfort. When I leave her flat, I find myself Googling signs from spirits and discover it at the top of the list. Part of me thinks that I have a lost the plot but I make a note of the others anyway, just in case.

The next day, I am sitting in a playground while my children play. I am talking to a friend about you when a beautiful butterfly lands on my hand, like I am some kind of Disney princess. It rests there for an absurdly long time and children come over to look. I remember that it is one of the signs on my list.

And then I start to find things: coins, pennies. I pick them up, figuring I need good luck. I find one every day for a week. It is on the list.

So, the next day, in the Botanical Gardens, I set you a challenge. If this is you, I say, show me something else.

And a feather floats down in front of me. Feathers are on the list. On the other hand, the Botanical Gardens is not an unusual place to find birds. I get up and start to walk towards home along the busy high street. There is a trail of feathers all the way along it. It leads me into the park. I need to get to school to pick up my children but I follow them anyway. The previous day (the day of the butterfly) my daughter had lost her school bag in the park along with her most precious cuddly panda toy which I need to find. I follow the feathers all the way to the cafe and go to the lost property box hoping to find her panda. Instead I find a book called *Revelations of Divine Love*. I'm not normally a thief but I pick it up and take it with me. I feel that it is for me. When I finally get to school my daughter emerges with the panda in her arms. Someone has found her bag while they were walking their dog and somehow they have tracked her down.

Is it a sign? I don't know but I know that it feels good and just now, that is enough.

The best first date ever

IF YOU WANT to stand out from the crowd, they say, plan an unusual first date. And our first date was as unusual as they come: we made a poker together.

Writers are always interested in learning new things. You never know when you might need to describe a blacksmith at work in a novel (and I'm sure one will feature in the next book I write) but the honest truth is that I wasn't really that bothered about learning the tricks of the blacksmithing trade. I just wanted an excuse to spend the day with you and it was the best one I could come up with. You'd said you would show me your blacksmithing skills years ago so it was an easy suggestion to make and one you were hardly going to say no to.

In advance of the meeting, you asked me a few times what I wanted to make and I had no idea (see above; I wasn't really bothered about making anything.) You said I could make a shepherd's crook and I confessed that Heidi was my dressing up costume of choice as a child. You called me Heidi for a while after that in your messages. In the end we settled on a poker even though I didn't yet have a fire.

I was nervous coming to your house for the first time. I got lost on the way and had to phone you to check where you lived. When I finally found it you were there at the bottom of the drive waving your arms and jumping around like a giant child. All of my anxiety dissipated when I saw you there. It was always like being reunited with my best friend when I saw you, even at the start.

It's funny how memories become like multi-sensory snapshots over time. What is it that makes the mind record just moments within the hours spent together? How does it choose them? What mechanism springs into action when we fall in love to say, stop, absorb this moment, it will be important later? This is what I recall:

You, the childlike giant, jumping about at the bottom of the drive, dressed all in black. The way you signalled the way to a parking spot in an empty field as if you had reserved it especially for me. That moment when you stood behind me and held my arm, helping me to hammer the molten metal and we both knew that something more than friendship was brewing. (The resolution at that moment that, no, the sexually submissive man with the 97% compatibility rating on OK Cupid was *not* the man for me. That the 3% incompatibility was crucial.) You, flustered, moving rapidly from one side of the forge to another trying to rescue me from danger. The smell of singed gloves as I picked up the wrong bit of the poker. You testing me, naming the parts that I've forgotten now though I remember your laughter and your voice telling me that I was the loveliest of distractions.

Your big black boots resting next to my purple boots on the railing of your veranda against a backdrop of fields and trees. Your straightforward appreciation of my company and the pivotal moment when you said something that made me sure of your feelings though the sound on that memory is turned down and I can't remember the words, just the glow of your warmth.

Drinking tea and eating flapjack, the staple refreshment of our time together. Me admiring your free-range lifestyle, you admiring my mind: 'You exude innate intelligence,' you said. How to woo a Beverley in one easy step. The conversation about my ex, the sceptic and our agreement that when he called me a magical thinker it was certainly a compliment. The hug as we parted. Me telling you that I'd had a lovely day. The promise that we would meet up soon. Perhaps a walk or something, you said. Or a bike ride. (We never did have a bike ride.) And, oh, I said, perhaps you could help me with some jobs? Like cutting the lock that held my bike to his bike in the yard. Symbolic, we said. And another excuse, setting the scene for us to get together again soon. Which we did. Really soon.

What I have loved I cannot hold

Your hands were soft and strong.
No, you had working hands, with rough nubs and
    edges.
But they were tender hands, kind hands, warm hands.
These adjectives aren't enough.
I search for the right words to describe your hands
and wonder why I didn't make notes sooner.
Why I didn't ask you to sit like a model in a life
    drawing class
while I took in every detail of you, so that I could
    recreate it now.
Why I didn't photograph your hands,
draw your hands,
imprint them in clay,
the way parents preserve the tiny hands of babies.
Why is it only newborn fingers we immortalise?

I didn't fully know you,
hadn't yet explored the back of your hand or the palm.
I hadn't made a map of hairs and freckles and veins.
I hadn't traced your lifeline with my finger,
didn't realise it was short,
just knew that your love line was strong.

What I do know is that you had big hands,
good hands,
hands that held mine snug and tight.
'Your tiny hand is freezing,' you said
as you sandwiched it between yours.

You were a furnace warming me from the
outside in, inside out.

I cannot hold your body next to mine,
cannot feel the flood of calm as you wrap yourself
  around me.
I cannot describe the exact feeling of your skin on my
  skin
or find the right expression for the way we touched.
I never stopped mid-embrace to write down exactly
how you tasted when we kissed,
but I can say this:

you felt like home.

Things not to say: 'The angels must have needed him'

'THE ANGELS MUST have needed him,' they say. But why would the angels need a blacksmith? Sure, he could fix gates, but he didn't work with pearls. Did they need him to be one of them? He'd look stupid with wings, in a floaty white gown. It just wasn't his style. And anyway, he didn't want to be an angel. He wanted earthly pleasures. He wanted to stay here with me. He wanted to spend the summer cavorting on hillsides and beaches with his sweetheart, making love in meadows and woods. He had plans. Big plans. Don't tell me that the angels needed him. I don't care how rusty their gates are. They could have found someone else to oil their hinges, taught someone else to polish their halos, someone older maybe, someone who was tired and done with living, someone who had no one to love. And please don't tell me this happened for a reason, that this is for the greater good because what you're telling me is that he and I deserved this shit and that it will all work out better in the end. There is no happy ever after in this narrative. This narrative is fucked. And I should know, I'm a writer for God's sake. No one would tell this story to make any kind of higher moral point. It is a horror story and a bad one at that. I'm not normally an angry person but if the angels come near me, I will tear their wings to shreds and twist their halos out of shape. Sure, the angels might have needed him but nobody needed him more than me.

Signs

I FIND MYSELF planning your funeral from a writing retreat on the Llyn Peninsula. I'm not sure I should be here but, in a world where nothing makes sense anymore, it seems as good a place to be as any. The children are with their father for this one week of the year and I am here amongst friends, cocooned by mountains in this place where a vast expanse of sea and sky calls like a siren over the garden wall. Daily I heed its cry, tramping over rough terrain to the water's edge. Walking, like writing, brings some release. It is a metaphor for something. Putting one foot in front of the other is a thing that I know I must do even though I want more than anything to lie in the surf and let the water carry me away.

Down on the beach, my friends stand at a respectful distance, leave me for a while sitting on rocks, searching the clouds while tears rain from my eyes as I imagine the beautiful photograph that you would have taken if you were here. Eventually, reluctantly, I walk back to join them on the path. Along the cliff a man with the largest camera I've ever seen, accosts me. 'My lady on the beach,' he says. 'I didn't expect to find you.' He tells me that he has just taken the most beautiful picture of me sitting on the pebbles. He shows me the photo and I cry. He says that he will send it to me later, when he is home.

Back at the house, I lean into the corner of my desk where there is phone reception and make another call to your mum. We debate again the merits of various poems for your service. I had thought your friend would read the poem your mum had chosen from my selection but apparently she's not happy with that poem and so we are back at the beginning again. It is not easy to make progress with half a signal and half a brain, halfway across the country, liaising with people I have only just met when all of us are shredded by grief and shock but I am doing my best. It has already been agreed that I am giving the eulogy, even though I have only really known you for eight months of your fifty-three years. 'I would stay out of it,' my brother says. 'Let the family do the funeral' – but it turns out that I can't. I cannot let some man in a suit who doesn't know you sum you up like some mediocre CV. I will not let you go out of the world in that way. And now your mum is asking if I will read a poem instead of your friend and I'm not sure. It is starting to look like I am going to be conducting the whole funeral, and I'm not sure whether I can do it. I'm not sure whether I am overstepping my role. I'm not sure whether to read one of my own poems or one of the more generic ones. It is hard to know what is for the best.

I put the phone back in my pocket and take deep breaths, wander into the kitchen to make a cup of tea. Someone asks me how it's going and I regale her with details of the debate over who should read and what and when. 'Ah,' she says. 'It seems like you're doing well. Keep buggering on.' And I smile because this is what you used to say to me, KBO, for short. For a moment I feel that you are in the kitchen with me. 'Funny,' she says. 'I never usually say that.'

It does seem like I am doing well, all things considered.

I have managed to drive myself and a friend across the country without crashing the car and I can maintain an appearance of composure for large chunks of these days which I spend walking on beaches, gazing at clouds, sleeping in crisp white sheets, writing to you. At dinner I am careful to sit between friends, their presence shoring me up, protecting me from small talk until one day, by accident, I find myself sitting next to someone I don't know. She tries to engage me in conversation but, as she is not talking about you, I cannot understand anything she is saying. I feel unsteady like I am on the deck of a boat on choppy seas but I smile anyway, trying not to let the mask slip, wondering if I can change seats without appearing rude, not sure if I can walk around the table without falling. And then a voice asks where the man in our group has gone. He's not here for dinner. Someone says that they saw him in the pub earlier. Someone else says he was on the drive not so long ago. Someone says, not to worry, he's a grown man and he can warm his dinner up later. And suddenly, the ship is pitching into deep waters. I am staring at the unused cutlery where the man should be and I can't believe that all these people are so callous and unconcerned by this absence. His body could be lying now on the road, his torso already swelling with death, fluids seeping onto the gravel. And I am standing up, knocking things over, saying incoherently that someone should look for him, that I'm sorry, that I have to go. And the room falls silent as I run for the door, trying to escape before huge sobs wrack my body.

My friends bring me herbal teas and tissues and I hide in my room, talking and crying for the rest of the night until my head hurts and my eyes can stay open no longer. I collapse into the sheets and hold onto your fleece like it is a life raft, tossed about on the waves again, sailing fitfully through the night.

Grief is everywhere

It is in the awful realisation of wakening and the
    curling back into night-time in search of lost
    dreams.
It is in the smell of your empty fleece, the small
    comfort of familiar fabric without the solidity of a
    body.
It is in the space at your side of the bed where I will
    you to appear as if I can conjure you by love alone.
It is in reaching out hopelessly to pat duvet furrows in
    search of limbs that I know are not there.

Grief is the card you gave me at New Year, wishing
    that all my dreams would come true.

Grief is in the view from the bedroom window, in
    the city lights that you loved to watch when you
    couldn't sleep, and in the morning sky.
Grief is played in the song on the radio as I make
    breakfast.
Grief is dragged like the weight of the bin that I
    bring to the side of the curb, knowing that this, like
    everything, is my job and my job alone.

Grief is every white van that drives by and every couple who walk hand in hand.

Grief is there when I gaze down my street and know that I will never, ever see you walking towards me again.
Grief is at the door when I open it and know that you will never be the guest knocking loudly, waiting to come in.
I let grief in instead.

Grief is there in the quiet, momentary forgetting and the loud remembering that follows.

Grief is in the playground at school where other mums share normal information and smiles as if nothing has changed; where I am the only one who knows that the whole world has been rearranged and all its parts put back in the wrong place.

Grief is knowing all of your hopes and plans that will never be.

Grief is every time I walk away from a friend knowing that I am walking back to an empty space, to a life where you are not there. Where you will never be.
Grief is sobbing my way towards home because I cannot tell you about my day.

Grief is trying to build your Meccano with my son
and not knowing how it works.

Grief is looking at photos from all of the years that I
didn't know you.
Grief is knowing that you wished I had been there.
Grief is feeling memories slipping away already and
trying to hold onto them.
Grief is the limbo of knowing that there is no way
back and no desire for the future.

Grief is your mum who rocks your t-shirt in arms
where her baby once lay.

Grief is walking where we once walked, remembering
how we talked.
A film, played backwards, snapshots of time being
erased until we are at the start and you don't exist.
Grief is the inappropriateness of sunshine, the horror
of spring.
Grief is everywhere. And everything.

Signs

WHEN I GET home from Wales I have a message from a friend. She tells me that she had a dream about you. You were in your own artists' studio looking young and healthy. She tells me that she spoke to you and that you told her that you were really happy with me and that things were going well. She says that, it sounds strange but you had a crown of tiny purple and yellow flowers around your head. She says that you told her that we shouldn't let our days and nights be mountains to climb but that we should enjoy life. She says she woke up crying.

The next day at my house we are sitting at the table drinking tea and she picks up the funeral celebrant's card from the table. She looks surprised.

'What's that card?' she says. 'Those were the flowers on his head in my dream.'

For the first time I notice that the motif on the business card is of tiny purple and yellow flowers. It is a strange synchronicity. And synchronicity is on my list.

The man of my dreams

I DREAMED ABOUT you again. How I have longed to dream about you. One of those gentle dreams where you might appear as if in a vision and offer me some words of comfort. Or the other kind, where you might just be there talking and laughing as you used to. But this dream was a dark dream. You were sitting, eating and your belly was swelling up as if each mouthful was inflating you like a balloon. And the next minute you were running towards some marble steps. You tripped and fell and then it was over.

'Be quiet,' I said to my children in another dream. 'I just need to send this message to Paul.' And I pegged colourful flags to a washing line, desperately trying to reach you with some kind of domestic semaphore.

I had spent three days frantically trying to reach you before we found your body. From time to time I re-read the messages now. They start casually with a 'Hey. How's you?' on Thursday morning and end with frantic pleas for you to get in touch on Saturday. All shades of emotion are there: humour, worry, fear, anger and despair. I left every kind of message: text, Facebook, voicemail, notes on your van and your door after all of my shouting and crying outside your house in the darkness had failed. You couldn't come to the door because you were already two days dead, lying on your bed, alone. I thought you might have gone out walking (it was quite normal for you to go wandering in the night), though my tears and shaking limbs held a different possibility and I knew already that there was no happy ending to the story. Either way I knew that I had lost you. I couldn't commit to a man who would disappear for days on end without warning and the only alternative (ridiculously far-fetched though it seemed) was that you were dead. In the end, though I lost your body, our love was restored when we broke down the door and found you there.

'Hey Jack,' I said, in one message that week. 'Have you seen Bert? I can't find him.' You were a man of many aliases. To most people you were Paul Harding, or Blacksmith Paul, but on Facebook you masqueraded as Jack Smythe. You were one of those Facebook sceptics, wary of giving too much away. Jack Smythe, the exorcist from Vatican City who studied at the University of Yangon and lived in Timbuctoo, California, born in Hong Kong. To me, you were also Bert Mulligan, the persona you inadvertently set up on your new phone in order to communicate with me via Messenger. You didn't realise that you could just connect to your old Facebook account. It led to some interesting exchanges. Jack, we saw as a vagabond and a pirate. An all-round ne'er-do-well. Bert was also a bit of a scoundrel, who worked the fairgrounds. They were bitter rivals for my love. Once I invited them both to my birthday party and they planned to resolve the issue once and for all with pistols – water pistols, of course, because the children would be there. Occasionally, our banter would get so convoluted that, eventually, I would have to ask if I could speak to Blacksmith Paul.

'I love Blacksmith Paul,' I said.

'At last, Beverley Writer,' you said. 'She's the one for me.'

When you woke on the Sunday morning before your death, you told me about your dream. You told me that in the dream I had walked off into a pub and that you had gone through a door and found yourself in a disused factory alone. I wonder if that is where you are now. I hope that, one day, you will come back to me in my dreams.

Signs

I GO TO your house again. It is a thing we do, searching through the rubble as if we are pillaging a bombsite, picking at the remnants of your corpse for an ounce of flesh. Yesterday your mum handed me some scrappy notebooks, telling me that there were some bits about me in them and it was like I'd found the holy grail. There it was. Evidence of the incontrovertible truth that you lived and that we loved. That it meant to you what it meant to me. That it was real.

I pick up a dusty bag of runes from the floor in the room that masqueraded as a living room ('where can Beverley sit?' you once mused because there was only room for you amongst the books and albums and scrap-yard debris). I remember the time on the beach when you were collecting smooth round pebbles to make your own runes and I think about bringing them home with me. But I hesitate and leave them on the floor. Like everything in your house, they are old and grubby; they would seem out of place in my suburban home.

But when I get back, my daughter is reading a novel in the window. She is talking to me about the plot and showing me pictures of runes in the book. I didn't know she knew anything about runes. I tell her that you have some and she is wild with excitement. So I go back to fetch them for her, like life is now some treasure hunt that I am compelled to follow. When I bring them back to her, she is fascinated. She picks one out, says 'this is Perthrow. It's my favourite.' I ask her if she knows its meaning and she shakes her head so we look it up on my phone. And this is what it says:

The beginning and the ending are fixed. What's in between is yours. Nothing is in vain. All is remembered.

All is remembered.

The road less travelled

THE FIRST DAY that we went out together feels like the happiest day of my life, though I know there must have been other happy days before it, in years gone by, memories faded by time. This one shone so brightly though, I'm not sure it will ever be eclipsed.

You arrived at my house, freshly shaven in your bright blue fleece and the shirt that became known as the 'Beverley Shirt'. You came equipped with tools on the pretext of sorting out some jobs but you didn't do much, just cut through the chain that bound my bike to his, set us free.

I made chilli and told you of my internet dating exploits, taking in the barely concealed look of disappointment on your face when you realised you were not the only man on my radar, though you were already the only man in my heart. And then it began. The first adventure. You took me to the reservoirs at Redmires, stopping the van by a derelict building to take pictures for the 'shack project' that you were curating on your laptop. Later you told me how mesmerised you were by the look on my face as I stood like a ghost in the house. You wanted so much to capture that look again, but I didn't know what it was. A mixture maybe of uncertainty and desire. A look that probably belonged just to that day. And then the real journey started, from the car park and up the hill. We went through the wrong gate from the moment we set out and strayed further and further from the path, but closer and closer to each other.

'We could make a coffee table book,' I said. 'You could take the photos and I could write poems to go with them.' You sent me your photo that you'd taken and I sent you a poem. 'A beautiful way to remember a magical day,' you said.

The Road Less Travelled

Two roads diverged in a yellow wood
and knowing he had but two choices,
Frost chose the road less travelled,
laying words along the path as he went
like a mantra for wise feet to follow.

But you have led me to a landscape
that dips and dives like the nameless birds
that swoop overhead in the September sky:
starlings, skylarks, swifts?
Here, I'm not even sure there is a path
and though you claim to know where you're going
in truth, we neither know nor care,
content as we are to wander and to wonder
side by side in the open expanse of the day.

Mostly we spring on tussocks,
tossing words and laughter as we go,
moving swiftly from grassy hump to hump,
topic to topic, to avoid getting bogged down,
marooned in the mire. And though we speak
sometimes of paths taken and not taken,
trod and untrod, we plant our feet firmly,
smack bang here in the glory of the present.

Then we spy a spinney, a copse, a triumph of trees
waving their branches to us from a desert island
in this sea of purple flowers and we know
without a shadow of a doubt that we must
abandon the path (was there ever a path?)
and head to this oasis, like pirates
(you do have an inner pirate don't you?)
on a quest for hidden treasure.
We join hands briefly as we tread on rickety rocks,
assail the barbed wire fence, go AWOL on the moors.

But then something unexpected happens
and one view leads to another and we see
a house – a solid pile of stone perched
above a tranquil pool, like a call to home.
Still in sync, we change track again,
cross the bridge from the past to the future
and back again. And we sit, side by side,
watching ripples from hidden fish on the water,
not knowing where we will go next
but thankful for the road less travelled today.

The Other Road Less Travelled

TODAY YOUR MUM and I went on our own adventure. Where she used to rest her arm on yours, today she rested it on mine. Where I used to hold your hand, today I held hers as we went on a voyage of discovery, searching for the hidden path down to the river. We were on a treasure hunt again, neither of us sure where we were going but somehow I helped her to find her way back to the memory you shared and she showed me a spot that you hadn't yet taken me to. We fed ducks, held back tears, searched for you in clouds. We shared our stories, felt your presence, mourned your absence. We watched the nameless fish beneath the water – trout, perch, carp? It seemed absurd again that you were not there. We don't know how to do this yet, without you. But together we took fairy steps into the light of the sun.

These days I wake up shivering

IT'S LIKE THE fear has set in before daybreak, consciousness shaking me out of the protective darkness of sleep. I curl, foetal, around the soft comfort of your clothes and shudder, wondering how to face the day. I get that tense, sick, nervous feeling that you get on the day of an exam, or a long journey, or the day of a funeral, every day.

I remember waking with you on the day of my mum's funeral, feeling myself curled tight, eyes squeezed shut, hoping to block out the day, not sure if I could face it. I managed to shuffle myself across the bed and snuffle my head onto your chest. 'I don't want to go,' I said. You wrapped me up in your warmth and at some point we emerged, donned the uniform of grief and prepared ourselves to face it.

On the morning of your funeral, I wake alone. Somehow I get the kids to school and then get ready to say goodbye again to your body, though I feel I have already said goodbye at the undertakers the day before. It had been a month since I'd last seen you and even though you were in a wooden box and I was unable to see your face, I was grateful to have you returned for a moment from hospitals and post-mortems and to sit by your side once more. I had talked to you and cried on that wooden box, resting my head close to where I imagined what was left of your head might have been and letting the words out: I'm sorry, I love you, I'm so sorry. Suddenly I felt your coffin lurch so violently that I thought it was going to fall off its stand. I was convinced you were trying to reach me and was terrified for a moment that you were trapped but I figured it was probably in my mind, or my body, that I had seen you dead and you had been through numerous tests in search of a cause. There was no way you were alive in there. If you were trying to reach me, I knew you would be telling me not to blame myself. There was nothing I could have done. I sang 'Somewhere Over the Rainbow'. It's the song I sing to my children, the one I sang to you on your microphone in your music studio the weekend before you died. It was like I was rocking our distressed souls with my voice.

I wear the new dress that I bought in Wales. It is a dress that I think you might like. It is a sober brown but rustic and pretty. No one has told me what to wear and I don't want to offend your family by wearing something bright but I don't think you would want me to wear black. I am becoming good at imagining that I know what you would think. I collect my notes and put the yin yang ball that you gave me on my birthday in my pocket. It seemed like a strange present at the time but I have carried it with me ever since. It jangles when I walk, keeps you close.

At the crematorium I stand amongst the small group of my assembled friends. They didn't really know you but they know what you meant to me and in this moment, in their loyalty, they have become the people that I value most on earth. Your family arrives next and I touch your mum's arm to let her know that I am here and then the hearse pulls up in the stillness and I notice the woodland wreath of roses amongst the family flowers and I am glad that I phoned back and said that, yes, even though you didn't seem like the kind of man who would want flowers, I wanted to be represented there.

Entering the chapel, I'm not sure where to sit. I am not family but I think I should be near the front because I am to speak. I hear your mum asking where I am and I move to sit behind her, trailing my entourage of friends with me, like a peacock's tail, feeling that we shouldn't be taking up so much room but unable to move without them. And very quickly, it seems, the man in grey has muttered some rote words and I am being summoned to the pulpit. I breathe deep and walk on shaking legs up to the front and begin speaking. It is the hardest thing I have ever done, standing up there, speaking to a congregation of people I have never met, telling the assembled people how much I loved you whilst searching the crowd of faces for your ex-girlfriends and step-children. It is the most diverse cross-section of society I have ever seen. Millionaires in cashmere coats sit side by side with labourers and hippies, your mum's middle-class friends in pearls and cardigans alongside people who could easily be homeless. I say my piece then I sit down and allow my tears to fall.

We have agreed to leave the curtains open at the end so that people can say goodbye. It seemed like a good idea at the time but after I have watched your family parade from the chapel I realise it is my turn. I walk to the coffin and suddenly my feet feel like there is a magnetic pull holding them in front of the wooden casket. I should be moving gracefully past but I cannot move. I touch the wood and then lean down to kiss it as if I am kissing your lips one last time and I am planted there, growing roots. I want to throw myself on top of the coffin and beg them not to take you. I look round in panic and see a friend striding down the aisle towards me, her arms outstretched. Gently she guides me away. And you are gone forever.

These days I wake up shivering. It's like the fear has set in before daybreak, consciousness shaking me out of the protective darkness of sleep. I curl, foetal, around the soft comfort of your clothes and shudder, wondering how to face the day. I get that tense, sick, nervous feeling that you get on the day of an exam, or a long journey, or the day of a funeral, every day.

And then my little boy's face appears at the bedside and I shove your clothes behind me and reach out for his morning softness and the shivers gradually cease. For him and his sister I will get out of bed. I will smile. I will go on. I am their roots and their strength. From me they grow.

Death has torn up my roots. My parents are gone and I stand alone, wobbly, unanchored and without you by my side. You were the one I clung onto. You held me firm, kept me upright. With you I was starting to grow. And you were growing too in symbiosis. But you were cut down overnight, in your prime with no warning and now my nourishment is gone. My parents were my roots, my past, you were the blossom of my future. I'm not sure I can grow without you. I'm not sure that I want to. I'm not sure I can love a world that can be so cruel. But I love them, the little boy and the little girl. For them I must live.

The smouldering ache of loss

YOU WERE A man of fire and the flames of love were strong, from the first date when we made a poker together on your anvil; hammering red hot metal, bodies close together, feeling the heat rising between us. You were overwhelmed by your passion. Almost ran away. For all the pain your death has caused me, I'm so glad that you didn't, so glad we shared what we shared together. You built me bonfires on the moors and stoked the flames of log-burning fires in holiday cottages. There was fire in our hearts from the moment we met. In the last poem that I wrote about you, I wrote of sparks turning into flames. And then, suddenly, just when the fire was blazing, someone put it out. Smouldering is the right word for this loss.

You'd planned to have a bonfire and, in spite of your absence, we go ahead and hold it in your memory out at your place the week after the funeral. It is a good opportunity to burn what remains of your belongings before the landowners reclaim the place that you called home. I am so numb that I find myself standing in the embers of the fire, melting the soles of my boots until the stones from your yard are embedded like jewels in metal. I take those stones with me now, feel their imprint as they dig into the soles of my feet. It feels fitting to carry that pain as I walk.

The truth is, it is easy for me to turn towards this pain. The pain is comforting. Because the pain speaks of love. I feel close to you, lying here, feeling this searing, smouldering heartbreak. It brands me with the knowledge of how deeply I loved. How much I have lost. Easier to feel it than to turn away, to enter into the cool worlds where the fire has gone out, where eyes glaze like pale marbles in artificial light. Stay here with me where the flames are still bright. They say that if you play with fire you will get burned. I played. It burned. It hurts. But it is real.

I didn't know

I DIDN'T KNOW what to expect when I started
writing. I only knew that writing would be something
to hold onto in the darkness, the only way out of the
swirling waters of grief.

I didn't know the waters would be so deep or so
violent. I thought I'd be pretty expert at this grieving
lark by now. After all, I am experienced – skilled, surely
– in the art of losing gracefully. But I was wrong.

I lost my innocence in a difficult childhood and the
stability of a family when my parents divorced. I lost
my first love when I too divorced in my twenties. I was
divorced before other people had even started to get
married. I lost other loves along the way. I had no map
for how to make things work. No solid foundations on
which to build.

I lost my father when I was thirty, watched him lose
his faculties and his grip on life for years. Lost my
inheritance in a courtroom battle with the woman he
loved. Lost my chance to say goodbye at the funeral she
orchestrated, and my chance to hold onto his memory
when she took all of his possessions, buried his ashes
behind locked gates, and went off down south with
the family photos.

I lost my second baby in the womb. Watched it fall
away in blood and pain, staining the sheets.

I lost my little one's babyhood. Watched him turn
limp and grey in my arms. Nearly lost him for good
but he was saved to scream through years of hospital

stays and diagnoses of rare diseases.

I lost his father in those years. Years of stress had taken their toll on a relationship that wasn't strong enough to hold. He couldn't hack it. Why would he? Who would want to have to deal with all those sleepless nights, all those worries, with a partner who was shaken to the very core. And then I met a man. A man I loved. And he left too. He took a piece of my heart with him when he left. I felt broken.

And then, who would believe it? There was some justice. You came into my life like some kind of knight to rescue me. You showed me how to live and how to love again. You brought sunshine and laughter into my rain-filled existence, made me believe that somewhere, there was hope, that maybe, just maybe, I was allowed some joy. You told me I was perfect, that I was everything, that you wanted a future with me, that it would all be okay.

And then she died. My mum. The person who had always been there. Who gave birth to me and gave me roots. Suddenly she could hold on no longer. She filled up with liquid and cancer crept up through her body, strangling her until she could no longer speak or look me in the eye. She turned away and left the room, left me an orphan with just you to hold onto, my anchor in this alien world. Just you and me and the children and a hope for a future. It kept me going.

And then you went quiet, didn't reply to my messages. I thought you were letting me down, like men do. And then I found you, inflated like a black balloon on your bed, with blood seeping out of your body and everything was torn apart. Loss is so familiar to me.

And yet still this grief has surprised me. The force of

it. The rage of it. Like the time I got caught in a riptide in California and was pulled out to sea. Even me, the strongest swimmer I knew, who thought I was invincible, was powerless against its force. Or in New Zealand where the waves pulled me with them and tumbled me over and over like I was so much washing in the machine, dumping me on the sand and dragging me backwards so that my knees bled. I learned afterwards that you can't swim against those kinds of currents. You have to swim sideways if you want to get out of them, or else you are pulled out to sea, dragged by the undertow.

I haven't been able to swim against this tide of grief either, have had to succumb to the force of the water, allowing it to pull me way out where the life rafts can't reach me, succumbing to the waves, emerging exhausted and bleeding. Writing is a way of surrendering, whilst not quite drowning. Sharing is a way of waving to the people back there on the shore.

I suppose, in the end, what I didn't realise was just how much I loved you. I had downplayed it, kept it quiet, thought that shouting about it might jinx it. I had learned the lessons of experience and waded in gently this time, letting the water creep up slowly around me rather than diving in headfirst. You were doing the same. Love swelled between us and then crashed, subsiding like waves on the beach and we retreated, regrouped and came back together, over and over again. We would always have returned. The pull between us was like gravity. Hopeless trying to resist that force. We knew deep down that we were destined to be. Now I am all at sea. No one really knew what you meant to me. I didn't quite know it myself. I hope perhaps you did. I hope you know it now. I do.

Have I told you that I love you?

Funny that I don't remember the first time you said
that you loved me or the time that I told you.
In other relationships, it had been a 'thing',
who said it first and when.
With you it just didn't matter.
I didn't need the things I used to fish for;
I already had the catch.
I knew you loved me, didn't need the proof,
just needed your presence.

I remember standing on my doorstep in the early days,
arms around each other, saying goodnight:
'I'm very fond of you, Blacksmith Paul.'
'I'm very fond of you too, Beverley Writer.'

And I do remember the feeling,
spooned in your arms one night
with you holding me tight, saying,
'and I've told you that I love you?'
Smiling into my pillow as I said that you had
and your voice in my ear saying, 'good. Good.'
Funny though that I don't remember when.

Signs

AT THE BONFIRE that we hold for you after your funeral, I seek refuge in the tiny makeshift bathroom at the back of the house. There are no curtains or blinds at the window and I have a view of fields and sky. I can see the makeshift hutch where your hens used to live before the fox got them and imagine you pacing the hillside reading poems to the buffalo that graze there. These are the kind of stories that your friends tell around the bonfire while they drink beer and laugh as if the world hasn't recently been blasted to pieces.

I see a scrap of paper on the floor and I pick it up. It is a 'to do' list and in amongst the names and phone numbers, there are some words. They look like a poem. I read to myself and imagine I can hear your voice reading to me.

Rain falling on glass. The white sky is over my head, winds across my mind. My body is thought. In time I will be stretched across space and fill the void. Is this not our reason?

Skies, winds, thoughts. These are the places that I feel you close. You have left a space, a massive void in my life but memories and strange synchronicities, sometimes, temporarily patch up the hole. Sometimes it feels that there is a just a small gap between life and death and that both of us reside in a strange in-between world, our souls connected though our bodies are apart.

Sometimes there is comfort to be found in this. And sometimes there isn't.

I want to remember, I need to forget

IT'S THE LITTLE things that set me off. Like, I'm in Marks and Spencers buying school uniforms and I find myself walking past the men's underpants and I feel this crushing weight descend on me. I have no one to buy men's pants for. I never bought you pants. I never will buy you pants. Maybe I never would have bought you pants. Maybe you weren't that kind of man. Maybe we would never have had that kind of relationship. But it makes me sad anyway. For the rest of the day, I am trying to remember what you told me about the kind of pants you liked. You'd found a shop that had the perfect fit and you'd bought a load of them. But I can't remember which shop. I want to remember the name of the shop. Even though I will never go there to buy you pants. Even though, I feel now, that I will never buy men's pants again. I want to remember it because it is a tiny memory and I feel them slipping away. I only had eight months of you. I want to remember every detail, right down to the pants. The pants that I will never ever buy.

I need to forget the way you looked when I last saw you, lying three days dead on your bed, but I remember every detail of it. I could describe it with great precision, twist my words and wring my heart out to convey the exact hue of your skin, work out the perfect simile for the smell. But I won't. Because I don't want to remember you like that. I don't want other people to see you like that.

This morning, for some reason, I woke up trying to remember where we had been on the first day that we kissed. Before the walk. Before the walk that I do remember. The walk where we kissed. I asked you in my head. I find myself doing that these days. I find you answering me. It makes me happy that I can still hear your voice. But you couldn't tell me where we'd been. You just told me how nervous you were that day.

We'd been sending each other messages that week, both of us wondering separately where this thing between us was going. And then you said that if I came out to see you that weekend, you would wear your blacksmithing smock. I challenged you, said I didn't believe you had a blacksmithing smock and that if you dressed up I would come as Heidi. I remember that you sent me a picture. You were wearing a leather smock and holding a sign that read 'Eastmoor Heidi Fan Club'. I remember how it made me smile. I remember thinking, yes, this is a man that I can love. I remember showing it to friends and the excitement, waiting for Saturday to come. I remember wavering, wondering if it was too much to dress up as Heidi. Would it seem kinky somehow? Was it too soon? And then, at the last minute, I did it, because this was how we were together. Playful. I loved your playfulness.

I remember that when I arrived, shaking with excitement, you were round the back of your house playing the trumpet. You called it your alpenhorn. You were rehearsing. Didn't realise I was there. You came out into the garden, if you can call it a garden, laughing. Your face lit up when you saw me in my straw hat and petticoat. I said the dog was my goat. You took a picture. I wish I could find that picture. I wish I could find your phone. I can't remember if we hugged.

I do remember the walk though. I'd changed in your forge. I wish I could remember what I was wearing. We walked up a soggy path under a canopy of trees, nervously, sometimes alongside each other, sometimes single file. We slipped and tripped. We were both clumsy, both extra clumsy that day. When the woods gave way to a grassy hill, you held out your hand to me and I took it. On our first walk together, we let go, but this time we held on.

'Do you mind me holding your hand?' you asked.

'No,' I said, my heart jittering in my rib cage.

'Good,' you said.

You gave my hand a squeeze and I could feel you shaking. You stopped under a tree. Did you plan it down to the last degree? I'd asked you before: if you were a tree, what kind of tree you would be and you had pondered, waited, said that you needed to give it proper thought. I liked that you gave it proper thought. I imagined you would be an oak and so did you but, no, you said, you were an ash. I can't remember why but I know that you said something about healing properties and that you weren't sure you could claim to have them. I wish I could remember the whole conversation but all I can remember is standing beneath that tree, I presume it was an ash, and me saying that perhaps, I thought, you might have healing properties. I needed healing. And we hugged. Or did we kiss first? I can't remember. But we definitely kissed and we were definitely shaking, like we were fourteen years old again and this was our first kiss. Yes, I remember that kiss.

Things not to say: 'How are you?'

HOW ARE YOU? Why do we say this every time we see someone? It begs only one response. Fine. Or other pointless rejoinders. And how many of us are really fine? When someone stops me at the school gates and says, 'how are you?' as they're pushing a buggy with one hand and looking over their shoulder at a toddler, what do they want me to say? That I am desolate today, thank you. That I'm struggling. That my eyelids are a fragile dam barely holding back the torrent of tears that are waiting to fall as soon as they turn their back.

Unable to say fine, I sometimes say, 'up and down' and immediately find myself wondering where exactly the 'up' has been. I'm a writer and a pedant. Inaccurate words won't do. Rough to putrid my dad used to say. Maybe that would work. Down to desperate, maybe? Or perhaps I should say that I'm swimming on, but that there's an undercurrent of sadness pulling me under from time to time. Or maybe I should try a meteorological reply. Say that, at the moment, it's mostly clouds with occasional downpours and the threat of thunder.

I know they mean well and that I am bitter and unforgiving. That, if everyone ignored me, I'd feel worse. That it's just a British custom, like talking about the weather. But at least the weather is something we could agree on.

'Nice day for the time of year.'

'Yes indeed it is. Horrible time I'm having but at least the sun is shining.'

I wonder what the right question is. I'm still not sure there is one. Maybe 'what's been happening?' might be better, though that sounds a bit too hip and happy. But it feels more like an open question that invites a response: I'm feeling blue or, this week I've been sorting through his things. Or, as a friend said, 'how has this week been?' At least it's a question that suggests that this week has probably been tricky and full of complexity and that maybe she has time to wait for a lengthy reply.

If there isn't time, I don't know, maybe let me just get the child to school without asking how I am. Observe the clouds and the thunder on my face and steer clear. Let me settle him on his carpet space with a smile and let the dam burst when he's gone. And maybe later, when you have time, I'll tell you what's happening and how I'm feeling and that today, it rained again.

The fear of forgetting

I GO OUT for the first time in public. I'm not sure if I I'm ready but it's worth a try. I have got my crying over in my bereavement counselling in the morning and I've written earlier in the day so I think I might be safe from public displays of grief, think I might be able to handle it. I go to an outdoor screening of Baz Lurhmann's *Romeo and Juliet* and sit on striped deckchairs in the freezing cold April night. It is almost fun for a while. I have a nice chat with a friend, drink a glass of Prosecco, eat vegan nachos and watch a tragic love story unfold. I can relate to tragic love stories. It is fitting. I feel okay.

But then, when things feel okay for a while, suddenly, I don't feel okay anymore. I start to panic. I start to worry that I might be 'getting over' it, getting over you. I don't want to get over you. I don't ever want to get over you. When you really love someone, there's an urge to want that love to last forever. That's why people get married. That's why Romeo and Juliet got married. I want my love to last forever too.

It seemed so unlikely at first, that our love could last the distance. We had what you referred to as 'the lifestyle conundrum'. You had no responsibilities while I was drowning in the drudgery of single parenthood, living in a 'proper' house, caring for a sick child and a mother with terminal cancer whilst trying to run a regional arts organisation. You tried to end things before they'd begun. You were frightened of losing me. I was frightened of losing you too. We were middle-aged. We knew that life is not a fairy tale. We knew that things go wrong. Things had always gone wrong. But sometimes, we allowed ourselves to dream. I know you dreamed of marrying me. You said so. I felt it too. Not long ago we were standing hugging in my kitchen and I said, 'shall we just get married and live happily ever after instead of splitting up? I think it might be nicer.' And you said, 'yes, let's do that. It sounds much better.' Till death us do part. Death us did part. Way too soon.

And then, suddenly it happens. The man on the deck chairs in front of me leans over and kisses the woman sitting next to him. And tears start spilling over my eyelids. I curl up in my blanket and let them stream down my cheeks. I will never sit next to you like that. Never hold your hand. Never feel you lean over to kiss me. I am alone, longing to hold onto the past, not wanting to ever love again. But not wanting this to be the end of love for me. In limbo. Unable to go back. Not wanting to go forward.

It might seem strange in this culture where we want to avoid pain, hold it together, keep moving, but I welcome the tears. The tears make me feel close to you. The pain is a reminder of how deeply I have loved. I don't want to forget my love. I don't want to move on.

So, I stay in the moment, as we always did. In some moments, I can smile. I had some of those today. I sat with a friend outside a coffee shop and talked of the future. I even laughed. I thought I was doing okay again. Five minutes later, I burst into tears on a relative stranger. It's just the way it is. I haven't forgotten. I haven't moved on. But maybe, gradually, there are more moments where I smile.

I remember

MOSTLY I REMEMBER the way you made me feel.

'You have warm feelings for the blacksmith?' said the therapist.

'Oh yes,' I said. 'I have very warm feelings for the blacksmith.'

I had always had warm feelings for the blacksmith. I just didn't know what they were. When you phoned that day, on Ed's phone, I felt joy bubbling up like a spring inside me. Like I was more excited to hear from you than from him, even though he was one of my oldest friends whose presence in my life I had missed. But I had missed your presence even more. I just didn't know it. I miss your presence now more than I could ever have imagined.

I remember seeing you a few years ago, outside the gig. You were helping to move the PA for the band. I felt it then, that feeling, the warmth, the way I lit up around you. You told me that Ed had divorced, sowed the seed, I guess, which would lead me to get back in touch last year. I remember saying that I had no idea how anyone stayed married. I was tied up in the rope of my own unravelling relationship, unable to break free, unable to breathe. You said later that you felt so sad for me and so sorry. You didn't understand how anyone could make me feel that way. How anyone could allow me to be so unhappy. You cherished me, cared for me like I was a rare and protected species.

'You're special,' you used to say. Not in the way any old boyfriend might say it but in the manner of someone who was an authority on the subject, like it was an inarguable truth. And yet, even though you held me so close, I could still fly. You were a free spirit too.

'I know my heart will soar with yours,' you said. And it did.

I remember seeing you at the pub on that night back in August. You were wearing a brown patterned shirt that was shiny and didn't fit you. It was a truly terrible shirt. I remember taking it in and wondering if I could fall for a man in such a bad shirt. I knew I was halfway there already. Turns out I could. It worried you, that maybe I didn't fancy you as much as you fancied me because I'd said I wasn't bothered if you cut your hair or not. The point was, not that I didn't think you were attractive, it was that how you looked was pretty much irrelevant to me. I was in love with your soul and your mind. You were the most beautiful man in the world to me regardless of your wonky teeth or your holey t-shirts. You can buy a man new shirts and I did. But you can't renovate a man's soul. And yours was perfect.

You used to call me perfect. I didn't like it.

'I'm not perfect,' I used to say. 'I'm flawed like everybody.'

'Well, you're perfect for me,' you qualified.

I couldn't argue with that.

I remember the way you made me feel. Special, perfect, cherished. I try to keep that feeling with me now.

Love is a seven-letter word

WHEN I DISCOVERED that you liked doing crosswords and playing Scrabble, my head nearly exploded with joy. How I had missed having a man to play Scrabble with. Once we had discovered this shared delight, we played many times, mostly at my house but also on the mini-breaks we had together; you would neglect to pack food or clothes, but always remembered the Scrabble. I'm sorry to say that, when you died, I was in the lead. I know this will displease you immensely and that it was something you wanted to rectify. I'm sorry you won't have the chance. You will be pleased, though, to know that your mum and I have plans for a game soon.

I remember the day that we first played Scrabble. It was September. I know the date because it was the day of my son's fifth birthday party. After our first night together had left us confused and overwhelmed, we had agreed to go back to being friends but there was no question that we were still assessing the situation, that we were on probation. That day you notched up a few more points in the wider game that we were engaged in. You were on call all day to help with the building of the Ninja Lego birthday cake for my allergic son and you fetched bouncy balls from Tesco's for party bags, delivering them just in time for the party – as usual, I was running late. And then you waited for the evening when the children had gone back to their father's and you came round after the party for Scrabble. It seemed a safe activity, the board keeping us at a respectable distance from each other like a chaperone, the words on the board taking the focus away from the unspoken words that hung in the air between us.

I was exhausted and longed to curl up in your arms but instead we just hugged for a little longer than was decent and then set about playing the game. We debated the rules. You'd never heard of blank replacement. We had a different way of totting up the score at the end. But we agreed on the important stuff: no looking up of words. In my tiredness I knocked the board over at a pivotal point in the game and impressed you with my ability to completely reconstruct the whole board. I can still picture the scene. You sitting across from me on the kids' dressing up box. You always looked big in my living room, like some kind of Hagrid figure who didn't belong in a normal house. When you died, I found a description in notebook of the game that you had written. Funny to think that, to you, I looked small.

Her son's birthday party has left her tired leaving our choices diminished. We hug for a long minute – her lonely, I needy. Small talk, pictures on laptops, then we play Scrabble. We appear close-matched. I sit opposite her over the board and she looks small suddenly on a big sofa in a big room whilst I observe disembodied a fact in the room, not sure what to make of things. The game ends. It couldn't be better, a kind of quantum superposition of victory: by my rules she wins, by hers I win. Perfect.

It was. You were. Perfect for me.

This is how you loved me

Like an archaeologist excavating the lost city of his
   dreams,
an artist gazing on his Mona Lisa,
an engineer fascinated by the workings of my mind,
a musician who heard the sweetest song in my words.
Like the reader of a book he couldn't put down,
a pirate who had found the x that marked the spot.
Like the sun whose job it was to warm my earth,
the magnetic south to my magnetic north.

Without your love I feel like:
clumps of scattered mud,
a painting hung in an empty room,
a scrapyard full of rusty cogs,
tumbling words falling from a cliff,
a book whose pages have been torn out,
a hole in the sand where the treasure once lay,
the dark side of the cold moon,
just a pole, alone, all at sea.

I didn't just lose the man I loved,
I lost the man who loved me.

How would you love me now?

YOU WOULDN'T TELL me to hold it in, this pain, this love. Big emotions didn't frighten you. You would open up your arms like a harbour to hold the swirling waters, stay present while I cried. When I cried about my mum's death or the past or the contents of my mangled brain, you would hold it all. 'I've got you,' you would say. Perhaps you've still got me, now. When it felt like everything might fall apart, I would say, 'keep hanging in there' and you'd mimic hanging from a cliff by the tips of your fingers with mock-terror on your face. You would make me laugh and feel grateful at the same time. I couldn't scare you away. You weren't going anywhere.

Anything I needed was okay by you. If I needed to talk, you would stay up all night listening and if I needed space and rest, you would happily make yourself scarce. Too scarce, that last week, as it happened. Why did it have to be that week that you went? But you'd tell me not to torture myself about that as well. You wouldn't want me to make things worse with all these 'what ifs'. Things are bad enough without me heaping guilt onto the fire. You were always so kind. You would want me to be kind too.

You would tell me to get some sleep and to eat properly. You would ask me to bake some flapjack even though you can't eat it anymore. 'Don't stop eating flapjack just because I died,' you would say. 'It's so nutritious. It will keep you going.' You would send me soothing music to listen to and tell me to watch *Neighbours* even though it's a ridiculous habit. You would, of course, tell me to 'keep buggering on'. You would bring me a crossword to do to stop my mind from going down dead ends and you would write me messages saying, 'send me a poem, Writer Beverley'. You would love that I'm writing my way through this.

You wouldn't mind that I'm blurting out the contents of my soul on the internet. It wasn't your style but you loved my writing and you would be touched by the comments of support, pleased that through my words, I can reach out to others and touch their hearts as well.

You would take me for walks in beautiful places that soothe my soul and you would tell me to spend time with the people who make me feel better, who make me feel good about myself. And you would tell me to have no care for people who upset me. At the funeral, one of your friends told me that something he'd learned from you is that you always left the party without saying goodbye. He liked the way you did your own thing. You left this earth in the same way, completely unexpectedly, with no warning, no goodbyes. You would encourage me to do what I need to do to feel okay. To be on my own if I want to and to duck out of social engagements if I can't handle them.

The last time we went out you made up a hand signal. Four finger taps on your palm meant 'I need to go now,' three taps was 'let's go soon,' two taps was 'let's make love'. I did two taps just for fun and you pulled me to you at the party and said, 'Really? Right now?' And then we left. We could only do so much socialising. We went home to be alone together with our love.

Now, when I'm out and it all gets too much, I will remember to say to myself, 'I've done well, but it's time to go home now, back to the harbour of my memories of your love.' And you will welcome me home and make me turmeric tonic and tuck me up in bed.

'Let me be to my sad self hereafter kind'

(from Gerard Manley Hopkins)

When she needs to cry, let her;
there's no shame in weeping for all she has lost.
When she needs to be alone, make her a comfortable
nest and let her hibernate in it.
Play her soft music or let her hear the peace in silence.
Protect her from harsh voices and cold wake-up calls.
Give her the strength to say no, again and again
and nudge her occasionally, when she's ready, to say yes.
Let her stare at photographs and write endless words
   of love
and pain if this is what she needs to do.
Take her for walks in the places he loved
and let her feel the sun on her skin,
the wind in her hair,
the cool caress of water.
And, when she feels she can't go on,
remind her to reach out to people who love her and say:
'this is too much for me to bear alone.'

The Grief and Soggy Flapjack Society

TODAY I LOOKED at the house I'm going to buy. It's the one I looked at with you the week before you died. I pictured you building bonfires in the garden or tinkering in a workshop in the basement. We joked about you living in a shed at the bottom of the garden or sleeping on a camp bed in the cellar. You had a thing for unusual dwellings. It was a bit of leap for either of us to imagine you living full-time with me but we hadn't yet ruled it out. It is ruled out now.

Instead of spending my afternoon with you, today I spend it in a community centre in Pitsmoor at a grief writing workshop. It's not unusual for me to be in a writing workshop but, as I pack my pen and notebook in a bag on a sunny Saturday afternoon, the absurdity of it strikes me. How, one minute, grief is a distant cousin mentioned in anecdotes every now and then, and the next it has moved in, not just into the basement but into the house. How suddenly grief is part of my persona and now I'm talking to literary festivals about grief writing events and discussing with the bereaved the etiquette of grief TED talks and blogging publicly about pain. Whose story is this anyway? Do I have the right to tell it? Does anyone want to hear it? These are the questions we ponder in grief writing land. It's like the Jane Austen book club. But really sad.

One thing we have learned is that there is no rule book for grief, although there are many books about grief on display and I take most of them. Knowledge is power, or something, or something to do. The man sitting opposite me says he doesn't get angry. He doesn't see the point. But others rage against death like they are Dylan Thomas and it is the only thing to do. Some people, I know, sob their way through every day. Others remain dry-eyed, unable to squeeze out even a single dignified tear. Usually, I'm not one of them but today everyone but me cries as they read. I remain cool and detached. Maybe they think this is just a writing exercise for me. I don't look sufficiently grief-stricken, I feel.

The man in the grief writing workshop tells me that it is five years, four months, one week and three days since his daughter died of an unexplained cause. (I think about the blood and your brain and wonder again if they will ever tell us for sure what happened.) I apologise for not being able to remember how many weeks and days it has been since you died. It hasn't seemed important. I know that you're not here and that time is passing. I thought it was enough to know.

When I come home, I make flapjack for the first time in ages. For some reason, now I am compelled to count the days. It is imperative that I know when I last made flapjack. I check the calendar. It is two months, one week and three days. I made my flapjack every Friday ready for your arrival. I haven't been able to make it since. But today, I do. Today I am sufficiently together to mix ingredients in a bowl and put them in the oven. When it comes out, it looks strange. It hasn't set. It is a congealed mess, singed round the edges. Something is missing. It takes me a while and then I realise, I forgot the oats. It is not the same, without the oats.

Pieces of you

WE SPOKE ABOUT ashes before we'd even got together. I've no idea why. No one had died yet. In fact no one's death was even imminent. My mum's cancer was still pretty much in remission. Your Auntie Joan was chugging along. We weren't anticipating having to think about where to scatter ashes for a while. But that was the nature of our relationship. We covered most of the important topics in a few short months.

We were up on the moors above Redmires Reservoir. You told me about the family arguments over your father's ashes. (We were never even allowed to argue about my father's ashes. They were buried in his wife's garden and then she moved down south with all of his money and possessions. But that is another story and this conversation was about your father.) You were uneasy about the fact that he had been scattered in different places. We joked about the various ethereal body parts struggling to reach each other, longing to be reunited. I think, now, that you wouldn't want your ashes to be split and sent to the four corners of the wind, although I know how much you wanted to travel.

I remember this as your family discuss where to scatter your remains but, as usual, I'm not sure what my role is. I'm not your widow. We weren't married. We'd only been together eight months. Although your family make me feel so welcome, I don't have any rights. And everyone wants a piece of you. Everyone knew a different side of you. We all have different memories.

'Tell us one of your memories,' your friend, Pete, said at the bonfire, as I cried onto his shoulder, saying that no one shared my memories, that my memories all belonged just to the two of us. That now they just belong to me. So I told him this story.

We'd been walking at Wyming Brook, walking and talking. There had been a lot of talking. We weren't yet having a relationship. We were in some limbo between friendship and love, wondering where we were going. We spent much of our time wondering. Mostly I had been talking and you had been listening. Your listening was intent, you were thinking hard. I was laying it all out for you – the sick child, the bad separation, my mother's cancer, the heart-breaking ex, how hard it all was. I know you were there alongside me, taking it in, weighing it up, wondering whether you were up for the job. I remember us standing on the bridge staring at water then sitting on a bench, gazing ahead at trees, afraid to look each other in the eye.

It was getting late when we arrived back at the campervan.

'We should be somewhere where we can see the sun set,' I said.

'We should'.

We drove to the car park at Redmires and raced the sunset up onto the hillside. We lay down side by side on the heath. I turned onto my side so that I could watch the slow descent of the sun on the horizon and you did the same. We were two spoons, lying a respectable distance apart. There was no one else around and all was silent, save for the sound of the breeze in the long grass, making a soundtrack to the movement of clouds across sky which gradually deepened to a rosy pink. The air grew cool as the sun sank. I shuffled back towards you to share your warmth and you put your arms around me. And we lay there until all the brightness had gone from the sky and I was starting to shiver in spite of the heat between us. And when we stood up, you held out your hand and we bounded down the hillside, joined together, the blacksmith and the writer, at the end of another perfect day.

If it were just up to me, I would scatter your ashes right there in that spot where we lay. I know for sure that there, in that moment, you were perfectly content. You told me so. Life doesn't get better than a moment like that. But you were fifty-three. You had other relationships, other lives, other beautiful moments. I can't keep you all to myself. And so the discussions about who should have your anvil and which tree should be planted where continue, and we talk about benches by the sea and by the reservoir, discuss whether to free you to the wind or bury you in one spot. I don't know where you will end up but I know this much: whatever we decide, there will be a piece of me that is forever yours and I will keep a piece of you forever in my heart. And that spot, that piece of ground, will be forever ours; that memory shared, now, by the people who read, by the people who listen.

Some days these are the only words

I really loved you.
I really miss you.
I wish you could come back.

How could you leave?

Ｈ OW COULD YOU leave when we were still in love, when passion hadn't faded, when there was still so much to do? We hadn't yet had time for familiarity to breed contempt or even indifference. I hadn't tired yet of your stories, you still hung on my every word. The air between us was full of longing, the magnetic pull between us so strong. It was like you ripped my skin off when you left, though no one could see me bleeding. And this longing still scrabbles about like a crab with no shell, searching for its home.

If you were going to die, couldn't you have left it, at least, until the trees were losing their leaves? So we could have seen all four seasons together. At least, that way, I could relive them each year on a rota. It would have been more poetic, a better title for whatever this is: *365 Days With the Blacksmith*, or *The Year of Love*. They could have a made a movie of it.

And why would you die in March? What were you thinking? Were you in cahoots with the grief police who think I should get this grieving lark over in a few short weeks? It would have been convenient. I could have grieved in the snow and been reborn in the Spring. April Fool. As if it could be so easy. Did you not consider how it would feel to see new life bursting out all over when all I could know was death?

And couldn't we at least have had one sunny day to paddle on a beach, one June night gazing at stars, one outdoor swim, one warm moonlit night, one festival, one camping trip, one barbecue? Is that too much to ask?

And, seriously, how could you leave me of all people? Me, who has been left and left and left again. Couldn't you have stayed long enough to understand that I have abandonment issues? Didn't you promise me that you had at least twenty years in you? That you were as strong as an ox? That, even if we weren't lovers, you would always, always be there for me, always be my friend? You did. I remember it. You promised.

We never even had time to have an argument, for God's sake. Just a tiny blip that one night when you rolled away from me in bed, your feelings hurt. Do you remember why? Of course you do. I was saying that I was worried because you were older than me that you might get sick or die. I didn't mean this year. I meant in ten years. Or fifteen. Or twenty. I started to cry and you rolled back towards me and held me tight because you understood. That I couldn't take any more loss. That I couldn't risk loving you only to lose you. 'I've got you,' you said. You said that if we got married we could have a pre-nuptial agreement, absolving me of caring duties. I'd seen too much of hospitals, cared for too many sick people. You said you would spare me any more of that. To be fair, you did. No hospitals, no sickness, no deathbed scene or slow farewell. Just a loving goodnight message. And then silence. And blackness. And a longing that has no home.

I know you didn't mean it. I know that leaving me and this earth was the last thing on your mind. I know now what I knew already, that there are some promises we can't keep, even when we want to. That it wasn't in your power to stay. And I know you didn't leave me empty-handed. You left me with our love still intact, went out on a high note, before anything could go wrong. You left me with a love story, short though it was; maybe a novella instead of a saga. And you left me with a love that continues beyond the last page. But still, how could you?

Because you love me

B ECAUSE YOU LOVE me, I will find the strength to carry on. Because you lost your life, I must somehow find a way to value mine.

One day, when time has passed, I hope that people will be able to look at me and see your presence instead of your absence.

At the moment, your absence is more tangible than my own being. I am just fragments of myself stitched together with pain. I am sad eyes, grey skin, tear-tracks and shaking limbs with a gaping wound where my heart used to be. Your loss is threaded through every fibre of my body. This body that you loved.

One day, perhaps the world will see the shape of you in the way I can keep loving even though I have no reason to trust love. In the way I will build a new life moment by moment and never give up hope even though life has let me down so many times. In the way I value myself, knowing that, at least once, someone whole-heartedly understood me and loved me and thought I was wonderful. That someone wanted to stay even though their wishes were denied.

You nearly gave up hope, but you picked yourself back up and started to live again. You felt I was your reward for your faith in yourself and in life. I know you wouldn't have missed it for the world even though life was so unbelievably cruel to you again. I wonder if you could keep going if it was I who was gone instead of you? I don't know. But I know that you would want me to keep on going.

If people could see you in me they would see a person whose heart was still open. Who loved and lived until the end. Who cherished the little things and a moment of beauty amidst the pain. Who kept on learning and exploring. Who laughed in spite of all the madness and sadness of the world.

I hope one day that will be me. It won't be today. It won't be tomorrow. But, one day. Maybe.

Love is knocking at my door tonight

She peeps through the window and sees me
sitting pale and silent in the old armchair.
She isn't sure if I will let her in.
Truth be told, I'm not sure myself.
I'm used to a different kind of visitor –
the uninvited guest who pushes past me
regardless and refuses to leave.
The house is already full of them –
sorrow, pain, death and loss hanging around,
putting their mucky paw prints on the furniture.
'I come in peace,' she whispers
through the letterbox.

I won't say I welcome her with open arms –
my arms are too tired –
but I unlock the door, leave it ajar
and she follows me into the kitchen
on a breath of spring air.
'You sit down, my sweet,' she says
and puts the kettle on and
while it boils she strokes my hair
and hums a soothing lullaby.
She can see that I have had enough.

'It's not fair, is it?' she says.
'It's more than one person can bear
to have a lifetime's sorrow in a few short years.
You seem like a really good person.
You didn't deserve this.'

I nod my head and let the tears flow
and know that everything she says is true:
not fair, too much, had enough.

She takes a tea bag from a box that I haven't seen before.
The label reads, 'For emergency use only.'
For some reason it surprises me
to find that it has come to this, a state of emergency,
but I drink it anyway and it soothes me.
Love wipes the dust from the surfaces,
arranges daffodils in a vase,
opens up the curtains a crack
to let the light in.

The doorbell rings and I start to get up.
'No,' Love says. 'You rest. I'll get it.'
She picks up a broom and sweeps the visitor
off the step before I have even seen them.
'It was no one important,' she says,
'The people that matter will come back tomorrow.'
I nod again and drink my tea.
Love seems to know what I need.

'Right,' she says. 'Off to bed.
Leave the washing up. It can wait.
You've a busy day ahead:
swimming, walking, writing to do:
the things that nourish you.
Oh, and those two, the little ones
with the curls, round cheeks, bright eyes and freckles.
You need your energy for them.
Keep them close and they'll hold you too.'

I get up from my chair and walk to the door,
prepare to see her out,
steel myself for the tears that always come now
when I say goodbye.
But she is sitting on the kitchen chair
with her feet on the table doing a crossword.
'Sleep tight,' she says. 'See you in the morning.
I'm moving in, if that's all right?
Someone needs to look after you.'
I nod again and smile.
'Goodnight.'

SUMMER

(JUNE – AUGUST 2016)

hanging by a thread

The wall of in-between

If you are the one who died,
why is it that I feel myself to be a ghost?
The sun's rays shine straight through me as I sit
like a spectre on the wall of in-between.
You opened a door to the other side
and now it won't quite shut.
I fear that if I close it,
I might lose you forever.

Sure, I know how precious life is,
I have seen first-hand how tenuous our grip
but how can I live wholeheartedly when half
of my heart is on the other side of the wall
and the only access to it is through that door,
the door I cannot go through,
the door I cannot shut?

I want to seize the day –
it might be my last after all.
But the day I want to seize is a day with you in it
and the days we seized together
are numbered now and finite.
There will be no more.

So I sit on the wall with the door ajar
and hope for a time when
I might keep your presence
with me in the whole of my heart
and be wholeheartedly present,
my outline solid as the sun sets again
on a day well-lived.

Swimming through clouds

TODAY IS SATURDAY again. Saturday was our day. From the first Saturday when we walked over Redmires and discovered our abandoned house, I have spent almost every Saturday with you. Until suddenly you weren't there to spend them with anymore.

On Saturdays, I still walk out onto my street and see you walking towards me like a mirage. I see you today, as on other Saturdays, but today I don't cry. Today, somehow, I have reached some new stage of grief, some kind of acceptance that Saturdays are no longer the days when I expect you to arrive. Your absence no longer surprises me. But I still see you there, parking your van and walking towards me smiling. And I still feel derailed for a moment by the remembrance that your solid form is gone.

Saturdays used to go like this. I would walk with the children to their drama class and take the dog in Chelsea Park and then, sometime after that, you would knock on my door. Loudly. You always knocked loudly, even when the children were in bed. I'm not sure you were a person who could have done anything quietly. You had a touch of the dramatic about you. In the early days of our relationship you had a habit of prefacing any announcement by saying my name in a booming voice that would make a drumroll of my heartbeat. I was terrified that you were about to break up with me. But usually you were warning me that you might need to leave half an hour earlier than usual or that you might need something to eat. It became a joke between us and I started to do the same. 'Blacksmith Paul,' I would say. And you would hold my hand and look earnestly into my eyes while I said something mundane such as, 'Would you like to go swimming with me tomorrow?' You would always say yes. I would always say yes. It was always easy to make plans because we always wanted to do the same things and neither of us much cared what they were anyway, so long as we were hand in hand.

I remember the first time we went swimming together. I took you on a free pass at the gym. You were already in there when I arrived at the poolside. We were still at that stage of the relationship where I would look at you curiously from time to time, wondering who you were and how we had come to be here. I had that feeling then, watching you swimming towards me. Instinctively, I dived underwater and swam like a mermaid along the bottom of the pool, feeling the tiles slide under my belly as I had done as a child. You did the same and we emerged, laughing in the middle of the lane and I had that thought again: 'Who is this man and what is this thing between us that needs no words?' It was like a dance. All of it was like a dance.

It was inevitable that, before too long, the dance and the swimming would merge and we would develop a synchronised swimming routine. We were in the pool at the holiday cottages at Brimham Rocks in February. We had three whole days together. (How precious those three days feel now.) We had the pool to ourselves and spent some time perfecting a manoeuvre in which you hoisted me above your head, with my arms outstretched and span me around until I was dizzy and laughing. I remember it vividly. The utter joy of it. The recognition of how rare it is to be so in tune, harmonious, melodious with a fellow human being. We sat under the stars in the hot tub and talked while the wind howled around us and our noses froze in the cold night air and we lost track of the time and nearly got locked in the showers.

After open water swimming, there are no showers. So says the trainer at the Yorkshire Outdoor Swimming Club where I go today. You have to get in slowly to allow your body to adjust to the temperature and get out slowly too. A hot shower, like a cold dunk, can send your body into shock. Or so he says. Grief can send your body into shock as well. It has been over two months and I still feel the vibration of grief in every nerve. The physicality of this grief has surprised me. It is unlike any grief I have ever known. And I have known a lot of grief.

We had planned to go to the club at Harthill together and I wonder today what you would have made of it. Neither of us are really 'club' people. Neither of us like following the rules. (Are/were, like/liked – I'm not sure still which tense to put you in). In the end there aren't too many rules anyway, but they do make me wear a wetsuit for the first lap of the orange buoys. It is so tight I can't breathe. They let me take if off once they have seen that I can swim and then I feel free. It's the way I like it, with the water against my skin. I hate things that interfere with my senses when I'm outside. It used to make you laugh, the way I wouldn't wear gloves to pick up snowballs, the way I won't wear sunglasses, the way I hate the idea of headphones. I want to see it all, hear it all, feel it all, just the way it is. Even when the way it is can be too much.

I swim off on my own into the water, leave the wetsuit crowd behind, dive down and resurface, looking up into the sky. I don't know what it is about this moment. It isn't the freezing water. It might perhaps be the lack of clouds or the brightness of the sky. Or perhaps it is the way I pause for a moment to pat myself metaphorically on the back for being here without you, doing something that I love. But I start to cry out there in the middle of the reservoir. I miss you Blacksmith Paul.

I miss you

When things go wrong, I miss you.
When things go right, I miss you.

There's a crick in my neck and I miss your hands
to iron out the bumps and knots.
And yesterday I went to the gym
and there were men there, your age
being alive and well
and I couldn't lift a thing because the weight
of grief is so heavy and my muscles feel wasted.
I feel wasted by sadness.
It is so hard to describe it,
so unbelievable,
the way in which I am still
shaking,
vibrating with it all,
the way in which sometimes all I can see is
that you are not there

and I couldn't hold back the tears again
because it was Tuesday
and you should have been there
meeting me at the gym for a swim
and you were not there.
You were not there.

And last night I watched singers sing
and it was beautiful
and I missed your hand in mine
so I held my own hand,
held myself together
and couldn't believe that you weren't there.
You should have been there.

And I have this thought every day:
Can we just stop this charade now
and can you please come back
so that I can stop being such a sad drama queen
and get back to living and loving you?
It is just farcical
that you are not here.

And, today, I got the best news
that the house of my dreams is mine
(fingers crossed, please help me,
I need it to be mine)
but all I can do is cry
because I saw it with you
and I saw you there
in the garden building bonfires
and I want to call you and tell you the news
and you are not there.
You are not there.
You will not be there.

The stories we tell

U NLIKE YOU, I have never been a reader of science fiction. I haven't studied quantum physics or
pondered the conundrum of parallel universes or time
travel. I was six when I last watched Dr Who. But suddenly I find myself wondering about these things now.

Today, I drive out to the Peak District with my children on the first really hot day of spring and imagine,
as I often do, the narrative in which you didn't die. In
this narrative, today, you come with us. I would have
introduced you properly to the children by now and
things would have been going well. For the first time,
perhaps, today, we are like a family in the making. I feel
you sitting next to me as we drive out of the city and
picture you paddling in the stream with the children,
trousers rolled up, a giant in a mini adventure of stones
and leaves and water. I see you studying the rocks that
my son collects, watch you carry the sticks that he finds.
You acknowledge to him that the big one is indeed like
an evil emperor's staff, the little one like a sword and
the knobbly one a walking stick. You demonstrate each
one in turn and agree that it is essential that he brings
them all home because that's the kind of man you are. I
imagine us sitting on the picnic blanket and you telling
me stories of your childhood trips to Padley Gorge and
you tell me the story about wrestling some dog in the
water, the story that Ed tells. We are like all the other
families out here today enjoying the sunshine. It is a
lovely day. Except for the shadows.

My memories of the last week of your life are plagued with shadows. I was about to introduce you properly to the children that week. But something happened on that last Saturday to make me question things. I remember it again today as I sit on the picnic blanket, looking up at Longshaw where we had walked. I was feeling sad that day and worried about your brain. I felt there was something wrong with you but we reassured ourselves that it was I was just grappling with memories of my dad with his brain tumours and my brain-injured ex who had left the year before.

A few days after you died, I had an epiphany and suddenly I found a new narrative and, to my grief-stricken brain, it all made sense. In this narrative, the whole of my life had been leading up the moment of your demise: the father with the brain tumours, the sick child and the heartache of the ex-boyfriend with the brain injury were all part of a complex plot. I had thought he was 'the one' but I had misread the signs. He was a red herring, a plot twist, a foreshadowing of the main event. You were 'the one' and all of these previous tragedies had been some kind of universal training programme. In fact, I was put on this earth purely so that I could recognise that you were ill and save your life. In this narrative I had failed spectacularly. I was hysterical in my kitchen sobbing on my brother's shoulder. I should have saved you. No wonder Joan Didion called her widow's memoir, *The Year of Magical Thinking*. My writer's brain was piecing things together, looking for a narrative that made sense. Even if it left me and my survivor's guilt as the villain.

The notion of parallel universes may or may not be magical thinking. Apparently, the theory has some backing by scientists who believe that consciousness outlives the human body and transfers into another realm upon death. I find this a more comforting narrative. In this narrative your death was simply the opening of a door from one universe to another, a fork in the road, a pivotal point in a Choose Your Own Adventure story. In this narrative, you slipped, in a moment, out of this universe and into a parallel one where you are living in some different form, exploring some different realm. You were an adventurer by nature and there is no question that you would have loved to explore a different dimension, although I still like to think that you would never have chosen that path over the one you could have walked with me.

You sometimes talked about the narrative you would have chosen. The one in which we got together at the first opportunity, eighteen years ago. In this narrative we would have got married and had children. We spoke about it in the campervan on the way back from Knaresborough. Unusually for me, I was the cynic, joking with you that you would have been too messy and disorganised and that I would have been stressed and impatient, worn down with childcare and housework and eventually I would have fought you for custody of the children. You didn't like my version of the story.

'What about my version?' you said. 'The one where I get to gaze adoringly at my beautiful wife and baby. The one where we live happily ever after?'

'It's better this way,' I said. 'This way we get to retire together and have the bookshop by the sea.'

'I like that version too,' you said, though you still wished that you had passed on your genome, the little genome with a pointy hat.

I think about the various narratives and think it might make a good novel or a film and then I realise it has been done multiple times: *Sliding Doors*, *The Time Traveller's Wife*, *One Day*, *The Versions of Us*. We've all wondered at times about the paths we didn't take, about the role of fate or chance in the narrative of our own lives. We all want things to make sense. But life is not a story and the ends aren't always tied up neatly. There isn't always a scene of redemption or a silver lining to the cloud.

Weeks after you died I sent you a message saying that I wished we could start again and do life properly. Did I think you could read it? Did I think we could travel back in time? Had my magical thinking come to this? The truth is we can't go back in time and do life properly. Even if we could, we've seen *Back to the Future*, we know the risks. We can't have the narrative that we wanted. But we did have this.

Today, a friend sent me an email. She'd been reading my blog and had to stop because she found it so painful. But she said the words of Raymond Carver kept coming into her head:

> *And did you get what*
> *you wanted from this life, even so?*
> *I did.*
> *And what did you want?*
> *To call myself beloved, to feel myself*
> *beloved on this earth.*

You were beloved and so was I. And as people keep on telling me, not everyone can say that.

Saturdays and Tuesdays with
Blacksmith Paul

I'm reading *Tuesdays with Morrie* at the moment.
I can only read about death.
I can only think about life and death and love.
I can only live in the heart of this pain.

I haven't been able to watch TV since you died.
I've tried a few times but there is nothing that doesn't
    freak me out.
Even *Neighbours* is too distressing for me now –
people keep falling in love or breaking up or being
    reunited
or getting sick or living or having accidents or getting
    married or dying.
Fictionalised, it's all too much for some reason.
I want to escape but instead I find more comfort from
    writing and reading,
even though it means diving headlong into heartache.

Turns out Morrie would approve:
By throwing yourself into these emotions,
by allowing yourself to dive in, all the way,
over your head even,
you experience them fully and completely.
You know what pain is,
you know what love is,
you know what grief is.

And then, maybe, one day,
what,
no, it's too soon
to even think about
letting go.

I watched a bit of *Anne of Green Gables* with my
    daughter,
tears spilling from my eyes.
My Gilbert Blythe is dead.
My happy ending is gone.
Nothing is safe.

Our days were Saturdays and Tuesdays.
Saturdays and Tuesdays with Blacksmith Paul.
It's not as catchy.
I need to work on a title
for whatever this is.

Every day we had was precious.
'One day,' you said. 'We're going to have a bad day.'
But we never did.

Life Interrupted

'C AN I GET a word in?' you would say.

'No,' I would reply, not used to being interrupted. I wasn't accustomed to being with someone who had so much to contribute to the conversation. You always had so much to contribute. You still had so much more to give.

'What can I contribute?' you said in a message. You were in a state of panic and self-doubt. It was the day after we'd been to the Yorkshire Sculpture Park. The poppies were on display there and we'd abandoned our plans to go to the coast in favour of a shorter day out.

We explored the landscape, walking and talking and taking photographs, recording the moments. You stopped to look at the birds circling in the sky, wandered off like a giant wading blacksmith-bird into the mud, regardless of the warning signs. 'Please don't sink,' I cried out after you, knowing that there was no way I could rescue you.

We covered a lot of ground: our grandparents' experiences of war, the price of metalwork, the wonder of sky. And the important stuff. You were auditioning for a permanent position in my life, though we were back to just friends and there had been no public advert, nor formal application procedure. We sat on a bench, enveloped in green, gazing at water and I asked you those all-important questions about your previous relationships, why you'd never married. You talked of your parents' divorce, your cynicism about true love, how you'd just never really wanted marriage, how engagements had never turned into weddings. You just hadn't quite seen the point.

'Do you ever just hear yourself, saying "will you marry me?' in your head?"' I asked later, one day, as were lying in a bed of love and the words were circling like birds in my mind.

'I do,' you said. 'All the time.'

You said you wanted it with me. You said it was the first time you'd really felt that way.

'I don't want something that just lasts ten years,' you said.

We walked up the path to the Long Gallery, hand in hand. (We were always hand in hand, though no contract had been signed.)

'What are we doing?' I suddenly blurted out, unable to contain it any longer.

'I think we're moving towards something,' you said, holding my hand a little tighter and gazing seriously into the distance, at the long view.

More than ten years.

You wanted forever.

Do you have forever now?

I sit in a cafe in Hay-on-Wye. We never came here but your presence fills every gap in conversation, every note of music, every bookshop shelf, every crackle of wood in the campfire. If you hadn't died, you would be here with me now. It would have been our longest stretch of time together. You would have loved every moment. I should read festival authors but, at night, I return to my books on grief, and the only words I write are memories of you.

'Don't look on it as a life interrupted,' says the author

I am reading, quoting astrologist Patric Walker. 'Try to think of it as a life completed and then you can take it with you for the rest of your life,' It resonates with me. I write it down. But it still feels like you walked off mid-sentence, sank into the mud, were snatched by the wind to fly with the birds where I cannot reach you. Maybe your life was completed but your death has interrupted mine. I don't know where I'm going anymore. I don't know who I am. I take pictures of heart-shaped clouds and iron bowls of fire and I keep you with me as I promised, waiting for a sign to follow into the future.

Through your lens

I'VE NEVER HAD a decent 'author' photo. It's been okay because I've never really quite seen myself as a proper author. I never thought I was good enough, as an author, or as anything really. I've always been plagued by self-doubt. It was something you and I had in common, along with the difficult fathers. But when I published my first book last year, I thought I'd better make a website and I struggled to find one of those suitably enigmatic portraits that authors have. So I cobbled something together using inadequate snapshots taken by friends. Sometime after we got together, I asked you if you'd take a good author portrait for me but you never did. Like so many things we had planned, we never got round to it. Or so I thought.

And then I found a photograph amongst the files on your laptop after your death and instantly thought that here it was, a gift from you to me – the author photo that you never took. It is extra special to me because, though you'd never shown it to me before, strangely, you had written about it in a message to me, the message that you sent me when you were wavering about whether you were good enough for me. It was taken in the Yorkshire Sculpture Park last October on the day that we got together (for the second time!) This is what you wrote:

I was looking at one of the pictures I took of you yesterday on the bridge where the poppies are. I could eulogise. I'm not going to though, except to say that one of the qualities I saw there seemed to be a tremendous maturity and yet last night as I looked at you I saw a completely different face, youthful, angelic almost, such grace. I am overwhelmed.

So am I, when I look through the photographs that you took of me. Somehow, looking at myself through your lens, I see a different version of myself. I can see myself the way you did. And the gift isn't just the pictures to put on my website and on the jackets of the books that I must now write, it is the gift of having been truly loved. I can see myself through your eyes and know that, just as you were, I am loveable. I am good enough. It is the most precious gift. Thank you.

In love with your ghost

I DISCOVERED 'our song' this week. It is a song by Martha Tilston, called 'Seagull', and I saw her perform it at the How the Light Gets In festival in Hay-on-Wye. It isn't a sad song about loss. In fact, it's a song that captures perfectly the confusion and excitement of falling in love and it reminded me vividly of our own process of coming together. And, even though you weren't physically there, I knew that you thought it was perfect too. And that made me happy. And I felt joyful because the feeling of being in love was, for me, so alive as I heard it. And I sang it joyfully at full volume about ten times while I was driving until the singing gradually got drowned out by the tears when I remembered that you're not here anymore and I am in love with a ghost. And then the tears ran dry as they always do eventually and I made a mental note to ask my bereavement counsellor if it's a bit dysfunctional to still be in love with someone who died three months ago or whether this too is a perfectly normal part of grieving.

I am discovering that it is a strange business when the person you are in love with dies. There isn't really anything quite like it. There are other deaths and other losses, but nothing like this.

When you lose a parent (and I have lost both), you're not expected to look for someone else to fill that gap. Your father is still your father and your mother is still your mother. You won't ever have another one and that's okay. There will always be a hole in your life where that person used to be but you will talk about them with other friends and relations and they remain there with their names intact: my mother, my father.

Some say the worst grief (and I can believe it) is to lose a child. I've only lost a tiny foetus and that was hard enough. It must be unbearable to see your child leave the world before you, even if your child is an adult. Nothing, not even another child, can replace the loss of the unique individual that you engendered. And you will keep their photo on the mantelpiece, maybe even keep their room as a shrine to their memory. They will stay in the same position in your heart for all eternity.

And if your friend dies, even your really good friend, you can still talk about that friend, maybe with other friends, and the gap will be there just the same because there will be some things that only that particular friend would have understood. But you will have other friends and maybe they can grow to hold the weight of the friend who is missing. Probably they won't feel too insecure to be your friend. Probably they won't worry that you loved your dead friend more than you love them. Perhaps some really good friends might even hold your gaze while you talk about your departed friend without looking away embarrassed or changing the subject. Because we want to honour our friends by remembering them. That's not dysfunctional. That's right and proper. But when the man you are in love with dies, what are you supposed to do?

I was forty-four when we met so, although you were certainly up there with the big loves of my life, I had been in love before. And being in love has always ended but not like this. Usually, in my experience, love is slowly eroded over time, by the attrition of arguments and resentment until you can't imagine that love was ever there in the first place, or until love is just a pale, sad memory, or the dim glow of embers. Separation usually follows and then there is sadness and pain, but soon the embers die down and there is just ash, or, if you're lucky, love is replaced by the fond glow of friendship that carries on into the future. Of course, for some really lucky folk, the 'in love' stage mutates into a deeper, long-lasting love – I'm not so experienced with that sort of love. And sometimes, someone leaves you abruptly with no warning and it feels like your heart has been shattered into tiny pieces. But there is still a sense to be made of it. Friends come round with bottles of wine and tell you that he didn't deserve your heart in the first place and though you might rail against it, at some point there is only that truth: he didn't love you enough so you must let him go, put your heart back together piece by piece and wait patiently for the man who does deserve you to arrive.

I did all of that. And then you arrived, on cue or perhaps a little too soon for my liking. I was still healing from that kind of monumental heartbreak and I wasn't ready but it turns out you had to arrive then otherwise it would all have been too late. And, it was just like that song, our song: true love flew in through the open window like a seagull. And it bashed about and freaked us both out and yet, we couldn't stop smiling. And like Martha Tilston we closed ourselves up from time to time and almost ran away. It was too big to handle. We had all those feelings: 'should I stay, should I go, should I even be here?' But in the end we opened up and we stayed and it was beautiful and terrifying all at once. And it is these words that I sing so loudly:

'you are beautiful, you're beautiful, you're beautiful, you're beautiful.' Because it is, in my head, the only word for you and I never told you when you were alive how beautiful you were. You were such a truly beautiful soul. And 'I love you, I love you, I love you, I love you, I love you, I love you, I love you. I really really do.' Because that is how it was and how it still is. My love for you doesn't diminish because you died, in fact, in some ways, it has continued to grow. Our love was growing, rising, expanding, full of energy and potential. And even though you are gone, I still feel your presence. And as I talk to your friends and family I am still learning about you. I am still in relationship with you. My love for you has not died.

And yet, you are physically gone. And joy is replaced by sadness again. And if I keep talking about you as my boyfriend or partner, people will think I am weird. And if I make a shrine to you, I will definitely be seen as weird. And when I talk about how much I loved you, how much I still love you, even now some people turn away and change the subject. I feel like there's an expectation that I should, somehow, get over it, look forward, move on. And even as I write about you I know that I am bringing you back to life again and then grieving all over again when I close my laptop. And I wonder if I could ever make room for another love and if another love could love me, the person who is writing publicly about this lost love. And yet, I love you, I love you, I love you, I love you, I love you, I love you, I love you, I really really do. We have moved from a lifestyle conundrum to a metaphysical conundrum and the process of grief is an unending cycle of joy and pain, love and loss. The seagull bashes about and freaks me out and sometimes, even now, when I remember you and when I feel connected to you, I can't stop smiling. And then the tears come again. I don't know when it will stop. When a love hasn't run its course, how can it ever stop?

The people we meet in heaven

THIS MORNING WE were running late for school. It was a sunny day and the dog needed walking and so I decided to breakfast in the park. Such are the perks of the freelance writer. While I ate, I sat watching a little girl chatting with her grandmother over breakfast. The girl had plaits and sunglasses. She was interested in my dog who was sitting at her feet salivating. The grandmother and I shared pleasantries about the sunshine and the dog. My mum must have been like that, I thought. I remembered all of the days that she had looked after my own little girl while I was working, the way she was so focused on the child, the way grandmothers are, like there is nothing more important in the world. There is nothing more important in the world, I thought. Suddenly I couldn't help myself. 'My mum used to look after my children,' I said. And, then, before I knew what I was saying, I said, 'she died.' And the woman said something about time being precious and no one knowing how long they had and she tried to wish me something positive, 'you have a nice dog,' she said. And I walked away crying, thinking about the precious time my mum had shared with my children and the influence she will have had even though her time with them was short.

It took me by surprise a little, this sudden grief for my mum this sunny morning. My grief for that loss has been eclipsed by this new grief for you. I had barely had time to process it before I was in shock, left reeling.

Your loss was so brutal, so visceral, so unexpected.

I lost my mum in stages. I had time to prepare. And yet it was still unexpected when it came. She had bounced back so many times and was so determined to live that even I sometimes thought that perhaps she would go on forever. Perhaps we are never really prepared even when we know that death is inevitable, unavoidable, a fact of life. It's a fact of life that no one wants to talk about, especially not my mum.

We never met each other's mums during our relationship. At our age mothers get jaded. They have welcomed too many partners. They raise their eyebrows when we mention a new one, wait to see if it's serious before they get too interested. This one was serious as it happens. Very serious.

Although you and my mum never met, you were often in the same building, separated only by air and doors and staircases. The narrative of my mother's death runs in parallel to our love story. It's impossible for me to believe even now that you are both on the other side of a one-way door, that you followed her so quickly out of this world. But I know it's true. I went to both of your funerals and your ashes sit in two separate jars, waiting to be scattered, memorials to both of you still need to be planned. It would be comforting to think that you have now met but my magical thinking only takes me so far and not to a world where you are sitting together taking tea and chatting about the good old days.

Your mum had never drunk tea, she tells me. She had a phobia about it. It used to bewilder you. But she has started drinking chamomile tea now. She wanted to have her first cup of tea with you. It's another thing she will never do now. So she drinks tea with me and we talk about you and the air is thick with love and grief and loss. We know a thing or two about loss. We are not fine. We are not getting over it any time soon. We're okay with that.

When your story first collided with my mother's it was not a good moment. We had spent the night together for the first time and that morning, you had sent me a message saying that you thought we should just be friends after all. I was shocked. I was so sure that you liked me. I couldn't understand what had happened to make you change your mind. And then, just as I'd got the children to school, my mum phoned to tell me that she couldn't breathe and asked me if I could take her to hospital.

The next time, we were 'just friends' again. We had talked things through, slowed things down. I had told you that I couldn't handle you being unreliable, not just now, with all this going on. We'd been for a walk on a Tuesday night. I was in the middle of cooking curry. You were playing DJ on my laptop, when my mum phoned again to ask me to take her to hospital. I didn't want to leave you, was overwhelmed with emotion. I walked over to you and half-hugged you, half-kissed you, not sure what I was doing. We ate tea quickly and said goodnight.

The way you stood by me and supported me is one of so many reasons why I loved you. I had a new boyfriend when my dad suddenly started dying, twelve years ago. I'd been to see him in hospital. He was brain-damaged and confused me with his wife. He started trying to take my clothes off. I went to see that boyfriend on the way home. I needed a hug. He dumped me after that. He said I was giving off 'negative energy'. He didn't want that in his life. But you sucked up that negative energy and left me replenished with your love. You spent Tuesday nights sitting in your van or in hospital cafes while I waited to see consultants. I kept saying sorry. You kept reassuring me. You had a book. You were fine. You were always fine so long as you had a book and nothing was more important to you than me and the mum that needed me.

You almost met at the launch for my first children's book. The chemotherapy seemed to be working and my mum was out of hospital and in good spirits. You were loitering in the background because the children were there. For such a big man you were surprisingly good at loitering unobtrusively. I wanted to introduce you but I was busy being an author and looking after the children and my mum was so proud and so happy to be out, chatting to my old school friends. The moment just never arose. The next time you were loitering was three weeks later at her funeral. In the same room again.

'I wish I'd met your mum now,' you said. 'She seems like she was really special.'

'What about your mum?' I said. 'Maybe I should meet her.'

'You will,' you said. 'Let's arrange it.'

Instead we arranged it ourselves, the week after you died, building new connections in our mutual grief – the ones who are left behind. I have lost a mother and lover. She has lost her eldest son. Nothing about it will ever be okay. But we reach out to each other across a sea of loss. 'I won't ask you how you are,' she says. 'We don't do that do we, you and me?' Instead we skip that bit and we sip our chamomile tea and we remember.

Perfect for me

'HOW DO YOU just keep getting better and better?' you once said, as we'd discovered yet another shared pleasure. It was something we observed regularly, this amazing compatibility we had and yet, when you re-joined the dating site that I was on, just in order to view my profile, I didn't even notice you, didn't actually recognise you, would certainly not have considered you as a romantic prospect. And yet, there it was, an irrefutable, wonderful, easy connection between the two of us that did just keep getting better and better.

'Are you like, just my perfect man?' I asked as we were walking along Ecclesall Road. 'You tick all my boxes.' I don't think you replied, just smiled and held my hand a little tighter, walking with an extra bounce to your step. You'd just told me that you'd quite like to learn to tango. I had always wanted a partner who would learn to dance with me. We hit a slight problem when you realised that the tango lessons would be at the Millennium Hall; you'd had an altercation with the manager having parked your van in the space reserved for religious officiates, but, hey, it was a small obstacle.

That week we had been exchanging letters. You had sent me your letter saying that you wanted me more than anything in the world and we had just spent the afternoon negotiating the terms of our new agreement, no longer just confused friends or lovers, but two people embarking on a proper relationship. We had walked along the road into town that evening chatting, holding hands, feeling content and we had found ourselves next to some kind of pub in a marquee where a band was playing and we'd stopped to listen. They were playing 'What's Up?' by the 4 Non Blondes and we sang along, muddling up the words and laughing at our mistakes, dancing together in the cold night air.

Next, I took you to a memorial evening for the poet, Ann Atkinson, testing you out in a strange setting (I was to take you to a few – book launches, literary nights, funerals, gatherings of mothers and small children). You performed beautifully. You chatted to my friends and members of the poetry world as if it were perfectly normal for you to be found sipping wine on a Saturday night in a room full of poets (you had ironed your only shirt at my house earlier and put on your smart trousers, not having learned at fifty-three that just because both garments were dark blue, it didn't mean they went well together). You sat in wonder all evening, absorbing the words of the poets, letting them fall like snowflakes around you, holding tight to me all night long as if you feared I might float off and never return. (I have photographic evidence. The only photos in existence of the two of us together). And at the end, when the poetry had stopped, my friend who was compering, suddenly said, 'I feel like we should dance' and as the band struck up the music to 'Dream a little dream of me', you immediately stood up and offered your hand in invitation. And I took it and we danced under bright lights at a poetry evening as if it there were nothing odd about it at all. And something fell into place that evening. The next day, my friends who had been at the evening were asking who you were, and my friend's mother-in-law spoke with confidence:

'He danced with you,' she said. 'that's a really good sign.' And it was. A really good sign.

Signs

PRINCE DIED RECENTLY. I guess you know that now. Of course, I like to believe that you are up there with him and Bowie dancing at some kind of celestial uber-party. It's what we do, a way to ease the pain. A sign of the times. Suddenly we believe in heaven and souls and signs, temporarily parking our cynicism and opening up to the possibility that our physical life is perhaps, after all, only one aspect of the whole. This is how it feels to me now.

Bodies may be separated but I believe souls roam free and sometimes I feel your soul is still in communion with mine. Sometimes I sense that you are close by and I see signs of you still in nature. The other day, I lay on the ground looking at clouds and asked you to do something for me and the clouds shifted to form a heart shape. And as I walked away, I saw a heron (like the gates you made) on the river and I just knew you were there. Don't ask me how I think you control clouds and birds as I have no idea. But I feel you when you are around. I read that psychologists call it animism, imbuing meaning into creatures and objects, the grief-stricken mind constructing a false reality. But what do they know really? They think love is all about wanting to marry your father.

I often feel closest to you when I'm outside, in the places that we went. A few weeks ago I took a trip to Redmires where we first walked. Just as I was arriving your mum phoned. She was pleased I was going there. She said you'd spent many happy days there as a family. We were talking about memorial benches and how she couldn't get in touch with the right department by the beach where we had discussed scattering your ashes. It's a long way for her to go and a big job. I said I'd have a look online when I got home. I got lost on my walk, didn't find the place I was looking for but as I was walking back along the road, I saw a man. He was about your age, sitting on a bench surrounded by daffodils, his head upturned to feel the spring sunshine, eyes shut. He reminded me of you, standing in the park, eyes shut, head upturned, basking in the sun. We should put the bench here, I thought, so that your mum, who can't walk, can come and sit on it and feel the sun. I phoned her and she thought it was a wonderful idea. I felt happy and I felt your happiness radiating down on me as if you were pleased that you had set me a riddle and I had succeeded. Yes, I'm sure that your soul is still in touch with mine.

Your mum feels your soul too. She tells me that she feels you are more at peace now and not quite as sad as you were at being torn away from this world. She doesn't know how she knows it but she says it is like someone has just told her and that it feels true. On your birthday, I take her out to look for a spot for your bench at Redmires and suddenly, out of the blue she says, 'Paul would have loved to see you dressed like that. I don't know how I know it, but he would. He would have called you his little wood nymph.' And she laughs at herself because the words feel so odd in her mouth. 'Wood nymph is a nice thing isn't it?' she asks. And we look at each other and smile because, of course, that is just the kind of thing you would have said. And I look down and realise that I am wearing the skirt that I wore when I dressed up as Heidi, on the day we first got together and that I haven't worn it since. And my heart sings with the closeness of you.

I tell my bereavement counsellor about some of the things I have felt. 'A lot of people tell me things like that,' she says. I tell her about the skirt and what your mum said. 'That must feel so real,' she says. And then she throws up her hands like she is sick of this charade. 'Well, it *is* real,' she says. We have slipped through that window again and we don't understand the science of it but some things are bigger than us, bigger than science. Love and death and grief are unfathomable. In our cynical, empiricist culture, we just don't have the words.

Stardust

Today, no cake,
just this ache

and space.

I write 54 words
instead of lighting candles:
53 for each birthday missed,
one for this day
missing you.

Blacksmith Paul is
in the Great Bear now
and stardust rains like
love below.

With memories held tight,
particles of light:
we form a constellation

of you.

Who can reminisce with me?

Y OUR MUM IS talking about your family, the people that I never met. She mentions Auntie Ethel.

'Did he tell you about Auntie Ethel?' she asks. 'She used to pinch his cheeks.'

I beam with delight and picture myself sitting on your knee and squeezing cheeks that were still pinchable even though you were fifty-three.

'Stop it,' you said, batting my hand away playfully, 'you're like Auntie Ethel.'

It thrills me every time I talk to someone who knew you and realise that, at least in some ways, we knew the same person. Another time, I am out in my campervan looking for a spot for the memorial tree with Rodney, who you used to plant trees with. He mentions the day that you planted the big tree in Broomhill. And suddenly you are sitting alongside me in the same campervan and Rodney is texting you and asking if you'd rather get up early to do the planting or do it late at night. I tell Rodney that I remember this conversation and we both agree that there was no question of you getting up early for anything.

These moments for me are rare and precious because, before your death, I only knew one of your friends and you barely knew any of mine at all. I hadn't met your family and you had only crossed paths briefly with mine. Nobody really knew us together. It makes me so sad that nobody knew us together. If we had had a few more years, even months maybe, I imagine things might have been very different. I imagine people telling me how great they thought we were together, how they could see from the way you looked at me how much you loved me. I could take things further and imagine them saying how they never believed you would get married and what a surprise that, at your age, you finally settled down. How you turned your life around – not that there was anything wrong with your life – but that you changed it, because of me.

Instead sometimes I have heard your friends say that you lacked commitment. People have questioned whether it could have worked in the long run. They're not sure, I know. Sometimes I'm not sure either. We weren't there yet. But I knew from the way you looked at me how deeply I was loved and I truly know how great we were together. And I know that you wanted it, all of it, and that you wanted it with me. I know that, for you, at least as you saw it then, I was the one.

But nobody knew us together. There are no wedding photos to keep on a mantelpiece, no shared stories of day trips or holidays with friends. Our memories are all just mine now and the only photos are five pictures of us captured in the background at a poetry reading. 'You look like you're the only people in the world,' your friend said when he saw the photos. And that's how it felt. And now it's just me. I am the one left behind. The only one who can tell the story. I reminisce alone.

Maybe that's how it always is. Maybe, even when we lose the same person as someone else, we actually lose someone different. My lover was someone else's child, someone else's brother, someone else's friend. We all lost something different. We all grieve alone. But how happy it makes me, just for a moment, to share that loss with someone else who lost you too.

Reconciliation to the impossible

I KEEP COMING back to the matter of time. If time is a linear concept, we had eight months. For you, they came at the very end of your life. I try not to wonder now about the length of my life, I don't have much taste for it. But the thought comes round now and then. What if I live until I'm ninety? What if this is just the mid-point and I have forty-five more years to live without you? What if, at the end of it all, I look back and think, 'that was the best bit', that you were the true love of my life. What if your image is still sitting there at the end of it all sparkling like a solitaire diamond on the plain platinum band of 'the rest of it'. What then?

'We're the right people at the wrong time,' you once said. I can't remember when you said it but it was a recurring theme, this matter of timing. It was certainly the wrong time for me. I was only six months out of the most heart-breaking relationship of my life. I wasn't ready to get involved with someone new. I was messing around on OK Cupid, flirting with virtual suitors, enjoying the ego boost of being pursued by hundreds of random men, just trying to forget him. But I wasn't ready for anything serious. It troubled you. This is one of the things you wrote:

26.9.15 – *Prior to going on a walk with Beverley*
I preface these remarks by saying I have never known a woman, indeed anyone, who has made me question my

relationships with them in such detail. I seem to have long periods of analysis and then a sort of summation. For instance, my latest one is 'Reconciliation to the Impossible' being the realisation of my unsuitability for Beverley. I am currently mulling over why a woman who seems to yearn for company has none, clearly she must be rejecting it. Surely not all of her admirers are unsuitable?

You certainly thought that you were. You couldn't see yourself through my eyes. You didn't see the funny, kind, intelligent, interesting, attentive, beautiful man that I could see. You only saw obstacles. You saw the huge disparity in our income and our responsibilities. You saw your eccentricities and foibles: your ramshackle living space, your unique lifestyle and peculiar habits (garlic sandwiches, midnight walks, sleeping with earplugs in after years of living in inner-city workshops, foraging in skips for fragments of metal). You didn't see that unique is amazing in a world of middle-aged men whose weekends are ubiquitous lycra and Netflix. Yes, those hundreds of men were unsuitable for me.

'You don't have to spend every Saturday with me,' you said to me on that walk. That was the week after we'd got together and then gone back to being friends. It was all a bit irrelevant really, whether we were a couple or just friends. A rose by any other name would smell as sweet and this thing between us was as sweet as sweet could be. 'I know I don't,' I said. 'But I want to.' There was nowhere I would ever rather have been than with you. I know you felt the same.

'Sometimes, I just can't see how it can work out,' you said. 'But I love being with you so much. And the things we do: the walks, Scrabble, collages (not just

153

the sex). It just feels so right and so good.' And it did. And knowing that something was 'right' and 'good' was new for me. It was something people had said to me so many times over the years. 'You just know,' they all said glibly, like they'd been to some secret school of Hollywood romance in which the hero is announced with an appropriate backing track and a big Cupid's arrow over his head. But it just wasn't like that for me. I never 'just knew' anything. I was still in therapy trying to figure it all out, trying to work out which things matter in a relationship and which things don't. I had made so many terrible relationship mistakes. Life and love have not been straightforward for me. So, of course, I still had doubts but I was working through them. As one friend said, 'But you doubt everything! I've never known you doubt anything less than your relationship with Paul.'

I got there in the end, wrote my closing letter to my therapist a month after you died. This is part of what I wrote:

Paul's death has totally clarified for me what I knew deep down all along. That it is the heart and soul of someone that matters and external success, superficial looks, money etc are of very little consequence to me. I'm absolutely sure now that he was plenty good enough for me and that I wasn't making any kind of horrible mistake. It is just horrendous for me to lose him now that I know that. I felt like I'd finally found the kind of love I needed and now it's gone again. He was far from perfect but he was wonderful for me and will be very very hard to ever replace.

It is true. You will be. Which brings me back, eventually, to the matter of time. We were the right people, no question. As for the timing. Who knows?

Maybe we could have had better timing. It turns out, perhaps, that you were a ticking time bomb. If it was already written, that you were going to die then, on March 10th 2016, how perfect, in your narrative, that I came into your life again when I did, that the last eight months of your life contained some of the best bits. That you went out on a high, knowing that you were truly loved and knowing what it feels like to truly love someone else. As for my narrative, it is I who am left now to reconcile myself to the impossible. I who is left to ponder the possibility that maybe time is not linear. That maybe quality of experience is more important than quantity. Maybe the quality of your love will last as long as I do and permeate all I go on to do. At least I 'just know' now what love is. A woman in my writing group was talking this week about a previous relationship and *The Eternal Sunshine of the Spotless Mind*, one of my favourite films. There are relationships that, if I could, I would erase from my memory. But not ours, not ever. It was beautiful, rare and precious, like that diamond, built up of perfect moments that shine out in their brilliance even now in the darkest days.

Because

Because you fetched bouncy balls for the party of the
  boy you hadn't met,
packed tiny, strange curios in an antique tin for his
  advent calendar.

Because you saw the beauty in my daughter's gesture
  and matched it with your own:
she gave her shells to her brother for their Grandma's
  coffin,
so you gave her the loveliest shell she'd ever known.

Because, when she died, you came Christmas
  shopping in Meadowhall
even though it was your idea of hell.

Because you brought me books that you thought I'd
  like reading
and shared music that I might like listening to.
Because you always, always listened to me too.

Because you carried wood and an axe up a hill in the
  dark
to build me my own personal bonfire for New Year.
Because you brought a paper lantern and a marker
to write to my mum in the sky.
This is why.

Because you gave me a lift home when it was cold and
    dark and I was tired.
Because, when I was with you, for once, I didn't have
    to be in charge.
Because I didn't care where I was going with you by
    my side.

Because you paddled in the sea in December
and walked through bogs without a care.
Because together we barely ever spent a penny
but knew there was no one richer.

Because you were strong enough to cry and show your
    feelings.
Because you left me with no doubts about your
    feelings for me.
Because you had a collaging kit and weren't afraid to
    use it.

Because, though you couldn't offer me a seat in your
    living room
you had the world at your fingertips.
Because you could play me a tune or show me the
    stars or read me a poem.
Because you knew what was really important,
what was important to me.
Because I knew how important I was to you.

Because you could accept me, just as I was.
Because you understood.
Because you were so very very good.

'You are such a lovely man,' I said.
'I hope you know that.'
It was the week before you died
and you were opposite me in my living room
though usually we were side by side.
You wavered, too humble to accept a compliment and
    then,
eventually replied:
'Yes, I think I do.'

It is true.
You were.
The loveliest man I ever met.
I don't know how I will ever replace you.
What am I supposed to do now
without you?

The tightrope of grief

EVERY DAY I walk a tightrope in the darkness over a gaping chasm. I have no idea where I am trying to get to as there is no light out there to aim for but I know I must keep moving, edging tentatively towards some kind of unfathomable future. It is a balancing act, I am told, between grief and recovery. Spend too long looking at the chasm and you risk falling into the blackness, never to return. But run too quickly over it and the darkness will eat you just the same, perhaps slowly or unexpectedly. Perhaps at some point in the future when you think you are sitting safely on the other side on a sunny patch of grass, the ground will open up and swallow you whole without warning. You can't escape from this kind of grief. The only safe way to go is carefully, inch by inch, breath by breath, word by word, day by day, putting one foot in front of the other, hoping (and yet I dare not even hope anymore) that one day you will be glad that you kept going, that one day you might reach the other side.

The best way to keep your balance on a tightrope is to focus on something directly in front of you which is fine by me because I can't look too far ahead; the emptiness is too overwhelming. So I put things in my diary, not because I look forward to them, but because they keep me looking forwards and, sometimes, looking forwards keeps me from falling. And sometimes I fall anyway. I don't yet know my limits in this new world. I have to test the rope to find out whether it can take the weight of me and this grief that I am carrying, this unwieldy monster that I haul around with me in the dark. Sometimes it is sleepy and well-behaved and I can carry it gracefully; the crowd don't even notice the beast on my shoulders. And sometimes, they notice it and are impressed that I can still tiptoe onwards with such a burden on my back. But sometimes, it is wild and wakish and it pulls me off-balance. And when this happens and the rope is slippery and the spotlights are too bright in my eyes, when the noise of the band and the crowds is too much, I go down. And you, my safety net, are not there to catch me. Luckily, at the bottom of the chasm there is water. Luckily I can swim. So far, I have not drowned.

I have started to compile a mental list of the things I can do so that I can put them in the diary and keep walking towards them. These are the things I can still do: writing, swimming, walking, talking about you, talking about grief, reading about grief, leading writing workshops, talking about work, reading stories to the children, getting children ready for school and bed, listening to music, playing games. I hope that I can move house. The new house is like an investment for the future, a pleasant place for some future self to dwell in some future life where there is joy. This week I added tennis to my list. I grew up playing tennis and the memory of how to play is strong: hold racket, move legs, hit ball. Repeat for an hour. Success.

This is the current list of things I can't do: keep the score whilst playing tennis, drink, go to the gym, watch TV, read normal books, make flapjack, manage money, listen to the news, listen to other people's problems, talk about other people's relationships, not talk about you, make small talk.

I have never been good at small talk but now I feel completely inept. I can't get my face or the tone of my voice to match my words and find myself smiling whilst explaining breezily to strangers that I recently found my partner's body and that my mum died too and that's it's all been a bit tricky. But, hey, I'm lucky that, because everyone is dead, I have money and so I get to buy a lovely house. And they don't quite know what to say and I try to change the subject and then they start talking about their families and I realise that I can't bear to listen to them. I try to join in with conversations about partners and I fall back on the conversational female staple of comparing experiences and then I remember that I'm talking about someone who is dead and that no one wants to hear about the sex life and domestic habits of someone who is dead.

And if people are talking about their divorces, I have no empathy anymore because death trumps divorce every time and I know because I've experienced both. I am positively, twistedly smug in my misery. It feels ugly and unkind and not at all like me. Even when people talk about illness I lack sympathy and for a moment I find myself thinking, hey, worst case scenario, they're only going to die and death looks pretty appealing to me compared to this farce. We're all going to end up there and right now, that feels like a blessing. Death holds no fear for me. It is living that scares me. I would have hoped that all this tragedy would give me empathy but at the moment I am self-absorbed and all off-kilter, tumbling off the tightrope under the bright lights while I feel the audience is staring aghast.

So, I walk home crying and long to curl up in your arms because you get me even when I'm weird, but you are not there and so I curl up with your fleeces again and realise that, for now, socialising is on the 'things to avoid' list.

And then I wake up and get back on the tightrope and put one foot in front of the other again, walking towards some unfathomable future. And as I walk I am so grateful for the people who walk alongside me and for the ones whose hands form a safety net beneath me and for the people who fill the gaps in my diary and listen to my self-absorbed, inept talk. And I am so grateful for you and your love, the tiny light in the darkness, that tells me that, even now, I am beautiful and wonderful and enough.

In love for the last time

BEFORE WE'D EVEN got together, you made us
a shared Dropbox. I liked the way our names sat
next to each other on it, like guests at a wedding feast.
First you shared photos of our days out but then you
started adding music to it, trawling your extensive
collection for songs and albums that you thought I
might like. And I did always like what you put in there:
music, like surprise parcels, waiting to be opened.

The first album I discovered this way was *Love for the
Last Time* by Experimental Aircraft. I listened to the
first track, 'Symphony', over and over again, carried
away on the melody, in sync with the lyrics, listening
out for a message in the words, a hint at your intentions.
Maybe it was there and maybe it wasn't but the words
haunt me now. I told you that I loved the song and you
agreed that you loved it too. I think we loved it for the
same reasons; we shared more than a Dropbox, even in
the early days.

We'd both had a fair few relationships. You were a
late starter so you'd had less than me but probably still
more than you would have wished to have. Even when
you were younger, you didn't realise how attractive
you were. At your funeral women from your past told
me how they had waited, hoping for you to notice
them, but somehow you didn't notice them noticing
you. You lacked confidence and took rejection badly,
found it hard to take the chance, but you told me that
you had never given up hope that one day you might

meet someone special. I know that you felt I was the someone you'd been waiting for. I'd never given up hope either but I was as scared as you were. We were a couple of old romantics who had learned the hard way that love doesn't always end with a happy ever after. When you get to our age, you become tired of endings, wary of new beginnings. Why even start something if it's just going to end? As Experimental Aircraft put it, *'We wanted to be in love for the last time, the kind of lasting love, we could not seem to find.'*

The other day I was driving in the countryside to meet a friend for a walk. I went the wrong way and almost reversed into a river as I tried to turn round. It is par for the course these days. I am not safe. When I'd rescued myself from the brink and we were walking, I found myself reflecting on my own death. 'Who would give my eulogy?' I asked my friend. I am the Queen of Eulogies. I did my grandma's, Dad's, Mum's, yours. I know how to make a funeral really special. I am so good at it that I have considered making a career out of saying goodbye. But I felt a sudden new kind of desolation (who knew there could be so many?) that, if I died, I would be no one's love. There would be no red roses on my coffin and you would not be there to mourn me, the way that I mourned you.

'He would still be your love though,' said a friend and, of course, she is right. Our love did exist. We might not have been married but we were together, at least until we were parted by your death. Other relationships had gone wrong but ours never did. This time we did not fail. This time, we took a chance on love and we flew. You were in love for the last time and, though you weren't wrapped in my arms when you went, you were wrapped in my love. Everyone who came to the funeral knew it, it was written in the local paper and now I write it for all the world to see: Blacksmith Paul, died 10th March 2016, beloved soulmate of Beverley. I don't know if it will be the last time that I will be in love but I am glad that, in some small and tragic way, you got what you wanted: a pure love, unbroken, that will last for all eternity.

Casualties of loss

THE TOW HOOK on my campervan is deeply embedded now into the metal bumper. I have reversed into things so many times since you died that I have lost count. Driving is another activity that has become hazardous. I remember the advice I read online for the recently bereaved: if you are crying so hard that you can't see where you're going, pull over. Once or twice I had to. But it's not so much the tears that alter my perceptions, it's that my whole awareness has shifted. My focus has changed. Objects in the rear-view mirror should appear closer than they are and yet I am looking so far back into the landscape of my memory that I run into them constantly. Reality hits me, like a brick wall, time after time. My eyes aren't on the road ahead anymore either. Instead they are looking into the past or searching for your presence – in clouds, in trees, in the faces of passers-by. I still look for you even now. Today, I actually stopped and walked back down the street and peered at a man in a red van. There was something about him. I just had to check. Maybe you hadn't swapped this life for the next, but had just changed your profession and the colour of your van. The driver nudged his mate and they laughed.

The week my mum died, I ran into the back of a man in a shiny white car. He was cross. It was a new car, he said, like this changed everything. He really didn't want to have it repaired. I apologised, handed over my details, explained that I was stressed. His car was the least of my worries, though I didn't say so. A few days later I put diesel into the tank of my vehicle by mistake. I ground to a halt a few yards from the petrol station though it took two young men from the local garage to suggest that perhaps this is what I had done. I sent you a message with a sad face and you replied immediately: 'stay there. I'm on my way.' I had never been so happy in my sadness as I was to see those words, to see your face when you pulled up alongside me, to feel your arms around me in your warm brown fleece, enveloping me with love and care. Being looked after is not something I am used to. It was a treat to see you during the working day and my tears turned into laughter as they always did when you were near. We sat in the campervan together, snacking on Waitrose provisions – stuffed vine leaves, chocolate rice cakes, millionaire shortbread. It was the closest we ever got to a camping trip, parked up at the end of Ecclesall Road, waiting.

You waited alone for the rescue vehicle while I went to see my therapist. 'You go,' you said. 'you need it today'. I didn't need to explain. You understood. You always did. The death had been a shock even though we had been waiting for it for six long years. I needed to talk it through. 'I'll be fine,' you said.

Later you watched with glee as the man pumped the fuel out of the tank, intrigued by the mechanism, asking questions while I hung about, content, just then, to be a dumb girl. I couldn't understand anything the man was saying. Grief can do that too. He taught you how to use the gas conversion and I let my mind wander, knowing that you had it covered. I have no idea now how to do it. I've no idea how to fix the pump either. That too has broken since you left. I thought it was broken once before and you said you'd have a look. While you were fiddling, I realised I hadn't turned the electricity on. We said you were the catalyst that made it work. You were a catalyst for a lot of things. I just needed to have you around and things were okay.

Since you died, it seems like everything has broken. It feels right somehow that things are grinding to a halt without you. First it was the TV. The reception went fuzzy a few weeks after you died so live TV was gone. Which made sense. Why should the TV be live when you weren't? Luckily we still had Netflix and On Demand, but some time ago, that went too. Turns out we can't always have what we want at the click of a button. We were down to watching the old DVDs but a week ago the DVD player froze. The drawer won't open anymore and *Rise of the Guardians* is stuck forever now. Now nothing plays at all. The silence is comforting. The landline went down in sympathy a while ago as well and though the broadband stutters into life every now and then, often it fades away, like it too is tired of the effort of keeping going.

My mobile is still working though I dropped it heavily soon after you died and the screen shattered so badly that I could no longer see what I was typing. I don't know when or where I dropped it. There are great holes in my memory. It is another thing that isn't working. My daughter and I have been playing Mastermind with a second-hand game but I have no recollection of buying it even though I know we haven't had it long. I often have no idea what I have been doing from one day to the next. I liked the shattered screen on the phone; the pattern had a certain beauty to it – like a butterfly or a spider's web. (I search for meaning in the strangest places now.) For months I have avoided repairing the phone as if fearing that somehow if I got it fixed it would be a sign of 'moving on', 'letting go', 'getting better'. I like the visible symbols of what your death has done to me.

There have been other casualties too. As if losing you were not enough, I have lost a friend or two. Not everyone is comfortable with broken things. Other friendships hang by a thread. I struggle to relate to people in the ways I used to and common reference points have fractured, though I have gained new reference points and new friends too. Some people come closer, while others retreat. My world is rearranging.

Soon after you died, I was crying so hard as I tried to phone a friend that I spilled boiling peppermint tea all over my thigh. I couldn't get up quickly enough, was in too much emotional pain to quite feel the urgency of the physical pain, too scared of my emotions to put the phone down. By the time I'd realised how badly burnt I was, it was late at night and my leg was swollen, raw and blistered. Hordes of friends on Facebook offered advice, while neighbours got out of bed to deliver aloe vera plants and people offered to babysit while I went to A & E. I was swamped with care. It is easier to help a friend with a burnt leg than a friend with a broken heart.

Today though, I fixed the screen on my mobile phone. One day I will repair the bumps and bruises on the van and maybe I can find someone else to fix the pump. Perhaps, when I am strong enough, I will even be able to sit for long enough at the end of the phone to find out, via the call centre in India, what is wrong with the broadband and the TV. But the scar on my thigh will always be there and the scar in my heart will be there too. Maybe I will move on one day and maybe things will get better, but I know I will always feel this pain. Because this pain is the other side of love.

The safe place

I SIT IN the counsellor's office and I cry as I try to explain, again, what I have lost. You have left great holes in the fabric of my life. My Tuesdays and Saturdays are blank spaces in the diary now and the ping on my phone no longer makes my heart sing, although I still check, sometimes, in case it is you. (They say the stages of grief are cyclical, not linear, and denial still shows up from time to time.) There is no one to say goodnight to now and no ongoing conversation. In each exchange with another human being, I am starting from scratch again. There is no adult that I speak to every day, no guarantee even that I will speak to any one person from one week to the next (except your mum, strangely, who I didn't even know in the before.) Mostly, I feel too tired to make plans, too grief-stricken to socialise, too absorbed in my sadness to relate to other people's struggles, too detached from the real world to connect. But I don't want to be alone because when I am alone your absence overwhelms me. And so I make those plans to walk towards even though really I just want to be walking towards you.

I miss my safe place, I tell her. It is the place where I don't have to work to be understood. Where I am automatically understood and where being myself is all that is required, where just being me is more than enough. I don't really want to go to the cinema, or the theatre, or to a gig or to the pub. I actually don't want to do anything. I just want a lazy day with nothing to do and you alongside me doing nothing too, in a world where we were like Piglet and Pooh and the only goal was honey. I want to lie in your arms all day and forget the real world. You were the real world for me.

I have often been told that I don't live in the 'real world' or that I have my head in the clouds. The phrase resonates more strongly now that I find myself gazing at clouds searching for your presence, knowing that our last words were about clouds, that you had your head in them too.

We were so alike, you and I, not from the outside but the outside is of no interest to folk like us. We live internally, we live from the heart and the imagination. Myers Briggs tests describe us as 'dreamers, healers, mediators'. We were both INFP (Introverted iNtuitive Feeling Perceiving.) I didn't know until this week that it was such a rare personality type, just knew that we were alike and that the thing we had between us was rare and special. Apparently only 4% of the population are INFP. Apparently, for our type, 'the risk of being misunderstood is high'. Apparently when we find like-minded people to spend time with the harmony we feel will be 'a fountain of joy and inspiration'. And it really was.

I don't want a busy social life or a full diary. For an INFP that would be stressful at the best of times and these are the worst of times. I just want my safe place, that rare and special connection, the place where I can relax with my soulmate from the tiny 4%. And so I find myself angry that you have been taken away and depressed about being alone and sometimes, I am back in denial, talking to the clouds saying, ' Are you there? Can you hear me? I miss you. Can't you come back? Please, can't you just come back?'

The reality of this grief

SOMETIMES I IMAGINE that my body is full of water. Someone has left a tap dripping inside me and each drip is full of grief and love and memories of you. They say the female body is sixty per cent water, but at the moment it feels more like ninety per cent. I am at least ninety per cent grief. Still. Almost four months since you died. Grief is my constant companion. I feel the water sloshing around inside me constantly and it makes me feel unstable. The noise of the dripping is like tinnitus that I can only drown out temporarily and I have to tread carefully to stop the water from spilling. The longer I go without talking about you, about it, the more the water builds up, the drips getting faster as the day goes on. Eventually, I am full to the brim with grief and it spills out in tears. I am still crying every day for you.

Today the tears came as I was standing in a sandpit at a children's party and a friend asked, with genuine concern, how I was doing. I don't know what I said but the tears and the words came unbidden and with them the relief that I feel when I am allowed to talk about it, to say to someone, 'this is how it feels', to share, just for a moment, the unbearable pain that somehow I am expected to bear, that somehow, I am bearing. I want to tell people about it again and again. I want to tell them how awful it was to find your body; how terrible it is to have to live without you; how painful it is to have loved you and lost you so soon; how horrendous it is to have been the person you shared your dreams with; how your unfulfilled dreams are carried in my body now, like the weight of that water.

But I have told everyone I know all about it. This isn't news. And yet, somehow, for me, the bereaved, it is. Somehow, when you have lost someone so close to you, that person dies again and again as you wake up each day and with every day, they just get more and more shockingly dead. It isn't getting any easier, in fact it is getting harder, I guess because denial has retreated and I am facing the reality that you are never coming back and that somehow, I have to build a new life without you.

When some people see me crying and hear me still talking about you four months on, they look at me with concern. Their usual response is to ask if I am still seeing my bereavement counsellor. They look relieved when I tell them that I am: at least the professionals are involved. Others ask if I have seen my GP, the implication being that perhaps I need some pills, that this sadness is not normal, that it is out of proportion to the loss. Sometimes I wonder if they're right. The professionals tell me they are not.

Part of the problem is the length of time we were together. We were only involved for eight months. Sometimes I remember the break-up calculation that someone once gave me. Theoretically, according to someone, it should take half the length of the relationship, to get over it. By this logic, I should be over it by now. How great that would be. To be able to put it neatly away in a box, along with the other failed relationships and move on. But this isn't the same. You didn't leave me for another woman, we didn't get bored of each other and we didn't hit that point where we realised that it just wasn't going to go anywhere. You died, completely out of the blue and disappeared from my life without warning. It is a huge loss.

And yet, I am not a widow. We weren't married. We hadn't even established whether we would ever get married, or even whether we could live together. For comfort, I read books written by widows and I see the difference. They describe the way in which family and friends descended on them with food for weeks and months on end, how they moved in with relatives or how relatives moved in with them. They describe not having enough vases and buckets for the flowers, their houses overflowing with letters of condolence. It wasn't like that for me. I got two cards and a bunch of tulips. A wonderful friend stayed for two nights and other friends brought food occasionally, listened occasionally, helped with the kids occasionally, but essentially, I was on my own. I am on my own. It is hard.

The professionals agree. My bereavement counsellor tells me that even if I had just found a stranger's body, I would still be in shock. It would be normal to still be reeling. And, as she points out, I didn't find a stranger's body. I found the body of the man I loved, deformed and decaying, three days after he had died. The memory haunts me still. It is natural to still be crying. And even if I'd had a happy life and then this had happened, that would be hard enough – but to have it happen on top of the loss of my mum and previous partners and the long-term sickness of my son, is really too much. 'No wonder you have lost your optimism,' she says.

And the GP says that, no, I don't need pills. I am having a normal reaction to a horrendous set of circumstances. This week I took the coroner's report to show her because I don't understand the medical terminology. She visibly flinched as she read it and acknowledged that she has had no experience of post-mortems, that she has never seen a body three days after death, that it has just struck her how horrendous that must have been for me. I remember the therapist I was seeing when you died and her reaction when I told her. She sent me home because it was too upsetting for her to deal with. The shock was unbearable for her. She had been listening to me talk about you for eight months and needed time to grieve herself. She had become fond of you and suddenly you had died and she was completely unprepared for this turn of events. She couldn't help me.

Only people who have been through similar bereavements understand how completely earth-shattering this kind of grief is because there is no widespread recognition of the pain of grief in our culture. In other cultures and historically in our culture, the expectations around grief are much clearer. People wear black or rend their clothes to visibly show the world that they are grieving. They are not expected to act normally. And there are recognised stages to the grieving process, that go on for months and years. No one expects someone who has experienced a close bereavement to socialise and after my attempts at going out and attempting to be normal, I can understand why. Yet, in our culture, we are expected to 'get over' someone's death once the funeral has passed and get back to normal as quickly as possible. My bereavement counsellor likened it to the way in which we deal with having children. These days, celebrity magazines show us photographs of women who are back at work with their bodies slim and toned, weeks after giving birth. We are meant to assimilate these huge changes effortlessly and are left feeling like failures if we acknowledge that birth and death have completely rearranged our internal and external landscapes.

I read about bereavement and am reassured and horrified in equal measure. I keep reading, with dismay, that the second year is worse than the first and that grief takes not months but years to work through. I read that uncomplicated grief, such as for the death of a parent in old age (uncomplicated because it is at least somewhat expected) takes four years to come to terms with where shocking death (like the one I have experienced) takes seven. I feel like I don't have seven years to lose to this grief, having lost so many years previously to other griefs and losses and sickness. And then I realise that grieving is not going to be the only occupation of these next seven years. I will live alongside the grieving process and there will be moments of joy amongst the sadness. But I read, also, that it will never go away and my bereavement counsellor tells me that this is true, that she is not in the business of making it better. I will carry this grief, like water, for the rest of my days.

And sometimes it will spill over. And I will need to keep talking about it. And I will write about it because spilling ink is as healing as spilling tears for me.

A friend recently sent me this quote from Elizabeth Kubler-Ross:

'Telling your story is primal to the grieving process. You must get it out. Grief must be witnessed to be healed.'

So I keep talking about it to people who listen and after I had cried in the sandpit, I felt a little more able to carry on again. The tears that spilled out made room for a little more pleasure and made the grief easier to carry. And now that I have written, I feel a little better, until tomorrow morning when I will wake up and realise that you are still dead and it will all start again.

Things not to say: 'I hope things get better'

SOMETIMES, IT GOES like this.

I'm having quite a good day, all things considered. The sun is shining, the kids are happy, I have ticked some jobs off my to-do list. I pat myself on the back. I am doing okay. And then I get a message from a friend asking when she can see me: 'I hope things are a bit brighter,' she says. And the sun goes behind the clouds for a moment and I feel a little bit less okay for some reason. Later a different friend sends me another message: 'I hope things get better soon,' she says. By now, it's raining and I feel thoroughly out of sorts and I still don't know why. These are my really good friends and they love me and love from friends like these keeps me afloat and yet, what is this feeling that they're leaving me with?

Yesterday I went to not one but three parties. This, you might call progress, or you might call it insanity. Since you died, so far I have been to two children's parties (and cried at both of them), to one disastrous night out in a pub (from which I walked home crying) and, other than that, social occasions have mostly revolved around you (it's okay to cry at those) or I have been one-to-one with good friends who have been there primarily to support me (while I cry some more). So, three parties was ambitious. I felt like a superhero to even attempt such a feat. If this kind of grief is like carrying a full glass of water all day long or walking on a tightrope, going to three parties is like trying to carry that water on a tightrope whilst making conversation with strangers. It is seriously impressive if you can pull it off. Mostly, I pulled it off.

The first party was the hardest. It was a street party on the road that the kids and I will be moving onto so we were meeting new neighbours. Luckily the natives were friendly enough. The kids had a nice time playing with other kids and I chatted to some other mums about school, about the house and the street. It was okay. For a while nobody asked about a partner but eventually one woman risked the subject and I had the thought then, that I could erase the episode where I fell in love with someone who died from my narrative and just tell her that I was separated. But I couldn't do that to you. I did fall in love and you did die, so I told her. 'I'm so sorry,' she said. 'You're very brave. To move on your own.' I felt it. Very brave.

The second party was easier, being at my brother's house and consisting, as his parties mostly do, of running around his garden trying to avoid being soaked by water pistols. In the kitchen he asked me briefly, 'how are things?' He stopped short of asking if they were better but the question hung hopefully in the air and I felt I had to give him something. 'Not too bad,' I said. He didn't have time to chat. And then a friend of his approached me and told me that she'd heard what a hard time I'd been having, and told me that she'd recently had a double mastectomy. It was like a breath of fresh air, in a stifling day of small talk. She wasn't okay either and there we were, standing like warriors on a battlefield, comparing tortures, eating nibbles in the sunshine, doing our best to keep living. Very brave.

The third party was fancy dress at the big co-housing project where you sometimes worked, amongst some of your friends: socialist performers and reformers. I walked there in twenties-style heels (talking nervously to you in the clouds, asking you for a sign of your presence as I walked, getting more nervous when the clouds kept moving and I couldn't see you). I was now walking on a tightrope, carrying water, in heels. I knew I was pushing it. But it was a beautiful evening. People sang and read poems and performed tricks. The people who knew you made me welcome as they always do and I chatted to other people I knew from years of working in Sheffield's third sector. As I sat talking to your friend (the one who found your body with me) the most incredible rainbow appeared in the sky and I felt your presence again with relief. The party host talked to me about the new house which is round the corner. We'd stopped short of moving into the co-housing project, though we had considered it for a while, just to be close to you. 'It's nice to stay loosely connected,' I said. And she corrected me, 'no, you are as tightly connected as can be,' and I was so touched. She introduced me to her cousin who lives on the street I'm moving into and he drunkenly asked me something about my marital status and I said, 'it's just me and the kids.' Just like that. So brave.

And then the activist singer-songwriter, Grace Petrie, did a gig right there in the central room in the house and she was amazing. And I sat there the whole time marvelling at how the world keeps turning and how people keep living. And I was thinking, 'is this it? Is this how you do it? In crowds of like-minded people, singing through the pain?' And then Grace sang a love song and I started to cry again and had to leave the room. Your friend put his arm around me. 'Are you still in pain?' he asked. And he is so kind and such a lovely man but there it is again, the bad feeling I get when he says that word, 'still'.

In amongst the parties yesterday, I chat to people on the Facebook group that I joined as part of my grief writing programme. They call it the 'Tribe of After', refer to each other as grieflings. I ask them why these words, 'better', 'brighter', 'still', have the power to bring me to my knees and they understand completely. They tell me that, of course, it is impossible to feel that the world is bright when my loved one is dead. And how can it get better? My loved one is dead. Unless someone can bring him back to me, it isn't going to get better. And, as if it wasn't bad enough to feel this way, my friends are, with absolutely the best of intentions, making me feel like I'm not doing this grief thing right, like it's not okay for me to feel the way I do. I am failing at grief. I need to change. Don't get me wrong, I want things to get better and brighter too. Sometimes I actually tell myself to snap out of it. But it doesn't work. I am grieving just as fast I can, healing as best I can in the circumstances. There is nothing anyone can do to speed up the process except listen and sit with me while I cry and acknowledge that I am in pain and that it sucks. I tell the Tribe of After that I feel like a superhero just for staying alive and they reply: 'you ARE a Superhero. You ARE.' One of them, in her own posts, writes: 'I don't have a hard life, I know I don't... but it does occur to me... that living is the hardest thing I've ever had to do.' Staying alive, without you, is enough. The kids are getting fed, I am managing to work, I am buying a new house for God's sake. I am a superhero. Please, I've lost so much, let me keep the cape.

When you're in love with a beautiful man and he dies – then what?

I THINK ABOUT that thing that teenagers do when they're first in love and on the phone. Maybe they don't do it these days. Maybe they just send multiple texts until their fingers fall off or they fall asleep drooling onto the screens of their smartphones. But I'm thinking of the way, in the olden days, young people used to find it so impossible to part that they'd say, 'you put the phone down first,' 'no you,' for about half an hour until a parent's voice would intercept the call and they'd have to say goodnight. We did that a few times, in an ironic way, of course, but kind of not.

It can be a shock to realise that you can still fall in love – I mean *really* fall in love – when you're a middle-aged man or woman, especially if you're a man or woman who has had a few relationships since those first heady days of youthful romance. Amazing to realise that you can still walk around in a daze, tripping over your own feet because your mind is always with your loved one. Wonderfully destabilising to spend your days waiting for the ping of your phone (because you too have entered the modern age) and your nights so enthralled with your lover's mind, body and soul that you forget to go to sleep entirely. Incredible to feel the kind of love where hours and days apart feel like torture and you can't wait to be reunited, where every parting is a wrench, a tiny grief. You are in the bonding phase of love, the enchantment phase, where you see only common ground and ignore differences. Love is blind, they say. Love is a form of madness, they say. Love is a drug. In fact, scientists have proven that being in love is like being on cocaine. You are bonded to your loved one by a powerful cocktail of hormones. You are attached to your beloved. You are, in essence, like Robert Palmer, addicted to love.

This week I joined WAY, a support network for people who are Widowed and Young. I consider myself neither widowed nor young (even though I am skilled at social networking and can drool on a smartphone with the best of them) but I realised that it might be helpful to talk to other people who have lost a partner and specifically people who have lost a partner before old age. Because the experience has been like nothing I've ever known and I don't know anyone in the real world who has lost a partner. I thought I might find people who understood. I've not been disappointed. I'd only been on the Facebook group for five minutes when someone said, in black and white, so clearly, the thing that I'd been feeling but not quite articulated: that there is a world of difference between losing someone you love and losing someone you are in love with. Suddenly it all made sense.

I've been careful in my conversations with the bereaved, to try not to suggest that there is some kind of grief hierarchy; everyone's grief is unique and incomparable and yet, this feeling has been nagging at me, that this grief is different, that it is violent, that it is visceral in a way that is unfamiliar to me. I've even been feeling guilty that this grief is so much more extreme than my grief for my mum who only died recently, or for my dad. And I get annoyed with friends who suggest that I am feeling so bad because this grief is cumulative, even though I know that they're right to some extent, because my heart tells me that, no, this grief is for you. My grief is commensurate to the amount of love I felt for you and my love for you, as it happens, was enormous. But there is something else going on here. I didn't love you like your family or friends did. I was 'in love' with you. Even when my mum was dying, I didn't think about her all day long. I didn't daydream about the beautiful future we would have together. I didn't pine for her until we were reunited. I loved her and I wanted her to stay in my life but I wasn't addicted to her. I was addicted to you and when a partner dies like you did, suddenly and with no warning, it is like going cold turkey. I am physically ill with grief. My body hums with grief so loudly that I'm surprised other people can't hear it. I am shattered by grief.

At the party when your friend found me crying, he thought he understood. 'Paul would have been here,' he said, like I was crying because I'd just remembered you because I was at a party with your friends. But the truth is that I don't just remember you at parties and I don't cry when something reminds me that you lived and that you are gone. I remember you all day long, the way I thought of you all day long when you were alive. I cry, or fight back tears, all day long, the way I fought back smiles when you were alive. I only forget you when I am distracted by something else for a moment. I am in agony, looking all day long for the place to rest my heart and it is gone. 'Are you still sad about Paul?' another friend of yours asked this week. 'Of course,' I said. 'I will be sad about Paul forever.'

Today I walked up to the spot where we first held

each other as we watched the sun set and I talked to the sky as I often do. 'How on earth am I supposed to do this?' I asked. You didn't talk back, though I do sometimes hear your voice in my head and when I asked you for a sign in the clouds, I found my heart again for a moment. Your love goes on but you are gone.

I think about those phone calls: 'You go first,' 'no you.' You went and I was calling you and there was no answer. You went first and you can't come back. You went and I am talking when the line is dead, waiting for a ping that will not come, rattling like a junkie coming off cocaine, on my own.

My heart has lost its home

THESE DAYS I find myself looking for hearts. I look for them in cloudy skies, in blossom petals scattered on pavements, in frying pans and puddles. This week, I found them on the beach, heart-shaped pebbles strewn across the sand, like stepping stones across the abyss. Sometimes I feel I am clutching at straws, searching for evidence that, though you are gone, love has not died. I am looking for you everywhere. I look for you in the faces of strangers, in the backs of men with broad shoulders, in male bodies in workmen's clothes. I send frantic messages to your friends and family. Sometimes they reply and sometimes they don't. It is just another form of looking. I am looking for evidence that you lived, that we loved, that it was real. I want someone else to say, yes, that happened. Though this is a nightmare, that wasn't a dream. Love existed. Love still exists.

I look for you on my arrival in Norfolk with the kids. This too is something that I do. With every coming and going, I am searching for my home, longing to tell someone – I arrived, I am safe, we are here. And suddenly I am crying in a strange kitchen as I look for spoons or cups or spaces on shelves, lost in a strange place where you have never been, where you would never be, where I wouldn't even have expected you to be, just because my heart is looking for its home.

Though a love of the sea was something we had in common, we only had one weekend by the coast. As it happened, it was the weekend before my mum died, but we weren't to know that then. I just knew that I was tired of the trips backwards and forwards to hospitals and that I needed a break, that I needed some time with you. After she'd died, I felt guilty that I'd spent that weekend away from her. Now that you have died, I'm glad I did. She would have wanted it that way. You took me to Sterchi's in Filey to buy chocolates for our mums. Though my mum never got to eat hers, I'm glad that your mum had one last box from you.

I try to remember every detail of our weekend but already it is blurred by time, already the memories are out at sea, like the waves at high tide and I feel them slipping away. We left early on Friday, I think, but then I think, no, surely you were at work on Friday and what did I do with the kids and it must have been late when we arrived. We listened to Neil Young, I think, but no, we were in your van, surely we listened to your music and the Neil Young CD was mine. I don't know anymore. I know that we arrived and that you made a fire. I know that we played Scrabble. I'm not sure who won. I know that we made love and that you felt that you had won that night. I know that you felt strange being away in a holiday cottage and that you looked too big in the low-ceilinged house, were out of place in the pure white bed linen. I know that the whole idea of renting a holiday cottage was alien to you. You were used to roughing it and not comfortable with me paying but I'd told you in no uncertain terms that I was too tired for camping in December. 'I'm going to book a cottage for the weekend, Blacksmith,' I said. 'It's up to you whether you come.' I'm so glad that you came.

You took me to some of your favourite places, to

the lighthouse at Flamborough and the beach at Thornwick Bay. We saw a seal. He peeped his head out of the waves, bobbed about for a while and was gone. We picked up pebbles on the beach then too. You were searching for smooth round shapes, to make runes from. We couldn't have predicted that you wouldn't have time to make them. We wouldn't have dreamed that the seal was a sign or a siren, calling you home, though you posed me like a mermaid on a rock, saw me like a wild sea creature, even though I was bundled up in waterproofs and a woolly hat. You were an artist then and I was happy being your muse. I loved the way you loved me. You didn't agree with taking naked photos of women having spent too much time around dishonourable blokes but you confessed that you wanted to then, as art. Maybe in summer, I said. But that summer never came.

Instead, this summer, friends and family fill the gaps in the diary and I write my way through the weeks, ride the turbulent waves of grief. Instead of making runes, I remember the old bag of runes that I found in your house and the message on the one my daughter picked: 'The beginning and the ending are fixed. What's in between is yours. Nothing is in vain. All is remembered.' I find the photos that you took on your laptop and read the signs in my face. I pick up heart-shaped stones on the beach with my children, pocket memories to store for later. We are still here. Love existed. Love exists.

Ancestral memory

I REMEMBER NOW what we did on the day we first kissed, before the walk in Eyam, before the kiss under the ash tree. You went with me to look at a property in Rowsley in the rain. You wore a long black raincoat, which somehow looked more like a wizard's cloak than protective outdoor gear on you. Afterwards we had lunch in Cauldwell Mill. We watched a rival blacksmith in the forge then stood by the old mill, watching the wheels turn, breathing in history. We talked about ancestral memory, the idea that somehow we might carry the collective unconscious of our ancestors in our minds and souls. We both felt it, the familiarity in the hum and whirr of industrial equipment. It was the same feeling we had with each other: breathing deep, drawing close, coming home.

Weeks later, together now, we held hands as we walked the Porter Valley, ambling along the river where Little Mesters once sharpened knife blades on millstones. We held each other, watching the flood and gush of water on the Shepherd's wheel, remembering those ancestors of ours. 'My great-grandfather made penknife blades on this river,' I said, casting my mind back for the fragments of stories my grandmother told. Later still, in Knaresborough, so deep in love that there was no way back, I idled the time by the River Nidd, leafing through books in an antique shop while you studied the markings on penknife blades, choosing one carefully for your collection.

The week that you died, I was meant to be leading a heritage writing walk along the banks of the River Don. You'd come with me a few weeks earlier to scope out the territory. You'd navigated the way by scrapyards, told me about a world that was alien and yet so familiar. My Sheffield is the Sheffield of green valleys and tree-lined streets, my accent polished like a fine knife blade, my only tools those of words and imagination. But my father and grandfather worked on that river. My father worked with oiled machines, big wheels and steel buckets. His father was a furnaceman who stoked the fires of the steelworks. My mother's father was a coal merchant, who sold the coal that powered the city. And here you were, a man of fire and iron, words and imagination, strong by my side, a bridge between the past and future. We talked about our future again on that walk. We'd been to see another house, the house I will soon move into, and we were discussing still the old conundrum: to live together or not together, that was the question. We never found the answer. We know it now. Still, on that river, we held each other tight and kissed to the accompaniment of gushing water and clanking steel, in the moment, melded together.

Yesterday, I walked back along the Porter Brook on a poetry walk and I remembered you, as I always do. I stood beneath an ash tree while my friend read a poem about the ash and looked up into the branches, remembering how you told me, on our first walk, that if you were a tree you would be an ash, remembering how you kissed me for the first time beneath an ash tree, later on that day when we first talked of ancestral memory in Cauldwell Mill.

My memories come full circle, my home town littered

with images of you now, strewn like leaves across the pavements. I walk my own heritage walk down memory lane, write my own poetic footnotes. Our memories are part of who we are. And you are part of me now.

I am thinking about what I have gained

'NEXT TIME, LET'S think about what you have gained,' she says.

I feel my hackles rise a little as they do every time some-one offers me some platitude about things happening for a reason, or your love being a gift to cherish. And I think to myself that I don't want to think about what I have gained. I don't come to this amazing bereavement counselling service week after week to talk about what I have gained. I come here to cry and to tell her what I have lost. I want to sit here and tell her again and again. Does she not understand how big it is? Does she not see yet just how much I have lost?

The truth is, I want to tell everyone what I have lost. I want to talk about it and write about it over and over until I have explained it in every possible way. I want to express it in poetry and prose, with pictures, signs and symbols. I want to find, each day, a new simile, a new metaphor, a new way to tell someone. I want to dance it, walk it, swim it. I want to spread this loss like a disease until everyone is just a little bit infected, until everyone has felt, just for one moment, a homeopathic amount of this grief. And yet.

Today I go out into the Peak District where you lived. I spend the morning with my writing group and then meet an ex, Chris, for lunch and a walk. We have a good chat. He listens while I tell him again how much it hurts and I accomplish my mission of making him sad too which always makes me feel just a little bit better: misery loves company. Together we talk at length about life and death, purpose and meaning. We talk about lack of purpose and lack of meaning too, about the way that, for both of us, sometimes, we're not sure where we're going, or why. The way that sometimes, we lack motivation.

For me, this sense of purposelessness has reached a new level since you died. My bereavement counsellor says that I am having an existential crisis. I am questioning the very point of being alive. I no longer take it for granted that existing is, in of itself, a good thing. Every moment now is framed by the knowledge of death. Big things and small things are seen through this filter. My ex is talking about buying a new sofa and as he's talking I find myself wondering why anyone would bother buying a sofa when we're all going to die. (And then I concede that while he's waiting to die, he may as well have somewhere comfy to sit.) We take it further. Why go to work? Why accumulate wealth? Why visit foreign countries? Even my writing feels pointless these days. A friend online says how important this grief writing is but I'm not sure anymore. I write because I can't think of anything else to do but I reflect to her that no amount of writing can bring you back and that feels like all I want. I could turn this into a bestselling memoir and then what? You still won't be here and I'm still going to die one day. It all feels kind of meaningless. The truth is, I tell Chris, when the person you love has died, you just want to go and join them. Without actually feeing suicidal, it's where you want to be and everything feels empty without them. At the beginning I felt that if I hadn't had children, it is where I would have gone.

I don't feel that anymore, I realise.

I am thinking about what I have gained.

I was always painfully honest but I am even more unguarded now. I say what I think. I speak what I feel. A writer friend tells me that writing online so openly would scare her. I tell her that sometimes it scares me too but what's the worst that can happen? It is only words. It is only truth. My truth is that grief has made me fearless. Grief has made me more me.

I am thinking about what I have gained.

I am buying a new house and I'm sure there is a multitude of things to be stressed about but I don't really care. It is only a house. It is only money. I have a different perspective now.

I am thinking about what I have gained.

Since you and my mum died, I have felt more alone than I have ever felt. I am no one's partner. I am no one's daughter. I am peripheral to everyone but the children. I tell my ex that I lack support because there is no one who is there for me day to day. But then I look at him, this old friend, who has caught the train to spend the day with me and I realise it is churlish of me to say that. Here he is, supporting me. I talk online to other bereaved people and I feel their support too. This week I told my Facebook world that I was worried about being alone without my children while they are on holiday with their dad, and friends flocked to fill my diary. So many people offered their company that I am craving alone time, that I have people on a waiting list to see me. I tell Chris that no one would care if I died and he says that perhaps I might be surprised how many people would care. 'I would care,' he says. People do care. I have learned to ask for what I need. I have learned that there is more than one kind of love. As I sit with my friend eating dosas in the sunshine at the end of the day I feel, for a moment, that I am glad again to be alive.

I am thinking about what I have gained.

I tell Chris that I can't think about the future anymore. Thinking about a future without you is too painful and so I have no choice but to live in the moment. While we are out, I find myself stopping to look at things more closely than I would have done before. I notice things more. I stand and observe the greenness of green, the treeness of tree, the cloudness of cloud. I see what is and nothing more. And I look at everything knowing that one day I won't be here to see it any more so I take it in. I learned that from you: the man who lived in the moment, who never planned for the future, whose future has been wiped out.

I am thinking about what we gained.

I tell Chris that it was fear of the future that made us doubt whether we could be together. We both knew that, in the moment, it was fantastic; it was the future that we couldn't see. I reflect again that if we hadn't overcome our fears and lived in the present, we could so easily have missed what we had. We took a risk, let down our guards, opened our hearts. We were fully present in each moment together. What we had was something real and brave and fearless. We had true love. I am thinking about what I gained. I am thinking about what I lost.

This time last year

I T I S O N E of the plagues of the modern age, that little trick that Facebook has of reminding you what you were doing or saying or posting last year, or five years ago, or in some different age when your life looked completely different.

It just happened to me and it wasn't even my post. A friend posted a photo of a gig that he was at on the first of August last year. It just so happened that I was there too. I remember it vividly. I was still feeling fragile from my last heartbreak but I was out in the world putting a brave face on, trying to be optimistic that things that might get better. After all, I thought, they couldn't get much worse.

I didn't know then, that you were lurking just around the corner. In two days' time, I would meet you again for the first time in years. I would be wary, scared to trust my heart to someone new, but gradually I would fall in love again. I would start to trust again. I would regain my faith in the future. I would have a wonderful time with you.

No one could have predicted that, a year later, I would be sitting here sobbing because someone posted a picture of a gig attended by my innocent self who didn't know that twelve months later, the love I hadn't yet met would be dead. No one would have known that my mum would be dead too. How much can change in twelve short months. From this week, every day will be an anniversary of a precious day that I spent with you. Until the day in March when Facebook will tell me that this time last year you died and all of my posts became memories of you, snapshots of heartache.

Cloud catching

T HE SKY IS beautiful tonight. If you could see it, you would capture it with your lens. Maybe you do see it. Maybe you made it especially for us. My daughter saw it, came bursting into the room saying, 'come quickly. You've got to come outside and see the sky. It is so beautiful. Can I borrow your camera. I have to take a photo.' She is right. Cracks of light shimmer like gold between the clouds and seams of sunlight jag across the sky like lightning bolts. But when we look through the camera, the tracks of gold disappear. We can't capture them on film. Instead we stand and marvel at them, checking with each other to make sure we aren't imagining these seams of light extending upwards in the dusk. We take some pretty pictures of the clouds anyway, running this way and that, looking from all angles, trying to catch the clouds: puffy ones, fluffy ones, clouds like feathers and angel wings. 'We should write a book called *Cloud Catchers*,' she says.

Like all of us now, she thinks of you when she looks at clouds. I tell her again about our last conversation, about the poem I sent and your photographic reply and your words to me: 'I love the poem, I love clouds and I love you.' She smiles and holds my hand and I feel a seam of light and goodness between us, between you and me and her – the girl you never really knew but knew so much about, the girl who only really met you once, the week you died, who rushed from the room to whisper to me, 'I really like Paul. Can he stay?'

Tomorrow we're catching a plane to France for our first foreign holiday in five years. I've never taken the children on a plane on my own and I'm worried that my grief-addled brain won't get us there. Yesterday we went to see your mum. She searched through her flat and gave them presents: an old toy dragon of yours for my boy and Auntie Joan's pretty scarves for my girl. Forgetting to give them the money that she'd intended for them, she threw it down from your balcony into the park where we were playing. 'I really like Paul's mum,' my daughter said in an echo of the words she said when she first met you.

I feel sad at the thought of flying off to the sunshine when you are no longer living, scared almost to leave you behind, scared to leave my laptop too. But then I realise that you are no longer tethered here and of course I will take you with us. And I think about the flight and how close you will feel when I look out of the window and see those clouds around us and below us. Thinking about the flight reminds me of the poem that I wrote the day before you died, the poem that you loved and I remember that, really, it was a poem about the rollercoaster of grief, written following the death of my mum. Today I feel we are heading towards the light but I know that the clouds will come and go. A few days ago I couldn't move for grief, couldn't stop crying. Today has been the first day I haven't cried at all. I'm learning to go with the flow of this grief, enjoying the moments of respite, before the clouds roll in again, engulfing me in blackness, spilling tears like raindrops.

I have the clouds in my head

THEY SAID I had my head in the clouds. But now, instead, I have the clouds in my head. They move in for hours or days at a time. Not the fluffy white, light as a feather, candy floss clouds, but a thick grey-white covering: smothering, suffocating, separating me from the rest of the world, blocking out the sun.

On days like this, life is a distant planet seen from the air, a world covered in tracing paper. I can just about make out the edges of things. Everything is hazy, muffled by the noise of sadness, the clouds of absence, the fog of grief.

Like the moment, last night, when we pushed head-first into cloud covering somewhere over France and everything retreated, pressure blocking our ears so that the only sounds were our own thoughts and all we could see was white. Neither the world below nor the blue sky above, just the blank bank of cloud, bearing down on us, suspended in a no-man's land of white nothingness, the fullness of emptiness blocking out the view.

My thoughts are all of you. Nothing else makes any sense. It is like I have crossed the channel and other people are speaking a different language that I no longer comprehend. Only the others in this Afterland understand how all-consuming it is to live with the clouds of the dead in your head. How exhausting it is to be looking all day through the mist of time, replaying conversations, retracing steps, wondering how one minute you were there and the next you'd gone, trying to figure out where you are now and how and what and why.

I stare at the sky, searching for you, looking for the blue between the clouds. And sometimes you are there and sometimes things sharpen and the clouds clear and I can hear for a while the song of birds, the hum of the traffic, the rhythm of the every day. At times like this I sit in the sun and marvel at how far I have come. And then suddenly, without warning, the sun is gone, everything is muffled and the clouds roll back in. All is distant except this pain. There is only relief when it rains.

Acts of kindness

I HAVE COME back from holiday and have no one but Facebook for company. No one phones to check we are home safely, no one is eagerly waiting to see us on our return. In fact, only the children's dad knows that we are coming home at all. And when he comes to pick them up for the afternoon, there is overwhelming silence, where once there would have been your knock at the door. I miss you and I miss my mum. Everyone needs a someone to say those words to: *I'm home.*

Eventually, yesterday, my sadness pushed me out into the sunshine and I walked, tears streaming, through the park, not caring who saw. He saw. I know he did. But I didn't meet his eye. It wasn't the time to stop to talk to the man who runs the fairground on a sunny day. I couldn't interrupt his patter and the chatter of sunshine children with my tears. I walked on.

I knew him vaguely before I knew he knew you. I've been wandering that park for years. He has a soft spot for a mum in a flowery dress, can clock the tired eyes of a single parent who has been on duty for too long. He brings me chairs and sunglasses, once even bought me a cup of tea. He lets the kids go on for free when I've forgotten my cash, doesn't mind if I don't pay him back. Though I do, usually, pay him back.

I only saw him with you once, saw the look of surprise on his face when he saw us hand in hand. You waved your greetings across the grass. You'd known each other years ago when you'd famously used your metalworking skills to make him a Klingon weapon. At your funeral someone wrote about it on the memory tree. There can't be many people who leave memories of fantasy weaponry behind them, but then there aren't many people like you.

He'd heard the bad news before I told him, strode out across the grass with open arms. Strange the way grief breaks down barriers, how I found myself hugging a fairground Klingon as if he were my own best friend. 'All the good ones are gone,' he said. He told me of his own lost love. We are bonded now in the club of broken hearts. Grief, the other side of love. Love, the other side of grief.

Yesterday's hug came from another club member who reached out to me when you died. She was in the park celebrating her late husband's birthday. Strange that my footsteps led me to her, that she ended up consoling me on her husband's day. I left her in the company of her own loved ones, sat on a stump in the woods and called your mum instead of mine. She is someone else I never knew before. So important to me now. We too are bonded forever in grief and love.

Today we go to the park again. I have the children in tow. I smile at him as I carry my tea and cups of water back to the playground, no time to sit today. Later, my daughter goes to fetch more water, comes running, beaming like sunshine back to my side, with a wand of bubbles. 'Paul's friend gave it to me,' she says, 'he filled it from his bubble machine. He said, madam, it's all yours.' And my spirits lift. Your gift to him, his gift to her, a gift to me. Small kindnesses passed on. He's like a kind of fairy godmother, we say. And we laugh, the way we did when we picked up the pure white feather outside art club on our anniversary and imagined you as an angel. Beauty comes in unusual packages. Love is as big and wide as sadness. Small things make a big difference. Surprising people welcome me home.

Moving forwards

TODAY HAS BEEN a strange kind of day. The first thing I saw this morning, after my little boy's face by my bedside, was a photo of my mum on a boat in Devon last year. Facebook helpfully reminded me that this time last year my mum was, as far as we knew, in remission from peritoneal cancer and we were on a family holiday with her. Of course, as she had terminal cancer, we knew it might be the last, but we were hopeful that it might not be. On the same holiday, I was texting you to arrange a date for our poker making. I wasn't even in love with you yet.

Fast forward twelve months and today the children and I get the keys to our new house. We move the first of our things in. The poker takes pride of place on the log burning stove and we bring a box of treasures from my mum's place too: a cherub and a moon-gazing hare for the garden, a bronze knight 'to guard the house' (according to the children) and some china and crockery. I bring her kettle and her teabags and even bring her mop to help me clean the floor. A new mop is precisely the kind of thing she would have brought had she been here.

But she isn't here. And you aren't here. And as soon as the children are upstairs arguing about their prospective bedrooms, I sit on my new balcony looking out over my impossibly beautiful garden and cry a mixture of happy and sad tears. It is the house of my dreams and if ever there was a house to have a happy life in, this is it. But it's not the life I wanted. Still, it is a beautiful house and a new chapter. People say it is a fresh start but of course it is not. I can't wipe away the past with a mop and a bucket of bleach and though there are all kinds of things I can't wait to leave behind, you are not one of them. Still, I must move forwards. Some things I don't have a choice about.

Language matters when you're a writer. It is important to get the words right. You are not someone I will 'get over,' like the flu, I won't 'get better' from this bout of grief and I won't 'move on'. I won't sweep you into the corner or toss you in the skip with the detritus from the old house. Instead, I will bring you with me as I move forwards into some kind of unknowable future in the beautiful house that you helped me to choose. I will think of you when I stand at the bottom of the garden wondering how to chop wood without you, and when the draft blows through the window that you observed was badly fitting, and when I poke my fire with the poker and remember how it felt when our hands first touched and the first sparks flew between us. And from the balcony I have a perfect view of treetops and clouds. I will watch them shift in the sky and move forwards. Though we want them to, the clouds and the clocks don't stop. Moving forwards, in grief, is all we can do.

I need to talk about Kevin

I FOUND THE book in the pile of unread novels on my bedside table when we moved. Little things like that turn up every now and then and throw me off course. One minute I'm blithely tossing paperbacks across the room into two separate boxes – keep, chuck – and the next I'm sitting on the floor fondling a book about a psychopathic child and his ambivalent mother because you gave it to me. Life is loaded with landmines, especially when moving house.

On the actual day of moving, I held it together pretty well. I watched the removal men carry the furniture from my mum's house without shedding a single tear and remained calm and collected as I ushered boxes into the new house. It was only later, when the supportive friends and the removal men had gone, that I fell apart. It was the Scrabble that did it. It was lurking there at the bottom of the box labelled 'Games', cradling score cards written in your handwriting and memories of contests gone by: BP vs WB. No more. Landmines.

Blacksmith Paul or simply Paul was the name you were known by. I'd actually forgotten your birth name was Kevin until I saw it embossed in gold on your coffin. I'm not sure you would have been pleased to go out of this world with the name you came in with; no one had called you Kevin for decades. I'm not going to start now.

But I do need to talk about you. I need to talk about you a lot. Not everyone gets this. Sometimes I wonder if people don't bring you up in conversation because they're worried about upsetting me. Maybe they think that if they mention you, they might remind me of my grief. Maybe they think I should be over it by now. Maybe they think there's no point in talking about you because you're not here anymore and I need to move into a future which you're not going to be part of. I don't know what they think but I know this: I need to talk about you.

Talking about you doesn't remind me of my grief because my grief is a constant presence, threaded through every fibre of my being, sitting like an elephant in the centre of my brain. It is much easier for me to talk about the elephant than to think of a topic that doesn't involve any mention of trunks and tusks and flappy ears. In fact, if they don't mention my elephant, I am liable, eventually, to bring it up myself: 'Speaking of grey school trousers, my elephant is grey...'

And not talking about you doesn't mean I will get over you quicker. Ever tried burying a live elephant? I'm no expert on grief but I am one hundred per cent sure that talking about you is helping, not hindering my healing process. (And anyway, I will never get over you. In time I might make friends with the elephant, or maybe shrink the elephant, or maybe grow so full of love that I can accommodate an elephant easily into my new life. But, get over you? Never.) Who knows what the future holds? I certainly don't. All I know is that, right now, I need to talk about the elephant. I need to talk about you.

And I can't move into a new future without revisiting the past. I only had eight months of you. I want to re-live every precious moment over and over. I will never tire of talking about you. No one can know me if they don't know you and don't know my love and my grief. I can't walk around with this elephant and not introduce it as part of who I am, who I have become, who I will be.

I haven't read Lionel Shriver's book. I've barely read anything since you died. I haven't watched anything either. How can anyone read a book with an elephant squatting on their brain taking up all of the space? The elephant has trampled on my nerves and thrashed its trunk around so much that whole chunks of my memory have been erased, so that I can't remember how a sentence began by the time I get to the end, so that words don't make sense. There's a great grey mass at the centre of my grey matter, blocking connections that I used to be able to make.

I wonder sometimes how someone who can't remember where her keys are, who just had to Google the author of an award-winning book, who doesn't know what day it is or which year, can manage to write. And then I realise that writing this is easy because writing is just doing what comes naturally to me and writing about you is as natural as breathing. Because my brain is ninety per cent elephant and it is such a relief to talk about it. I need to talk about Kevin. I want to talk about Blacksmith Paul. It might make me cry but it will also make me smile. Ask me about it. I want to talk.

I really liked you too

IT TOOK A while to find the right spot but your hooks are back up on the wall. They're the first things I see as I open the front door. Not in a cupboard this time, but on full display. Not in the background but in the foreground where they belong – where you belonged.

It's not long since you last put them back up in my old house. They'd been in the cellar since I moved there, hidden from view though I had carried them with me through four house moves.

I tried to remember when you put them up the first time, the time when I didn't see what was in front of me, when we were just two people who hung around with Ed, whose paths crossed occasionally in pubs and kitchens. I asked Chris, my ex, if he remembered them and he did. He took them down when we moved fifteen years ago and told me how the then purchasers had asked if I would sell them. 'You wouldn't hear of it,' he said. It pleased me to learn this. I knew those hooks were important.

We used to talk about it sometimes. You would shake your head in disbelief at the chance we missed all those years ago. 'What was I thinking?' you would say. As you put the hooks back up, you shook your head again. 'I can't believe I gave them to you for free,' you said. 'I must have really liked you.'

I really liked you too, Blacksmith.

I really liked you too.

Hanging by a thread

A T TIMES, ON this journey, death has felt more real to me than life. *Life is short*, they say. *You're a long time dead*, they say. *You only live once.* To the uninitiated, another's death is a call to life: live for the moment, carpe diem, follow your dreams. But when you have looked death squarely in the face and your dreams are of the faces of loved ones drained of life, it is not so simple anymore. Where once death was a call to life, sometimes now it feels like a call to home. There is so much love on the other side for me now. The pull of death is strong.

With the pull of gravity, grief comes like swirling waters in the plughole, dragging me down. It is hard to resist such a force. I see myself as a spider clinging to a silver thread, battered by waves so strong that they make me catch my breath and lose my mind. But I climb slowly upwards out of dark waters and towards the light. I am hanging by that thread, spinning a web of blind faith and love, even though I know that one careless swipe of a finger could bring it all crashing down at any moment. The instinct for survival is strong too.

I exist now in parentheses. But there is love on this side too and slowly the balance tips towards life again. 'You don't strike me as a person who is ready to give up,' says my friend.

The love on the other side will wait.

For now, it takes all my strength
but I climb upwards,
move forwards,
hang on.

AUTUMN

(SEPTEMBER – NOVEMBER 2016)

letting go

Letting go

SOMETIMES I WONDER if there is a part of us deep down that has some inkling of our life's narrative before it is complete, if we know somewhere in our unconscious the way that things are going to pan out. I find myself wondering about premonitions and feelings of déjà vu, about me and you and the way you told me before you died that a heavy, sad feeling had come over you from nowhere as you drove into Sheffield one day. And about the time, when we were lying in bed and I asked you what you were thinking, when you told me that if I left you, you would have to join the foreign legion. 'You're the woman I want to die with,' you said. Or about the dream you had on the last night we spent together where you watched me walk through the door to a pub while you diverted into an empty factory. I didn't attempt to analyse it at the time, but I wonder now. I sit here in my new house, looking over at the 'Stardust' print that you bought me for my birthday and it looks obvious from here, that swirling pathway to the stars that you said epitomised the journey of our love. It is an image of a journey up into the cosmos where I search for you now.

With hindsight it seems there were portents all along the way. It is in the films we watched together: *Truly Madly Deeply*, *It's a Wonderful Life*, *Finding Neverland* and in the poems that I wrote. I wrote about journeys taken in which we didn't know where we were going, spoke of doors that we would never walk through, talked of racing time around the bend. We didn't know how little time we had but somehow it feels like it was there in the way we cherished every single moment that we were together. In the moment, we were always so very happy. We only got confused when we tried to talk of the future. It was like we couldn't see it somehow. It didn't exist.

Last week I watched one of those films again. It is the first film that I've managed to watch since you died. It was *Truly Madly Deeply*, my favourite film of all time. And there they were, Juliet Stevenson and Alan Rickman gazing at clouds, and there she was, sitting in a therapist's office sobbing, 'I miss him, I miss him, I miss him,' the way I have done so many times. I wonder now why I have always been so drawn to that film and why we chose to watch it together in tears during the early stages of our relationship. Did some part of me know that my narrative would be one of gut-wrenching loss even back in 1990 when I first watched it, nineteen and full of hope? Did we know as we cried, that we would lose each other too?

I remember how back in Knaresborough in February, a month before your death, we stopped in an antique and book shop by the river. You bought yourself a penknife and a book about sailing. You bought me a second-hand version of *The Penguin Book of Love Poetry*.

'Open the book randomly,' I said. 'And the first poem we see will be about us.'

The book fell open at a poem by E.E. Cummings. It went like this:

it may not always be so; and I say
that if your lips, which I have loved, should touch
another's, and your dear strong fingers clutch
his heart, as mine in time not far away;
if on another's face your sweet hair lay
in such a silence as I know, or such
great writhing words as, uttering overmuch,
stand helplessly before the spirit at bay:

if this should be, I say if this should be –
you of my heart, send me a little word;
that I may go unto him, and take his hands,
saying, Accept all happiness from me.
Then shall I turn my face, and hear one bird
sing terribly afar in the lost lands.

'I don't like that poem,' you said.

I tried to think of an explanation, scanned the page for a different poem but it was already done. Enough of the magical thinking, we said, switching our romantic heads for the heads of cynics to suit the moment. But I wonder now. It was a poem about saying goodbye, about moving on and letting go.

As I packed up my old house and my mum's house this month, I have been forced to think a lot about letting go. I have sat in both houses weighing objects like snow globes, looking at days and years gone by through the mist, wondering what I should keep, what to relinquish. I have sifted through love letters from the ghosts of boyfriends past, stared at wedding photos from marriages now dissolved, packaged up the remnants of my grandparents' lives in tissue paper. I had already moved my precious mementos of our time together to the new house and eventually, only your toothbrush remained, still sitting in the cup on the washbasin. I wasn't sure if I could leave this mundane reminder of the life you lived behind, or if I should bring it with me into my new life. What would a new partner say if he saw your toothbrush sitting there? Could there ever be a new partner after you? Can you really love someone new when you still love someone who died? As I pondered these questions I looked up and saw my stickers still clinging to the wall of my old study – an image by Banksy of a girl watching a heart float like a balloon into the sky. When you love someone so much, how can you ever let them go? And did I know, when I bought it, that this would be my story?

I think about the film again and the ending where Alan Rickman watches Juliet Stevenson pack her own toothbrush as she embarks on a new relationship and the poem he recites to her, not Cummings this time, but Neruda: 'My feet will want to walk to where you are sleeping, but I shall go on living.' So often I have longed to join you on the other side, in the clouds or the stars or wherever you are. So many times I have cried, saying, 'please, can't you just come back?' But however much I love you and however much I cry, I can't bring you back. My magical thinking only gets me so far. I left your toothbrush behind. You don't need it where you have gone and I don't need its reminder that you are no longer physically here. Your absence is already as strong as your presence.

Yesterday, at our house-warming party, I watched my little boy playing with the inflatable helium balloon that he got for his birthday. There he was in the garden, next to the logs that you said you would chop, six years old and full of hope. And when he lost his grip on the ribbon and gazed after it as it tumbled and danced over hedges and trees and up into the sky, I held him close while he cried and thought of that girl again. Nothing is permanent. Sometimes it seems to me that the whole of life is a process of letting go. I turned back to the house and left the balloon to join you and Alan Rickman in the clouds. Your physical body has gone somewhere that I can't reach it and, though I don't like it, I am returned through the pub door of your dream to keep living.

I love you too

IT IS SIX months today since your heart stopped
beating. That is the official verdict. Not an aneurysm
after all and not a heart attack, just some wonky signal
that didn't get through. I picture your blood travelling
like a train down a track: pump, pump, pump, pump,
then bump, it is stuck in a tunnel, slowed down
maybe by the furrowing of an artery and it doesn't get
through. It only takes eleven seconds for a heart to
stop beating. They say you wouldn't have felt a thing.
We have pieced together the evidence and all we know
is that you weren't feeling well, that you went home
from work without a backwards glance, that when your
mum phoned, you told her you had a headache. For
all we know, after that, you lay down on your bed and
died. It was three days later that I found you there.
Sometimes death is a slow decline over weeks and
months and years. Sometimes it takes eleven seconds.
One moment you are alive, the next you are dead. Just
like that. No time to pick up the phone, no time to say
goodbye. Just gone.

I didn't pick up your phone. Instead they sent it
through the post and it arrived today as a ghoulish
present on this significant day. It has taken six months
of correspondence with Derbyshire police to finally
get your property returned. There is no longer an
investigation. The case is closed. You died of natural
causes. Nothing untoward except for the abomination
of a heart filled with love that stopped beating one

random night in March. There were no suspicious circumstances, nothing untoward. Just an unexpected death. Completely unexpected. (The counsellor looks at me from across the blue room of Bereavement Services. 'You have downplayed the shock,' she says.)

I had to lie down after I unwrapped the phone from the bubble wrap. That inanimate oblong of plastic and glass had been such an integral part of you, an integral part of you and I. It was the link between us when we were apart, sending signals back and forth across the hills. It was the camera that used to take photos of me on country walks. I'd watched you hold it to your ear and listen to your mum's voice, heard you banter with Ed, listened as you made arrangements for work. I'd seen it regularly flung to one side on my bedroom floor with your clothes. You carried it snug in trouser pockets. Maybe it was the last thing that you touched. I clutched it to my heart and lay foetal on the bed sobbing. Later, I plugged it in at your mum's house and we waited to see if it would spring to life but the signal wasn't getting through. The battery was run down and you haven't been paying the bill. It lay lifeless on the carpet. I left it there with its red light glowing when I said goodbye.

Part of me longs for it to revive and part of me is scared to hear the series of pings that would follow if it came back to life. I know it holds within it precious memories that I want to unearth, photos of days that can't be relived except in my mind. But I know that it holds other things too, the evidence of those in-between days, when I didn't know where you were, when I started to wonder where we were. It holds the messages I sent: jovial, casual at first, then worried, almost accusatory. And the messages of the friends that I asked to phone you, just in case, for some unknown reason, you were ignoring me. I look at the last message I typed to you before I knew, still held on my own phone: 'I'm not sure if you're avoiding me, down, lost phone or dead but not liking not knowing. I care about you and miss you and just want to know that you are okay.' I see the subtle change from 'love' to 'care'. the downplaying of the emotion. I didn't, for a moment, think that dead was an option. I wasn't sure anymore that we were going to survive. How could I commit to someone who was out of touch for three days when he knew how worried it made me?

Sometimes I imagine that there might be some technological glitch and that there is a message on your phone that didn't quite reach me. That maybe it is still hanging in the air somewhere over the Peak District. That maybe, there was a moment in those eleven seconds, when you tried to call. That I might turn on your phone and find that in your final moment, you were thinking of me. Not that you had any amends to make. Your last message to me was perfect. You said the all-important words, 'I love you' whilst I danced off onto another topic. I just wish, with all my heart, that my last words to you had been, 'I love you too.' I have told you so many times since your death but I don't know if my words still reach you. I don't know where you are. I said them again to the clouds today as I walked crying down my street. I miss you and care about you and just want to know that you are okay.

I will always love you

IN THE FINAL stages of his life, my father was
brain-damaged. His last round of surgery to remove
his brain tumours had failed and though he was still
irrefutably himself, he was a simpler, milder version of
his old character. The truth is, we got on better when
he didn't have all of his faculties intact. My memories
of the last stages of his life are amongst my happiest
with him. We'd had chance to sort things out.

I remember this moment like it was yesterday. We
were in his kitchen. He was sitting in a high-backed
chair with his wife behind him. He asked me, as he
regularly did, if I loved him. It was on his mind, always,
the distance that had been between us, his failings as a
parent of a daughter who, though she shared so many
of his characteristics, didn't fit his mould. And, feeling
relaxed and happy, I held his hand and started warbling
the words of Whitney Houston: 'and I-I will always
love you-oo, I will always love you…' I can still picture
him laughing with tears streaming down his face. It
was my last good moment with him.

Fast forward a decade or so and I am walking the
dog in the cemetery. I have been talking to your mum.
She's asked me to write a poem that she can read as we
scatter your ashes later on that day. I'm feeling grateful.
I've just read it to her and she loves it. I am pleased that
I have been able to do something to help her, to help
you. I feel a momentary rightness. It happens from time
to time, when everything feels aligned and clear, like

sun shining through the fog. I pick up a feather from the pavement. Silly, maybe, but I do this when I notice them, when I am thinking of you. Most of the time, I am thinking of you. Some people believe that feathers are sent by spirits to comfort us. Do I? Do you?

On this day, I am thinking again about letting you go, this time in the physical sense. I have had a difficult week knowing that this moment is ahead. I have been crying a lot and shouting at the children. My whole being is screaming that I do not want to do it. I do not want to scatter your ashes and I do not want to let you go. I want to go back to the life that we were building together. I don't want to be here, being an angry single parent again, feeling lonely. I don't want to be spending my day writing poems for memorial ceremonies, finding new ways to say goodbye. I want to be living and loving and hoping. I want to spend my Saturday like we used to, gallivanting over the moors, laughing and loving and feeling alive.

'He replenishes you,' my friend once said.

You do. You did. You topped up my tank with your love so that I had energy for the children in the week ahead. Now Saturdays are spent crying, leaving me tired when they return.

And you cannot return. And as I walk I acknowledge that maybe I am gradually moving into that mythical place called acceptance and that this is yet another kind of torture. Denial was easier. At least with denial I could imagine that we might still be together somehow. Acceptance means recognising that you cannot come back and that one day I might love someone else. And I don't want to love someone else. Nor do I want to be alone forever. I feel guilty for even considering a future with someone else, even though the someone else is only in my mind and not in my life or my heart. My mind is on a loop, on the fence, still wondering how to hold onto you, how to let you go. And then I hear a song playing. It is Whitney Houston. I stop and listen to the words, feeling that maybe you are speaking to me. It goes like this: 'I hope life treats you kind, and I hope you have all you dream of. And I wish you joy and happiness, but above all this, I wish you love. And I-I will always love you.' I look around to see where the music is playing from but there are no cars or houses with open windows. And then I realise that the song is coming from my bag. I reach down to my phone and it is playing from my iTunes. But I don't have Whitney Houston in my library (I don't even like Whitney Houston). I study it for a moment, trying to work out how it is playing and then I give up. Who cares? If ever there was a man who would send me a message in music, it is you, even if it is Whitney Houston. I remember my dad and I smile.

Later, I scatter your ashes with your family. Your mum reads my poem and we toss roses onto the ground. Bad planning and logistics mean that, after we've put part of you on the ground by the reservoir at Redmires, I have to run at great speed along the road to our spot with the rest of your ashes in the green, plastic container and leg it up the hill because I don't want to leave your mum out in the cold for long. I trail your ashes like I am Gretel trailing breadcrumbs, all the way up the hill, singing 'Somewhere Over the Rainbow' the way I did the week before you died, before your loving heart stopped beating one cold March night. I sing between gasps of breath until I reach our spot, the spot where we first watched the sun set the summer before, and I lay my final rose on the grass. And then I turn immediately, laughing, with tears streaming as I gallop back down the hill over the heather and gorse, saying to the clouds:

'Do you remember? How we ran hand in hand down this hill, like we were kids?'

And I know you do. And letting go of your ashes is fine after all. Because your ashes are not you. You are always with me and just at that moment, you are literally a part of me. In the wind your ashes have covered me so that my hair is stuck with particles of you, my eyelashes are crusted, my hands are grey and I am crunching you like sand in my teeth. And I am happy to merge with you again just for a moment.

You are gone. But you are not gone. The love continues but not in a physical sense. I know that you would want me to be happy one day, if I can. You showed me what love is and the bar is high now. Wherever you are, I am sure that you still love me and, even if one day I love someone else, I will always love you.

As we scatter your ashes

You loved the earth,
you loved the sky,
you were loved at birth
and when you died.

We release you now,
you're free to fly,
through clouds of love
up in the sky.

Farewell, we miss you
but won't say goodbye.
You are part of us all, still.
Love cannot die.

The future doesn't exist

I WENT BACK to see my old therapist last week. It was a routine follow-up from the sessions I had when we were together. She was the one who was helping me to trust again, who encouraged me to take a chance on love with you. She told me that no one is perfect, that nothing is permanent. Love is like a cup of coffee, she said. It always ends. Someone will always leave or die. All we can do is enjoy the coffee while it lasts. When you died, she acknowledged that she didn't expect my coffee break to be so short. (I'm not sure if I ever told her that I don't like coffee.) I start crying as soon as I walk through the door, remembering all the conversations we have had in this room about you. I cry as I tick the boxes on the routine form asking me how often in the last two weeks I have felt anxious, or sad or hopeless (most days, every day). I cry when she asks me if I think a lot about you (most of the day, every day). I cry as my pen hovers over that box that asks if I have had thoughts that I would be better off dead, as I explain that I have no plan to kill myself (I love my children) but that, often, when I am exhausted and drowning in waves of sorrow, I still have that thought that I would rather not be here anymore. Dead would be easier than living with this pain. It is natural, surely, to want to be with your loved one, and dead is where you are. I cry when she tells me that my scores are lower than when I started seeing her eighteen months ago, and that, according to some clinical diagnostic criteria,

I am suffering from moderate to severe depression, that my anxiety levels are high. She suggests antidepressants and some online CBT. I leave feeling worse than when I went in. I'm not just grieving anymore. I'm now mentally ill. Someone in some central NHS office has created a downloadable test that tells me so. It must be true.

I try not to let it get to me but I wonder again if I should be over this by now. I have passed the six-month milestone after all. I logged it as it went by and hoped for some respite. We were properly together for six months so six months seemed a reasonable length of time to mourn your loss. And I'd read somewhere that if you're 'functionally and significantly impaired by grief symptoms' six months after being bereaved, then you move into the territory of 'complicated grief'. And I remember the TED talk that I watched in March that told me that happiness is all in the mind and nothing to do with life circumstances. Apparently, six months after trauma, in most cases, the trauma has no bearing on levels of contentment. Evidently, I am not most cases. (Mind you, I have been through a whole heap of recent traumas. I have covered most of the most stressful life events in the last three years – sick child, ill health, separation, death of a parent, death of a partner, massive change in financial circumstances and I threw in a house move just to finish me off.) But I am complicated, still suffering, doing it wrong.

It was the mindfulness teacher who suggested the group watch the TED talk last time. She recommended it again this time, as I restarted the course six months after your death. 'Take it gently,' she'd said to me, 'see how it sits'. And it was sitting okay until she mentioned that talk again, and my mind was flung back to that evening when we were apart and I was telling you about the dude on TED and his theory that happiness is all in the mind, all about living in the moment. 'That makes sense to me,' you'd said. 'Longer-term thinking is more vague and uncertain, more likely to lead to anxious thinking.' Twenty-four hours later you were dead.

The therapist asks me the question that other people ask. 'What have you got to look forward to?' She's like a hairdresser asking me if I'm going somewhere nice tonight or if I have holiday plans, as if a night on the town will fix it all, as if things might look better from the top of the Eiffel Tower. My mind draws a blank. I can't see the future any more. The future now is vague and uncertain and reflecting on it leads to anxious thinking. I shake my head and she adds up my scores and shakes hers. I am failing again.

I leave her office seventy pounds poorer and seventy per cent less happy. Rather than head to the GP for some pills, I think of the words of the mindfulness teacher and ground myself by asking questions that I can answer, the questions writers often ask: what can you see, what can you hear, what can you feel, what can you smell? I see my daughter's freckles, speckling cheeks that are rose-petal soft to my touch. I hear the rustle of autumn leaves underfoot. I feel the water supporting my weight in the pool. I wake up and smell the coffee, even though I don't like what I smell. I do as she suggests and watch my feelings like clouds in the sky. I name them, as writers like to do, welcome them in. I see you, Pain. I feel you, Anxiety. I know you, Grief. Ah, Loneliness, you too. I remember you. I label the emotions, refuse to take on the label myself. I have moments, hours and days of unbearable depression but I am not depressed. I am grieving but I am not just grief. Yes this grief is complicated and cumulative. I have been through a lot over a lot of years. It will take time to recover.

A few days later, I get a message from my daughter's school. A girl has died. She was nine years old, healthy by all accounts. She contracted meningitis and died suddenly, just like that. I have to lie down and cry when I hear the news. I feel it fully now. It cracks open the rift in my broken heart again. I can't bear to imagine the carnage in another's life of such a brutal loss. This wasn't in anyone's plan. In six months' time, I wonder, will her parents have recovered? Will they be as happy then as they were last week? Will they be back to normal? Dr TED can say what he likes but I don't believe him. When death explodes into your life like that, there is no normal any more. Everything has changed. Everything is rearranged. Life will never be the same again. They will never be the same. I am not the same.

But it is not all doom and gloom, not for me, not now as I approach seven months without you. I reflect again on the therapist's questionnaire and wonder where the other questions are? The ones that paint a balanced picture. How many times in the last two weeks have you felt joy? How often have you felt love? How many moments of calm have you experienced? Did you see today, the beauty of the trees? How many times this week have you held something precious in your hand? Most days, every day.

I am living in the moment now, like you did, like we did. I take notice of each moment and hope that, perhaps, the future will take care of itself. Yes my moments of sorrow are many and as deep and dark as the deepest sea, but I have moments of joy too, and these moments are brighter now and more precious. At night, I hold my children tightly, marvel at freckles and fingers and locks of hair. I know that this moment might be our last. Life is made up of moments – unbearable beauty alongside unbearable loss. This moment is all we have. The future doesn't exist.

The autumn of grief

The family tree is broken,
the main branches diseased and fallen.
Only this stump remains.
This tree has been pruned too far back.
You can kill a tree with too much pruning;
some varieties just want to grow
free.

This tree once had dreams,
wanted to be a palm on a distant beach,
dripping with coconuts and
swaying to the beat of a calypso wind.
But now she stands like a lump of lead,
dormant in the damp earth
on the brink

of autumn.
Dormant but not silent,
she whispers in the dark,
tells grim tales of long winters
and deforestation.

I tie her to a stake,
smother her feet in fallen leaves
and water them with tears.
I watch them break down
to feed the soil.

Just now this tree cannot grow,
so she lies low,
waits for spring.
New life will surely come one day
not too far away.
Not today.

My brain has been blown to pieces

HERE'S SOMETHING I never knew until this year. When someone you really love dies suddenly without warning, it is not just your heart that gets broken. Everything is broken. There is not one tiny corner of your life that is unaffected. It is like a bomb has exploded into the centre of your reality and smashed it all to smithereens. Nothing makes sense anymore. It is like you've gone out for the day and come home and someone has changed the locks and rearranged the furniture. Everything looks wrong. The person who was at the centre of your world has randomly disappeared and it's like they've taken huge chunks of you with them. The bits that they haven't taken have been smashed into minute fragments and scattered who knows where. Some of them you might find gradually, close by, in the weeks and months following the explosion. Maybe they're just stuck in the waste disposal unit or down at the bottom of the garden in the compost. But some have been blasted into space and I'm not sure they ever return. Sometimes, you might find a corner of something that looks vaguely familiar and feel pleased that you're starting to piece things back together but when you try it for size, it just doesn't fit anymore. Then you remember about the changing of the locks and the furniture and realise that you're going to have to start from scratch.

Here are a few things that go missing when someone close to you dies without warning. Your sense of order: if people can just vanish overnight, anything is possible. Anything might happen at any moment. Your sense of justice: it turns out really bad things happen to really good people. If this is the case, is there any point in being good anymore? Is there any point in anything? The illusion of control: why plan for tomorrow when tomorrow might not even happen? Friends and family that you thought you could rely on: turns out not everyone wants to be close to a disaster zone. Your belief system: if you thought there was a benevolent God before, chances are you find yourself questioning their benevolence now. If you didn't think there was a God perhaps you start looking for one. It's all very well believing that one life is all you have when you're twenty-one and studying philosophy, but when your soulmate has just disappeared, suddenly, that philosophy seems sorely lacking. Your sense of narrative (important if you're a writer): the end just happened in the middle, redemption and resolution seem impossible and, frankly, the narrative trajectory is stuffed. Your empathy for other people: you either have too much or not enough. You can't watch the news anymore because one more bit of sadness could tip you over the edge, but when your friend is moaning about her husband or her job you want to bite her head off because she has no right to complain when her partner is not dead. Your sense of self: this angry, confused person is not the person you're used to being. Your memory: you can recall precise details about your time spent with your loved one but everything else is obliterated. Your brain: your brain has been blown to pieces.

Sometimes I think my brain has been more badly affected than my heart. I just can't remember or process things in the way that I used to be able to. Basic tasks baffle me. Emails go unanswered, bills go unpaid, bits of paper disappear on a daily basis and information, rather than going in one ear and out of the other, goes in one ear, bounces off this huge boulder of grief and goes straight back out the way it came in. People ask me if I've had a nice a weekend and I genuinely have no idea. I mean, I know it probably wasn't a nice weekend because those don't happen anymore, but I don't know what I did. Often, I literally don't know what day, week or month it is. My daughter corrected me the other day when I said it was 2017. Turns out I was wrong. The children correct me a lot. I get my words muddled and can't add up. I look at the stats for my blog and can't work out if something has been read a hundred times or a thousand or ten thousand. It's like my brain just looks at numbers and starts malfunctioning. Computer says no. It has taken me six weeks to assemble the six administrative pieces of paper necessary for me to run my school writing group. I forget to invoice for work that I've done. Frankly, if I had a proper job, I would have had to leave.

I have a theory as to why this happens to brains experiencing extreme shock and grief, and it goes like this: when something so enormous has happened, all of your brain's energy goes on trying to make sense of it. Your brain goes into its habitual problem-solving mode and sets to work. This is one hell of a problem so it needs all the brain cells you've got. It is scrambling about trying to make the narrative make sense, trying to find the missing pieces, trying desperately to make this okay. We've been programmed to believe that it is all down to us, the universe is ordered and if we just work hard enough we will be rewarded. And so our brains work overtime trying to make it so. But however hard we try, the pieces are still missing and, eventually, our brains pack up and go home, defeated in their efforts.

Grieving takes up most of our energy. And then there are other questions to grapple with. Big questions. What is the meaning of life? What happens after death? Where has the person I love gone? What the fuck am I supposed to do now? All of which doesn't leave much brain for anything else, especially if there are kids to take care of. So, my brain is ninety per cent this big boulder of grief and the rest of it is looking after the kids. Outside of this, only the areas where I am naturally accomplished still function. I can still write, so long as I'm writing about you or grief and I can still teach. I wasn't a naturally ordered person to begin with and now my ability to be ordered has been obliterated. It is coming back slowly, as I find those pieces in the garden, but, seven months on, processing this grief is still taking up most of my brain cells.

I've been away by myself this weekend. I went on a trip down memory lane, walking the path that we once walked, visiting the jeweller we met who has promised to make me a ring with the silver that you left. And, just this morning, I was congratulating myself on achieving several milestones. Firstly, this weekend, I read two chapters of a book that was not about grief. This is miraculous. I have not been able to read since you died; I can't concentrate for long enough and I can't see the point in stories that aren't true. I also read at least three articles in the newspaper (skim-read but progress, nevertheless) and completed all but two clues in the crossword. I felt quite proud of myself. I left the holiday cottage feeling positively smug until I got halfway down the road and realised I'd forgotten to leave the keys. I drove back and posted them through the letterbox. Slowly but surely I am putting myself back together. But when I got home and tried my key in the lock, it wouldn't work. I was back at square one: the locks had been changed, the furniture rearranged. And then I looked at my keyring and realised that I had posted the keys to my own house through the letterbox of the holiday cottage and was trying to force the holiday cottage key into the lock to my house. Turns out I still have a long way to go.

Keeping on

I WAS LOOKING through your photos yesterday, searching for a photo for my blog, when I came across the photos that you took last year at the Yorkshire Sculpture Park. I noticed the date: 10th October 2015. It was the day we properly got together (for the second time). It was a year ago today.

I notice every month when the 10th comes round. The 10th is the day that you died. Seven months today.

I notice other anniversaries too, noticing often what I was doing this time last year. Today is one of those for another reason. Tonight I am reading with other writers in The Red Deer pub as part of the Off the Shelf literature festival. I read there last year with the same writers. Last year I read from a romantic novel that I was writing, smiling at you in the audience, proud to have you there cheering me on. Tonight I will read from my grief blog and try not to notice the gap where you were. I have switched from fiction to memoir, in a relationship to single. Narratives aren't always under the writer's control.

I miss your support during this festival season. Last year you were my groupie, my cheerleader, my photographer and my chauffeur. You even helped me choose my outfits for my book launch. You were so proud to be with me and I was so proud to have a boyfriend who, for once, was behind me and everything that mattered to me. I introduced you to my friend,

Anni, who shook your hand and told you fiercely, to 'look after Beverley'. You promised that you would. You did. You were neither overly-impressed nor threatened by my writing, just loving and admiring. You were the perfect writer's partner.

I remember the conversation we had about my writing and about ambition. You said you were glad that I didn't need you to be ambitious because you weren't sure what to be ambitious about. 'I've never seen myself as a front seat sort of person,' you said, 'and nor am I a back seat sort of a person. More the kind of person who makes his own seat.' I loved that about you. In the same conversation you said that you knew that big things would happen for me in my writing career and that you were right behind me. Or maybe you were alongside me. And maybe now, you are somewhere above me, in your own seat. 'Keep on trucking, girl,' you said. I will. I do. Even without you. And even though I don't recognise myself in the photos from last autumn, I know that the optimistic author is still in there somewhere and that one day she will return. You helped me on my way, Blacksmith Paul. Thank you.

Shipwrecked

Some days, some parts of days, I am buoyant, afloat.
Some days I even think I can steer.
Some days I think I can see the shore.
Some days I am brave. I push the boat out.
Some days I push the boat out too far.

M ONDAY WAS ONE of those days. I thought I
could do it. I thought I could stand up in front
of an audience and read the words straight from my
broken heart. And I did. And it was awful, not because
of what I was reading (though maybe that was part of
it) but because all I could see was that you weren't there.
And all I could remember was that this time last year
you had been cheering me on, that this time last year I
was full of hopes for the future: I had a wonderful new
boyfriend, my mum was alive and I was launching my
first book.

As it turned out, the convergence of my reading with
the day we got together was too much to take and I was
thrown back into disbelief again asking the same old,
unanswerable questions: How could you have been
there just last year? How could you disappear, just like
that with no warning? How could the ending happen
so close to the beginning and how am I supposed to
face the future now? I stood up there trying to listen
to the words of my fellow authors but all I could hear
were the words of the letter that you wrote to me at

this time last year, when you talked about all that you wanted our future to be, our future together that has been wiped out. I cannot believe it still. On the way out of the pub a man smiled at me. It surprised me to think that a man could find me attractive still; evidently my exterior doesn't look like my insides. The man had a laptop and a nice face. Maybe he was a writer and a kind man. It surprised me to realise that I was available, and that, at some point, if I don't want to be alone forever, I am going to have to consider other men. I smiled back at him and then walked out of the pub crying. I didn't want him. I don't want someone else. I want you. I want to go back to the life we were building together, the life that has been destroyed.

On Tuesday I woke up crying and didn't stop. I cried through my mindfulness class, tears seeping out from beneath the eye mask as I tried to focus on my breathing and not on the gaping hole of the future. I sought refuge at your mum's and cried some more. I was back to searching again, for a piece of you to hold onto and your mum held out her hand like a branch at the water's edge and I clung on. I cried as I drove to my friend's for tea, cried into the nutritious stew she'd cooked. I went for a massage and cried into the towel, face down on the table. I came home, lay down on my bed and cried some more. I cried as I messaged a friend, cried down the phone to her when she rang, as I told her again how unbelievably unbearable this pain is. I cried myself to sleep.

Now I am shipwrecked, exhausted, washed up again on a small island of calm, unable to move, waiting for the wind.

Grief is not linear and sometimes all the emotions

strike at once: anger, shock, denial, depression, pain, guilt. I am in the eye of the storm and all I can do is cling on for dear life even while my whole being is screaming that this is impossible, that this is more than any human soul can survive. The pain now is no easier to bear than the pain at the beginning. Sometimes it feels worse. Maybe the contrast is bigger now between the moments of lightness and the depth of the dark. I don't know.

From my island of calm now, I look back at my life this week and it seems ridiculous. I am so privileged. What did I actually do: read a few words to a few people, had a drink with writers, lay down on a mat watching my breath, spoke with friends, had a massage, ran a couple of writing workshops. But, inside, I feel like I have been out on the high seas at night without a rudder or a map or a compass, when the waves are titanic and the winds are whipping across my face, utterly alone in the storm.

Grief isn't linear.

I'm not sure it's even cyclical.

Grief is exhausting.

Today I am shipwrecked.

Counting

These days I find myself counting,
I am always counting.
I count breaths, days, months,
log the seasons as they go by:
spring, summer, autumn.
Only winter lies ahead.

I don't know why I count,
don't really know what I am counting.
Life is upside down and back to front
and I'm not sure anymore
if I am counting up
or counting down,
if I am counting towards something
or away.

But I count the days,
tick them off on the calendar
labelled 'After';
you ended as it began.

I don't want to count:
every day takes me further
from a day spent with you
and a day closer to

But I count anyway,
watching time pass by,
amazed by the number of
days survived,
amazed still that you died,
amazed I am still alive.

Lost

I saw him in the park a while ago, your old friend who runs the fairground, who told me of his own loss soon after you died. He didn't ask me how I was. (I appreciate that in a person now.) He just gave me a hug, looked me in the eye and said, 'you're in the lost zone, aren't you?' I nodded. 'It takes a long time,' he said with a wisdom that only comes from experience. 'It will take a long time.'

I'm not sure what 'it' is. Some people might call it feeling better. Some might call it recovering from shock and grief. Some might talk of getting over it or getting back to normal. I'm not sure any of those things are possible. I don't think I can return to the place I was in before. I'm not sure that 'it' is even a destination I want to go to. The truth is, I'm not sure where I want to go at all. All I know is that he was right. I am in the lost zone. And 'it' is taking a long time.

Funny that lost used to be a good place to be. When I was with you, for our twenty-four-hour periods together, there was no time, no destination. We meandered through the day, often through the wilderness, aimlessly content, always happy to stray from the path. We didn't know where we were going from the day we set out together and most of the time we didn't care. Neither of us knew how we were going to be together but we knew we couldn't live our lives apart. 'I can't imagine you not being in my life,' you said and I felt the same. I still can't imagine my life without you now but somehow

I am living it. Having you by my side is no longer an option. There is a huge empty space where you used to be; a vacancy that I'm not sure how to fill. It is a lonely life being a single parent and an orphan. It is not a path I would choose to go down. But it is the path I am on.

I reflect sometimes that it's not just a partner that has gone missing since you died. Huge parts of me have gone too. My world has shrunk to this tiny zone of grief. It reminds me of being a new mum, when the world seemed to be encapsulated in a tiny fingernail. Only this time my focus is death instead of life, overwhelming absence instead of overwhelming presence. Focus shifts when lives come into and leave this earth. Everything is re-evaluated. I'm not sure anymore how I want to fill my days. So much of life feels pointless. So I lean towards the things that keep me sane, that bring me joy: writing, sharing my words, teaching, nature, my children. And love? Love has always been what I value above all else but I'm not sure I even want it anymore, not that kind of love, not the kind of love we had. Love like that doesn't come around every day.

Still, I reactivated my OK Cupid profile yesterday, just for five minutes, just to see who was still around, just to see how it felt. Crazy to think that it's only a year or so since I deactivated it. I turned it on just long enough to watch a few people watching me, to watch the numbers of my 'likes' go up. Counting again, I re-read my profile, wondered if it was still true, wondered if I was still the same person, found that I am not. Found that none of the men on OK Cupid were you. Read about men who want someone who 'doesn't take life too seriously', who 'likes going out'. Found myself deactivating swiftly. Confirmed that I am not ready.

I wonder what I would write if I were to re-write my OK Cupid profile now. It might look something like this:

My self-summary
Heartbroken writer, lost since March 2016, seeks a new direction. Still sincere and quirky, just very tired and sad. Doesn't like going out. Tried it last Saturday and had to stave off a panic attack. Might consider nights in with someone who gives good hugs and is attracted to women who cry a lot and talk about previous partners all night.

What I am doing with my life
Mostly I am wondering how the fuck I ended up here again. When I'm not wondering about that, I'm wondering what the point of anything is and writing about my lost love and grief. Attractive huh?

I'm really good at
Okay, I am still good at writing and teaching and swimming and talking, just that I am mostly writing and talking about sadness.

Favourite books, movies, shows, music and food
Truth is I haven't read a book that isn't a grief memoir for the last year. I don't watch TV or films either (can't concentrate for long enough and don't see the point). Listen to the occasional sad song and eat whatever is in the fridge (so long as it's in date and free from gluten, dairy, eggs and sugar). Feel too wobbly to drink alcohol. Living life on the edge.

The six things I could never do without
Writing, my children, nature, oh, and that man that I am doing without. Can't think of two more.

I spend a lot of time thinking about
Death and how to live a good life in the face of devastation.

On a typical Friday night I am
Crying.

I'm being slightly facetious, of course. It's not quite that bad. Still, I wonder what kind of man would fall for a woman like that? Only someone strong and brave and true. Only someone like, well, like you. I know that, even now, you would take me as I am and love me anyway. You weren't afraid of tears. I think of the words of my bereavement counsellor: 'The worst grief is when the person who would have made it better is the one who died.' She is so right. You made it all better. Without you it is all a lot worse.

I've been thinking of the words of another mentor this week as well. Megan Devine runs Refuge in Grief and she doesn't believe in recovering either, but she does ask this question: 'Given that what I've lost cannot be restored, given that what was taken cannot be returned, what would healing look like?'

This week I found it a helpful question and I started to wonder, knowing that wondering is the first step on a long road to who knows where.

This much I do know: I'm not ready for dating yet. So instead I will keep holding onto your fleeces instead of your body at night and I will talk to you in the clouds instead of face to face. It's not the same but it will have to do while I am still lost and wondering which path will lead me to a future. Other things I know are that I can feel the path beneath the undergrowth, that you will help me to find my way and that slowly I am moving forwards. This week, at least I started looking for a path. I don't know where my journey will take me but one thing is for sure: it will be a road less travelled. And it will be different to the one I would have walked with you. I am different now. Two roads diverged in a yellow wood. You left me at a crossroads and I don't know where I'm going anymore. But I will keep going anyway because what else can I do?

I want to go home now

THIS IS WHAT happens. Sometimes I'm with friends and maybe I'm feeling okay for a while. I'm chatting about something else, in the world together with other like-minded souls and it's not so bad anymore, this grief malarkey, it's manageable really, just a background hum, a touch of interference, a slight buzz of low-level anxiety, like an irritating fly that I can't quite block out, a dripping tap in another room.

And then someone says something. Maybe a friend mentions their partner or their summer holiday plans. Perhaps they ask me what I'm doing for Christmas. Or perhaps someone walks by with the same build as you, the same smell, the same clothes. And the noise is a crescendo building, anxiety rising up from the pit of my stomach and soon there are flies swarming all over my skin and the water is pouring out of the tap and flooding the system. Eventually there is so much water that the flood activation alarm sounds and the building has to be evacuated. So I go outside, take deep breaths and find myself thinking, again, that I just want to go home now. I have done well. I've made it through another day. But now, please, can't I just go home?

It reminds me of when I first had a proper job and I came home every day exhausted. Just finding the toilet or working out which teabags I was allowed to use was like climbing a mountain. And I felt proud that I'd got through it and then realised, in horror, that this was my new life and that I had to go back and do it again, and again, and again. It was too much for me. I went freelance. But there is no escape from this life of grief, this new life of mine. And though I'm doing well, all things considered, I am so tired of getting out of bed every day and carrying on.

So, I watch the friends turn back towards their lives, pick up phones to send messages, walk towards cars that arrive to collect them. I wave them goodbye and as they retreat into the distance towards their homes, I remember that I am locked out of mine. When they get back they will relive the moments of their day, continue the ongoing conversation of their lives and I will turn towards the gap where you used to be. There is no one to ask me how my day was, no one to recount my stories to. Life is a series of unconnected scenes with no plot, no backdrop, no audience.

It is cold outside and I think about calling someone but there is no one to call for help because you had the key and my mum had the spare. And I know that this is loneliness. And this is my life. So I walk all night, looking for a way back home, even though I know that I can never return. It is tiring, all this walking. And all of this noise. I want it to stop. I want to rest now. I just want to go home.

Raising the dead

I'VE NEVER BEEN a fan of Halloween. As a child, I went to every Halloween party in a tutu, waving a magic wand made from tinfoil in the hope of protecting myself from all the black magic in the air. I could never watch the scary films either. I was traumatised by *Bambi* and *Watership Down* and never progressed onto anything harder. I didn't like any mention of death. In fact I often had nightmares as a child about dying and about losing everyone I loved. Halloween and I were never going to get along.

Since I've had children myself, I've got into the spirit of it a bit. It has seemed like harmless fun, just a chance to dress up and eat sweets. Until this year.

This year, the sight of smeared make-up has been giving me flashbacks to finding your body. This year, I paused before purchasing a scythe for my weapon-crazy six-year-old; I don't need reminders of the Grim Reaper. This year I felt physically shaken standing in front of the Halloween decorations that line the supermarket shelves as my children pleaded with me to buy skeletons that lurch out from plastic gravestones. Dead bodies don't come back to life.

I drew the line at the plastic gravestones and we stuck with bats and spiders. I'm okay with bats and spiders. In fact, I like bats and spiders and 'Dead Bat in a Tin' is one of my most treasured possessions since you died. That bat was precious to you. So precious that you loaned him to me for a writing workshop but insisted

I give him back. Your brother found him above the visor in your van. 'Why would Paul have a dead bat in a tin in his van?' he asked. Why not? That's just the kind of guy you were (plus I had only just returned him the week that you died). I keep him safely now and still use him in writing workshops: imaginations grow wings and fly when presented with a dead bat, nestled in an old tin.

I have been thinking for the last few weeks about Halloween, about the irony of our death-averse culture that makes such a big deal now out of celebrating death, just on this one day of the year, with no reverence for the actual dead. And about how Halloween has become almost as big as Christmas, almost as commercial, an environmental disaster of throwaway plastic crap. I've thought of writing about it, but I haven't. I thought about writing about it today, but I won't because mostly, today, I just found myself thinking how much I wish that I could make a tinfoil wand, don a tutu and bring back the dead.

Last night I found myself hugging your jumpers again and talking to you before I slept. 'If I could bring you back,' I said. 'I would never let you go.' It took your death to make me realise just how precious you were. Sometimes I want to be able to show people how it feels to lose something, someone, you love so much. I want them to feel, just for a moment, a tiny fraction of this pain so that they will hold on tightly to their loved ones and never let them go. I want to tell them that everything can disappear overnight, without even a puff of smoke. And to the people who daydream about someone they're not with, I feel like saying, *don't wait, you haven't got forever*. And to the people who aren't

with the right people, I want to say, *grow wings and fly.*
Life is short. Wear a tutu.

I wrote a poem about the destruction of my fairy wings
when I was in an unhappy relationship and I sent it to
you one day. Late at night you would often write messages to me saying, 'send me a poem, Beverley Writer'.
You said my poem made you cry and then you said that
it also made you smile. 'I know my heart will soar with
yours,' you said. It did. And mine with yours.

I look at the bat in the tin, stroke his downy fur and
imagine the scene where I can blow gently onto his
body until his wings take flight again and he can flitter
across the night sky, as bats should. Imaginations take
flight. Writing is the only way that I can bring you
back to life.

Remember Remember

THE MEN ARE out on the green outside my new house, building a bonfire. They are hefting logs around, dragging bags of leaves across the grass, and the air rings with the sound of hammer and nail as they erect a structure fit for the king of all the Guys. I walk past and wave, picture you for a moment, amongst the group, hoisting old kitchen cabinets on your shoulder, hammering with mock vigour, laughing in camaraderie with the other men. How you would have loved to be there, I know. I kick a pile of leaves, talk to you in the clouds again, and walk on with the dog. I phone your mum, call to see your friends. As usual none of them can fill the gap.

I remember last year. I was sad that the children were with their dad on this, my favourite day of the year. I shed a few tears on your shoulder while we tried to decide whether to go out to a bonfire anyway but, in the end, we just lay in bed in my attic room, watching fireworks explode over the city from my window in each other's arms. I remember us listening to Jamie Lawson's song, 'I Wasn't Expecting That'. It wasn't our kind of music but those words resonated for us both. We hadn't expected to find ourselves so deeply in love, not at our age, not with each other. We weren't expecting the ending of the song when it came either, it was so abrupt, the way she dies and the song stops. We weren't expecting it to happen to us.

I didn't go to the bonfire with your friends the night

after, though the kids and I were invited. I was too scared to introduce them to you. I knew they would love you, like they loved the last one who left. I didn't trust you yet to stay. But I remember that you sent me photos of the bonfire and a video of your friend juggling fire and that you learned to Facetime. I can still picture your face looming into view, your laughter over the crackle of the fire, the wonder of you, marvelling at the wonder of it all.

Afterwards I said, come round, the children are in bed. And we sat on my sofa and you smelled of wood smoke and sparks and all was warmth. How lovely it was to see each other unexpectedly, we said, on a Sunday night.

Tonight I will watch the bonfire go up in flames and watch the guy collapse and I will remember; not the man who wanted to blow up parliament, but the man who lit up my life with a spark that burned so brightly, then fizzled and died, leaving just a trail of love like smoke in the air. I will imagine the feel of your arms around me in the darkness and write your name across the night sky.

Tomorrow, I will go to the bonfire with your friends and, this time, I can take the kids. Together we will remember you, the blacksmith, builder of bonfires, a man of fire. On this day, and every day, I remember you. On this night, and every night, I miss you.

What a difference a year makes

THIS WEEK, FACEBOOK has mostly been showing me photos of my book launch which happened 'this time last year'. I can't be the first person to wish that Facebook would stop helpfully reminding me of the past.

This time last year, I had two book launches. The first one was in London on the Monday. It was a magical day, partly because I was launching my first book in Waterstones in Piccadilly but mostly because I let my daughter bunk off school to spend the day in London with me. Even more magical with hindsight, was the fact that my mum managed to persuade her two sons that, in spite of having only recently come back out of hospital, she was determined to go. I don't know if she knew that she wasn't long for this world but we certainly didn't. This time last year they caught a different train to me and went out for a different lunch and then we all travelled home on the train together. This time last year my daughter sat with my mum playing Scrabble on the iPad with my brother while I slumped exhausted in the next booth. This time last year, we all posted the same photo on Facebook. This time last year she was alive. Three weeks later, she was dead.

This time last year I did a fashion show in my kitchen for you. For some reason I was a nervous wreck about this stupid book launch and about what I was supposed to wear. I tried on different outfits and you took photos of me, pretending that having photos would make it easier for me to decide, although really, you just liked taking my picture. You said the purple dress was your favourite but that you didn't want other people to see me in it because it would make you jealous. So I picked two other outfits, one for the Monday (the one we thought my mum would like best) and one for the Wednesday. I love looking at the photos that you took of me, not because I love looking at me but because I love looking at me looking at you looking at me. I can see your presence in my eyes.

On the Wednesday, everyone was there again and this time you came too, in disguise as a friendly photographer. My children were there and I hadn't told them about you yet so you hung about casually taking pictures. You were wearing the dark blue shirt and trousers that you wore every time you needed to look smart. You wore short sleeves even when it was freezing, partly because you didn't have anything smart to wear on a top of your shirt and partly because you were a raging furnace all day long. It was as if you'd absorbed the heat of the forge into your very being. In Waterstones I managed to surreptitiously introduce you to a couple of friends who loved you immediately, observing something that I loved about you too, that you were a man who was comfortable in his own skin, who made other people feel comfortable in theirs. I didn't need to take care of you; you were happy in the background observing. I kept thinking that I should introduce you to my mum but my mum was on cloud nine, running around taking her own photos, feeling proud and liberated, happy to be out on the town, happy to see her daughter finally succeeding at a dream. The moment never arose.

The children remember you from that day though, even though they didn't yet know who you were. My little boy, jumping about excitedly with his shiny blue balloon, let it go so that it sailed high up onto the ceiling of the bookshop. You climbed up onto the table and fetched it down for him, handed the string to him in the manner of a magician, your big hand meeting his little one just for a moment. 'Paul fetched your balloon for you,' my daughter reminded him the other day. 'He was really kind.'

You never showed me the photos that you took of my book launch, for some reason, but I found them after you died. They were the best photos taken that evening. I especially like the one of me and my friend Anni. You liked Anni from the moment she shook her finger at you and told you that you must look after me. She liked you from the moment that you shook her hand and promised her you would. It's not a great picture of Anni but it makes me smile to see the light in my eyes as I'm smiling at you.

In all of the shots of that evening, there are none of you and none of my mum. You were both behind the camera. Neither of you would be around for long, not nearly as long as you should have been. But this time last year, you were both alive and I was in love and things were good. What a difference a year makes.

In which we plant a tree

I THINK YOU would like your tree. It's outside an old shared house that you lived in, the one where you played hide and seek with the landlord when he came for the rent. It's an oak, not an ash. I know you wanted to be an ash but I think you would understand that we couldn't plant an ash because of the problem with ash die back. You should understand; you planted trees for the last couple of years of your life, just on Thursdays and Fridays. It gave structure to your week and a regular income. You enjoyed the camaraderie and the being outside in nature, though you hated getting up early and the restriction of your freedom. You were a man who needed to be free.

It was something both of us have struggled with in relationships, this desire for intimacy and the need for autonomy. Living with partners hasn't worked out well for either of us and you weren't sure you could do it again now. I wasn't sure that I needed you to, although I told you that I was sad to think that by spending my life with you I might never have that again. It was a work in progress. 'I just know that I want more of you,' you used to say. The last time we discussed living together was when you'd come with me to look at a house that I was considering buying, the house that I am now living in. We joked that if we lived here together, you could have a camp bed in the cellar or a hut at the bottom of the garden. No character from fiction reminds me of you so much as

Hagrid and a hut in the garden would have suited you fine. When we got back to mine, we discussed it more seriously and considered the idea that you could keep your own place (you would have needed a workshop anyway) and sleep there occasionally but spend most of your time with me. It was a compromise we were both happy with, perhaps the compromise that we would be living with now, if you were still living. Just in case you are wondering, living without you is no kind of compromise at all.

I remember discussing your need for freedom early on. We were in my campervan. I'm not sure if we were even a couple yet. You said that sometimes you found relationships difficult because you had things that you needed to do. 'What is it that you need to do?' I asked, wondering if it was something I could accommodate (I struggled with the partner who needed to play computer games and watch TV, and the one who needed to go up mountains). 'I need to make things!' you said with obvious delight. And I beamed at you. The need to create is a need that I totally get, it's just that I use different tools.

It is an interesting assortment of people that assemble in the park to plant your tree. Many of them are the same people that congregated at your funeral. We write messages on tags and plant bulbs around the base of your tree, then hold hands in a circle and remember you. I think of the stories people tell later and imagine their heads full of those memories as they stand there, gazing at your tree and remembering the different aspects of you: 'mullocking' Paul, stripping pipes out of derelict buildings; Glastonbury Paul, attracting crowds with a loud-hailer, wearing nothing but a cardboard box; Blacksmith Paul, showing countless friends and family the alchemy of metal; tree-planting Paul, who could lift and dig and banter while he worked. To most you were a friend, to some you were a brother or father figure. To me, you were something else. You were the centre of my world. As I stand amongst the crowd of people who knew you, in some ways I feel more alone than ever. The centre of the circle is just a tree and the people in the circle are not really my circle. No one remembers you the way I do. No one knows what we shared. I feel again all the same old insecurities, imagining that your friends must look at me and think that it could never have worked, that it must have been a casual thing. We know that it wasn't. We know that it did work. We might not have looked it but we were so alike on the inside.

As people share their memories, I see aspects of the Paul that I knew though and aspects of me too. 'He was a man you could tickle,' says one friend, which makes me laugh, picturing you laughing with me as I pinch your cheeks 'like Auntie Ethel'. 'He was great at crosswords,' someone else says, and I see us one Saturday, holed up in a cafe, racing to fill in the grid, blissfully content together. 'When he went on holiday, he just packed books,' says your sister and I remember myself as a child, trying to ram just one more book into my bag. 'He would give you things that he thought you'd like,' says another friend, and I think of all the things that you gave to me and the things you gave to my kids, even though they didn't know you. You were endlessly generous with your possessions and your time. And then someone says this: 'The thing I loved about Paul was that he made his own way'. I smile and nod.

'That's why I loved him,' I say.

Today, I find myself mindlessly looking again at dating profiles, not because I'm ready but just because I am trying again to imagine loving someone new. I swipe left over and over again on Tinder until there is no one in my region that I haven't discarded. It all seems so hopeless. Everyone is unique, of course, but there is no one like you. I don't want to spend my time with someone whose profile shows them holding a pint, or standing by a fancy car or bungee jumping off a mountain. I don't want someone who watches TV or plays football. I really don't want one of those people who doesn't take life seriously; we're just not going to get on at the moment. I want a man whose face lights up when he thinks of making something, who delights in words and clouds and derelict buildings. I want a man who doesn't worry about what other people think, who is full of love and kindness. I wanted you.

At the end of the day, we go back to the co-housing project where your friends live, and I read a bit of my blog to the people who remain. It takes some courage. I wonder, as I often do, if your friends think I've lost the plot, reflect that I probably have. 'I worry that people think I'm weird,' I say to your friend as he's leaving. 'We're all weird,' he says. And I think then that maybe people do get it. Maybe it's the thing all of your friends have in common. They all walk their own unique paths. I am reminded of the list of Dr Seuss' 'Rules to Live By', that I used to have stuck to my office wall. The last one feels fitting:

'We're all a little weird and life's a little weird and when we find someone whose weirdness is compatible with our own, we join up in mutual weirdness and call it love.'

Our mutual weirdness was the best. I don't know if I can ever find that kind of love again, but I download those quotes again and realise that I am still left with the others. They can still be my rules for living. I stick them back up above my desk:

'Be who you are and say what you mean, because those who mind don't matter and those who matter don't mind.'

(Who cares if writing a blog about you is weird?)

'Today you are you, that is truer than true.

There is no one alive that is you-er than you.'

(The me I am is the me you loved. I'm okay with that person.)

'You have brains in your head and feet in your shoes. You can steer yourself in whatever direction you choose.'

(It is still true. I just need to choose a new direction.)

I can't go where I wanted to go, but I can speak my truth and walk my own path, as you did. I don't know where the path will lead me but I know that sometimes I will walk to the foot of the oak tree and imagine that you are moving like the wind in the leaves.

In the end, you were getting tired of the tree planting and the moving people and the odd jobs. You wanted to make things again. 'Break free, Blacksmith!' I said to you the night before you died. You did. You are a free spirit now. And so am I.

Grief is like Snakes and Ladders

YOU START AT square one in a state of shock and disbelief. Time is a blur and you move along in a horizontal line, counting days like squares. And then one day, you land at the foot of a ladder and you start climbing upwards, out of the gloom and towards the light. You feel that maybe you're making some kind of progress in this new world of grief. You feel you're heading in the right direction, you're taking short cuts and zooming forwards. You start to imagine that you're winning. And then something happens and you step on the mouth of a snake and go tumbling backwards. Sometimes you are right back at the beginning again. This happened to me yesterday.

When I set out yesterday, I was really doing pretty well. I had plans for how to spend the day and, for the first time, plans for the future. It had even been about three days since I last sobbed my heart out which is definitely a record. But then I decided to call and see your mum, because I was round the corner from her flat and I thought I'd pick up your phone while I was there. It came back from the police station a little while ago, but we've not been able to get it working. After I'd seen your mum, I took the phone to the shop down the road to see if they could bring it back to life. They said it might take a few days but by four o'clock they had fixed it. So I drove back to collect it.

I thought about waiting until I got home but I couldn't bear the suspense, so I sat in the car and opened the screen. I was hoping to find some photos that I took of you on our trip to Brimham Rocks but there were hardly any photos on it at all. It turns out that when you were telling me something about your two phones and the relative quality of the photos and the cock-up with the two contracts, you were probably telling me that you had decided to keep the old phone for taking photos and were just using this one for calls. It looks like the photos I have of you will stay in my memory and never be shared. Instead, I just have the one of the rocks. Who wants a photo of rocks? Rocks will be there for all eternity. You were not.

I knew what would happen if I looked through your calls, but I did it anyway. Seventeen missed calls while you were lying dead, about six of them from me. I couldn't listen to the messages because there was no signal anymore. But it was the text messages that did it. And there it was: the last message that you sent. It wasn't a message of love. Instead it was a message about an eBay transaction. You were cancelling an appointment to collect something that you had bought. You said that you couldn't make it that Thursday evening because you were feeling really ill and that it was getting worse as the evening went on. 'I'm not sure I'll be better tomorrow, either,' you wrote. And that was the moment when the snake swallowed me.

I was back at the start again, like I'd slipped through a portal and gone back in time, picturing you lying ill on your bed all alone, willing you to pick up that phone and call an ambulance or call me, wondering what you were feeling, what you were thinking, if you knew, at any time, what was happening to your body. The next message in the list was from me. Just an everyday, late at night 'hello' that you never received. It seems likely that somewhere between seven and ten, you died.

I was shaking so much that I couldn't go home to an empty house so I went to see a friend. While I was parking I reversed into a lamp post and then I must have opened my door into a passing car because there was a man shouting abuse at me as I got out. I had no idea what he was talking about or why he was shouting at me. At first I didn't even realise it was me he was shouting at. There was just an angry voice coming out of a car telling someone to be more careful and to think of the kids and did I want to get killed? I had a cup of tea with my friend and when I got home I sobbed to myself in the bath and later I sobbed down the phone to a friend again. I started re-reading your post-mortem trying to understand, again, how you could have had a headache and memory loss but have died of heart disease. I still don't understand it. Today I have walked around with panic echoing in the background, fear rising. I have been casting about again for something to hold onto. I am back at the beginning, like it just happened yesterday. I can't bear the thought that you died alone and that there might have been something that someone could have done to save you. I tell myself that it's pointless thinking these thoughts. Nothing can change what happened. But I do it anyway.

I found myself thinking again about a friend of yours who said that it was inevitable that someone like you, who was independent and lived alone, would die alone. But I wanted to argue with her. You weren't a single man. You were with me and deeply loved. I just wasn't there when you needed me. I don't blame myself anymore, there is nothing I could have done, but it still it hurts beyond belief to not have been there when you died. I know though, that you weren't truly alone. It consoles me and destroys me at the same time to know that you were carrying me in your heart when it stopped. A part of my heart died with you, though somehow it keeps on beating.

I am back at square one. I roll the dice and edge forwards again, hoping for a six, praying for another ladder, knowing that there are snakes round every corner.

Turbulence

The upping and downing,
the almost drowning,
the black and white,
the dark and light.
The ebbs and flows,
the round it goes.
The toss and turns,
the friction burns.
The holding tight,
the letting go,
the taking flight,
the going slow.
The sinking and swimming,
the ending, beginning.
The future, the past,
the nothing lasts.
The darkness dragging,
spirit flagging.
Gravity pulling,
world dulling.
The waters swirling,
memories whirling,
time passing,
waves crashing.

The senses sharpening,
brightness startling,
the search for home,
the all alone.
The turning towards,
the turning away,
the leaving behind,
the wanting to stay.
The longing, the missing,
the searching, the wishing,
the dreams fading,
heart aching.
The fear of morning,
new days dawning,
the wanting to die,
the staying alive.
The almost sailing
then falling, failing,
faint hopes growing,
keeping going.

Everything I ever wanted

I WAS LOOKING through your photos again last week, putting slideshows together for your memorial, and I came across one I hadn't seen before. Sometimes I think I have looked through everything that you left behind – but then I find, perhaps, a hidden folder within a folder and there is something new to discover. I am still uncovering the evidence, discovering new things about you, falling more deeply in love even though you've now been gone for longer than we were together. It is eight months now and counting, always with the counting, still with the crying, still not better, not fixed, not over it. Not over it at all.

This photo was taken at exactly this time last year. Our initial quandaries about whether we could be together had been resolved and we were going out together to a party. It was a kind of coming out. What had been private was becoming a little bit more public. Even though it is a photo of something so mundane, this photo touched me more than most, because I have some inkling why you took it. I was upstairs getting changed and I'd left a card for you to sign. You had evidently done so and then liked the way our names looked next to each other and taken a picture. Beverley and Paul. Side by side. A couple.

We had a lovely evening that evening. The party was at our mutual friend, Ed's, house. It was really special for both of us to be there together. You danced with me properly for the first time that night and I remember being surprised that you had rhythm. Later, we sat holding hands, in that first phase of love when it is hard to let go. And afterwards, we walked, still hand in hand, down the park in the dark, chatting happily about the evening, deconstructing events, the way couples do. I can still feel the comfort of that rhythm as we fell into step so easily, side by side, a couple. We walked past the space where your tree is now planted and into our future together. We fell a little deeper that night.

Sometimes I am so lonely and missing you so much that I find myself searching for your name again in the list of friends on Messenger (I have to search now because your name is so far down the list of recent messages). I scroll back through the months, from the messages that you never read to the ones we sent in the early days. It is a form of torture that I indulge in from time to time, to bring you back to life in this way and then to feel the full force of your absence again when the messages run out.

I read again the messages that we sent on the day after the party. I was worrying that you might still have doubts. 'Scary stuff, this falling in love,' I said. You reassured me. 'You're everything to me,' you said. 'I want you to know that. I'm just realising the importance of what's happening.' What was happening was really important. We were falling in love: deeply, completely in love in a way that felt new for both of us even though we were middle-aged. 'Somehow, you seem to be everything I've ever wanted and never quite had,' I said.

And, as I read, a crack opens in the universe and I fall headlong through the gap, tumbling into blackness. The past has vanished and the present and future have merged into a gaping chasm. I am crying so hard that I can no longer see the words on the screen, feeling that I can't breathe, sure that I can't survive this pain any longer. I am falling faster and faster into the darkness, clutching your clothes to my chest as if they are the life raft that will save me. Eventually I fall asleep with my phone cast aside on the bed and when I wake, I feel shipwrecked again, the ground like shifting sand beneath my feet, my body water-logged, the sun too bright in my tired eyes. The tears are poised again, waiting to fall.

I let them fall as I sob my way through my bereavement counselling again, as I talk about how precious you were and how impossible it feels to imagine ever finding that kind of love again. Of course I had known real love before, but it was twenty years ago when I was too young to understand what I had. It didn't last for long. And now it feels like it took me forty-five years to find you and just eight months to lose you. The equation is all wrong. I talk again about how private our love was, how so few of our feelings were public because it was still so new. I talk about how upset I am that some friends don't seem to understand our relationship. 'Why do you need other people to validate what you had?' she asks. I can't answer but for some reason, I do. Maybe it's because we never had a wedding or a public declaration, that the closest we came to going public, was a party last November with our names side by side on a card. Perhaps I make our relationship public now because I need someone to understand what we had and what we lost. That this was not something small. That this was monumental. I search your files and our messages to remind myself what it was. I share them to show other people. I am digging up the past, looking for evidence that you lived, that we loved. Thankfully, she, at least, understands. 'You know, the more you talk about him,' she says, 'the more I realise how perfect he was for you.' She is right, you were. You were everything I ever wanted. And now you are everything that I have to live without. In some ways it should be easy; I am used to doing without. But how hard to it is now to live with the knowledge of what we might have had.

They will not give you back

They will not give you back
though I have prayed to gods that I don't believe in
and screamed from the top of the highest hills.
Though I have sobbed until my pillow
is soaked with tears from rage-filled clouds.
No, they will not give you back.

They will not give you back
though I have tried my best to rewind time,
turning clocks back further,
just a little bit further still
as the nights draw in.
No, they will not give you back.

They will not give back to me
those days when love was an endless river
and time stretched long like summer shadows.
They will not give back your arms,
your eyes, your smile, your voice.
They say they have no choice.
They will not give you back.

Though my arguments are valid,
though it is clear and understood
that I do not want to live without you
and that if they could just please return you,
I will be very, very good,
there is no loophole,
the verdict is final.
They will not give you back.

WINTER

(DECEMBER 2016 – FEBRUARY 2017)

a rock and a hard place

We're going a life hunt

(after Michael Rosen)

We're going on a life hunt.
We've got to find a new one.
What a beautiful day!
We're not scared.

Uh-oh! Sadness!
Thick cloud of sadness.
We can't go over it.
We can't go under it.
Oh no!
We've got to go through it:
Stumble, trip.
Stumble, trip.
Stumble, trip.

We're going on a life hunt,
Don't want to find a new one.
It might be a beautiful day but
we don't care.

Uh-oh, numbness!
Brain-dumbing numbness.
We can't go over it.
We can't go under it.
Oh no!
We've got to go through it!
Eating.

Drinking,
Overthinking.

We're going on a life hunt.
We've got to find a good one.
Want a beautiful day!
We're not impaired.

Uh-oh! Memories!
Deep, creeping memories.
We can't go over them.
We can't go under them.
Oh no!
We've got to go through them:
Sinking, drowning.
Sinking, drowning.

We're going on a life hunt.
We can't go back to the old one.
It was full of beautiful days.
Life's not fair.
Uh-oh! Anger!
Hot, mean, anger.
We can't go over it.
We can't go under it.
Oh no!
We've got to go through it.
Storm, rage.
Storm, rage.
Storm, rage.

We're going on a life hunt.
We've got to find a future.
Just one more beautiful day
with someone else who cares.

Uh-oh! Guilt!
Icky, sticky guilt.
We can't go over it.
We can't go under it.
Oh no!
We've got to go through it:
Sorry, sorry.
Sorry, sorry.
Sorry, sorry.

We're going on a life hunt.
They say we've got to move on.
Make our own beautiful days
if we dare.

Uh-oh! The future!
The yawning, dawning future.
We can't go over it.
We can't go under it.
Oh no!
We've got to go through it.

Tiptoe, tiptoe, tiptoe.
WHAT'S THAT?
Minutes, hours and days ahead,
got to keep getting out of bed.
IT'S A LIFE!

Quick.
Back away from the future:
tiptoe, tiptoe, tiptoe.
Back through the guilt:
Sorry, sorry, sorry.
Back through the anger:
Storm, rage, storm, rage.
Back through the memories;
Sinking, drowning, sinking, drowning.
Back through the sadness:
stumble, trip, stumble trip.

Get back to the past,
open the door,
up the stairs.

Oh no!
We forgot to shut the door.
Back downstairs.

Shut the door.
Back upstairs,
Into the bedroom.

Into bed.
Under the covers.

We're not going on a life hunt again.

(Well, not today, anyway).

I don't cry every day anymore

IT IS OFFICIAL. I have been grieving for longer than we were together. Somehow, eight and a half months have gone by since you died. We were only seeing each other for eight.

A lot has happened in that time, Blacksmith, much of it directly related to your death. Just on a practical level, it turns out there is a lot to do when someone you're in love with dies unexpectedly. I've written eulogies, helped to sort your possessions, catalogued photos, analysed post-mortems, scattered ashes, planted trees, organised memorials and, finally, managed to arrange a suitable location and inscription for your bench. Who knew it could be so hard to get someone to authorise the placing of a simple seat? Each different location that we've decided on has had to go to a separate authority for consideration and most of them have been rejected. But it's sorted now, I hope, finally, eight and a half months on. I think you will be pleased with it, when it's in place. I won't tell you where it's going to be yet, though perhaps you already know.

The words, of course, were a challenge. How can a man like you be summed up in the kind of space you'd get on Twitter? Brevity is not my strong point, as you know. I remember how it used to infuriate you when we were messaging each other, that I could type so much faster. By the time you'd replied to something I'd said, I was already two steps ahead. In the end, we settled into a familiar rhythm of a three to one ratio. I still miss those messages.

Now, instead of typing messages to you in the evening, I type messages to the bereaved on Facebook and write blog posts about love and death. I can't really write anything else at the moment. Other projects have been abandoned and now it feels like my life's work is to write about you and about loss. I've joined a new, international community of broken souls. There is a comfort to be found in being amongst people who understand. Most people, it seems, really don't understand. And why should they? It turns out that there is a big gap between empathy and experience. Still, empathy is a gift to be cherished and I have found it in surprising places.

If you're looking down on the chessboard of my life, you'll notice that the pieces have all been rearranged since you died. It's not just the King that is missing. People that were close have moved further away and others, that were on the periphery, have moved closer. Some people have all but disappeared entirely. And there are people there that I didn't even know before, some of them your people – your precious mum, some of your friends. And others, those broken souls. I look into their eyes and see myself reflected there.

Grief, you'll notice, has settled itself into the centre of my life now. It is not as scary as it was at first, no longer the unwanted visitor that I sought to banish, battle with, defeat. You can't fight with something invisible, nor run a sword through absence. You can't retreat from grief either. Even when I moved house, it followed me in, insinuating its way under ill-fitting doors and windows, creeping through the gaps in floorboards, settling into silences and empty spaces, making its presence felt when the world goes quiet. I wouldn't call grief a friend, but it is familiar now, comfortable almost. Grief is a haven from the madness of normality.

Normality is creeping back in though, slowly but surely, in little ways. I can bake flapjack now and I mostly eat proper meals. Fragments of my brain are realigning and I am probably remembering fifty per cent of the things I should be remembering, rather than the ten per cent I was remembering back in March. I've read a few chapters of books (not consecutive, not the same books) and I am starting to take on new projects (some of them not even grief-related). And yesterday I tried to watch TV again. I thought I'd start with *Neighbours*, just twenty minutes of something familiar; I've watched *Neighbours* religiously for decades. It didn't go well. I was out of touch with the characters and plot lines (a lot can change in eight months, even in Soapland). But it wasn't the onscreen drama that that felt wrong, really. It was the step towards more normal behaviour that felt wrong in itself, like trying to return to a place that doesn't exist anymore. The assertion of normality feels like attempting to close a door on this awful episode, which in turn feels like closing a door on you. It is the dance of grief again: the desire for a future, the lure of the past, the need to keep living in spite of the awareness of dying.

Today, as I walked down the stairs at my daughter's school, having run my lunchtime writing group, I thought of you as I always do in the gaps between activities and remembered those early days when I would walk down those stairs crying. In those days, appearing normal for an hour was a monumental feat.

I could only hold back the pain for very short periods of time. Today I didn't cry at all, just went home and made sandwiches, filled in my tax return. In the early days socialising was impossible. But last weekend I went out for an evening (albeit with really good, empathic friends) and I held it together for several hours. There was just one moment when suddenly the floor seemed to tip and I felt I was underwater, unable to hear what people were saying, when I felt the panic rising. But I kept breathing and held on and it passed. Things are improving. I don't cry every day anymore. In fact, when I look back at my blog, I realise that it is a whole week now since I was last in the grip of a proper grief storm. Without question, the periods of calm are getting longer.

In some ways I miss those early days when you were the only thing on my mind, when the whole world was a storm. But it is getting easier now. Not better. No less sad. Just easier. I know you would want it to be easier on me.

Grief is exhausting

D ID I SAY it was getting easier? I lied.

Of course, I didn't mean to lie. Anyone who knows me well knows that I genuinely can't lie. I have to tell people the truth, the whole truth and nothing but the truth, regardless of my relationship with them or the length of my acquaintance. It gets me into no end of bother. I blame my dad. Like an archetypal Yorkshireman, he called a spade a spade, and being on the receiving end of his truth was like being hit soundly around the head with one. I try to be a bit more gentle with other people's feelings but still, for some reason, unless I'm writing fiction, I am compelled to always tell the truth.

And the truth about grief, or about this kind of grief (for I believe there are different kinds) is that grief is unpredictable and temperamental. Just when I think I've got it under control, BAM! It hits me round the head again, like that spadeful of truth and leaves me reeling. Suddenly, I find myself struggling to breathe again, feeling dazed and confused like a cartoon character with stars around my head, in a grief bubble, detached and cast adrift from the rest of the world. And, as if this isn't bad enough, it's then that the panic starts, because I can't believe this is still happening and that there is no escape from the truth that what happened, happened, and that this is my life now. I feel that I can't possibly live the rest of my days with this gaping hole at the centre of my being. I want to run away from that hole but the hole is part of me and there is no escape. It feels that, at any moment, what's left of me might collapse inwards and fall through the crevasse or that I might be sucked into a vortex of oblivion. Seriously. I'm telling you the truth. It feels that bad.

But sometimes, it feels like I can dial my grief down so that it's just a background hum. It is always there, like a constant baseline to the music of my life, but the baseline has become familiar now, maybe it even adds depth. It is irritating, living with this interference, but it is manageable. Sometimes I can even hear a tuneful melody playing alongside it. New instruments are introduced and the different parts harmonise for a while into something beautiful, something that sounds almost like the soundtrack to happiness, almost like hope. And I think, this is nice, it's getting better, things will surely be okay. And it is usually at that moment that grief turns the baseline up so loud that I can barely hear anything else; grief, it seems, doesn't like to be ignored. And so grief asserts itself until the deep, throbbing baseline is so over-powering that the other instruments can't hear themselves playing anymore and everything is discordant and out of tune. Eventually, the melody is obliterated and the orchestra packs up and all that's left is the overwhelming noise of grief. Seriously. I'm telling you the truth. Day after day, week after week, month after month (don't talk about the years, please don't talk about the years), it feels that bad.

'No one ever told me that grief felt so like fear,' says C.S. Lewis on the opening page of *A Grief Observed*. He is right. It does. Grief feels horribly like fear. I wake up every morning with a tightness in my chest and a kind of lurching feeling as if the bed has been moved in the night and I am emerging every day into a strange new world. Gradually, as the daily routines take place, those feelings of terror recede but they return periodically throughout the day, often with no notice, often with no root cause that I can trace. It is like my mind and body are on red alert, waiting for catastrophe to strike even though the worst has already happened, even though, in many ways, I feel I have nothing to fear anymore. 'I am not afraid,' C.S. Lewis wrote. Neither am I. But grief does feel like fear, and feeling afraid all the time is exhausting.

Yes, more than anything else, grief is exhausting. It is a battle every day to reach for goodness, to climb up a shifting mound of sadness towards the light. It is so tiring to get to the end of the day knowing that tomorrow I will have to do it all again. And again. And again. I am so tired that I am shaking. I desperately want to relax but nothing is relaxing. I want to lose myself in a good film, but I can't concentrate. I want to read but I can't follow the plot. I want to write about something that isn't you, that isn't grief, but I can't make up stories at the moment. I am wedded to the truth. I wish I could get drunk but I can't stomach alcohol anymore. I wish I could go out and drink and dance and socialise but I can't do it.

I did go out on Saturday night though (I couldn't have done that a while ago). I went out with a friend to a street market and I floated around like I was an alien in a spaceship from another planet, observing people living their strange lives in a strange world, where all the men had hipster beards and ate food from trays in the freezing cold, in an industrial warehouse with music blaring as if this was the new fun. I felt dislocated, old, out of place. I drank a warm glass of punch, stared at flames in rusty bins, browsing Facebook and Twitter to feel the protective presence of fellow grievers. I read a quote by Emily Dickinson: 'I am out with lanterns, looking for myself.' Exactly. Most of the evening I hung out by one of the hipsters who was stoking the flatbread oven, watching his hands and his forearms, wondering if I found him attractive, longing for male company but not able to think about being with anyone else. 'He's like Paul,' my friend said. And I realised she was right and that I was just standing watching him move the iron in and out of the fire, like he was a blacksmith at a forge.

What I want, of course, is to relax by curling up in your arms in front of the fire and doing nothing. We hardly ever went out. We had no need. What I want is to feel the calm familiarity of your body, your presence, your understanding. But there is a hole where you were that another man can't fill. So I fill it with activity, with exercise, with my laptop, writing until the words blur on the screen, building a fragile bridge across the gap with truth. Writing brings me calm. But it is tiring.

Grief is horrible. Grief is boring. Grief is exhausting.

Hibernation

Sometimes, I wish I was a bear.
I would gather nuts and berries now, in the last flush
   of autumn,
hoard my store while the air is crisp and clear
and then withdraw, hunker down, hibernate.
I would hide in the darkness
as the nights draw in
and sleep, deep in a drift
of white feathers and daydreams.

Someone please anaesthetise me
while these dark days pass over.
Wake me in the spring,
when I can recall the love of sunshine,
when I am ready to live again a full life,
not this half-life of grief.

For now, just let me sleep.

Life goes on

I DIDN'T REALLY rate Auden's funeral poem until this year. Aside from the fact that it's hard to take anything seriously once Hugh Grant has been associated with it, it always seemed a tad melodramatic. All of those pleas to cut off the telephone and silence the dogs annoyed me. Why should the rest of us be denied access to all the wonders of the earth and the cosmos just because one tiny speck of a human being has gone? People have died before and will die again. What makes your grief so special, Winston? That's what I used to think. That's what I thought when we looked through funeral verses when my dad died. That's what I thought when my mum died. But when you died, those words weren't strong enough. 'Stop all the clocks.' I get it now. I really do.

But the clock went on ticking and life continued regardless.

When you died I wanted everything to stop. Time lost all meaning and all of life seemed pointless. I know it was hard for the people around me to witness; I have two beautiful children who are the epitome of goodness and hope and yet, for me, for a long time it did seem that 'nothing now can come to any good'. For the first time in my life, I really and truly just wanted to die, not as a momentary thought but as a pervasive day to day reality. The agony I was feeling – that I still feel sometimes – seemed impossible to bear. I wanted it to stop. I wanted time to stop. I wanted to be where you were.

But the clock went on ticking and life continued regardless.

Even so, my sense of time has gone AWOL. It is nine months since you died now but I can conjure you so vividly in a heartbeat, that I can almost believe that you just walked out of the door and will be back at any moment. And yet, at the same time, each of those two hundred and seventy-five days has felt like a metaphorical trudge across a barren desert, feet sinking into sand, dust in my eyes. Or like crawling up a mountain on my hands and knees in a gale, slipping across frozen wastes, with frost biting at my skin. So many clichés. All so true. These nine months have been both the longest and the shortest of my life.

The clock went on ticking but time was a concertina, stretching and contracting.

I went to see the osteopath the other day. I'd been once before since your death and I thought I'd better go back for another check-up; writing non-stop for months on end has had repercussions on my neck and my spine.

'It's been a while,' he said, when I walked into the room.

'Not really,' I said. 'About three weeks, I think.'

'No, five months,' he said, checking his notes.

The clock had been ticking and had left me behind.

Although it is only nine months since you died, I have been grieving for a year now. My mother died at this time last year, from a cancer that had always been terminal, even though it seemed, at times, that she might out-run it. Eventually, unexpectedly, the clock stopped for her at 6pm on 10th December 2015.

But for me, the clock went on ticking and life went on regardless.

I got the call when I was bathing my children. She'd gone peacefully in the arms of her sons. I'd seen her earlier, known that it was possible that she wouldn't have long. But the consultant had said that she might have forty-eight hours or maybe a few weeks depending how she responded to the medication that they'd given her in the hospice. I'd sat with her and held her hand while he'd tried to tell her that there was nothing more he could do, while she pretended not to hear.

'I'm here,' I said.

'I know,' she said, though she wouldn't or couldn't open her eyes. As far as I know, they were the last words she spoke. She was asleep when I left, but I told her anyway that I had to fetch the children, that I loved her, that I would be back. The children needed picking up from school and the Christmas Fair was on. You can't miss the Christmas Fair just because your mum is dying.

The clock went on ticking and life went on regardless.

I hadn't told the children that Grandma might be dying. How could I? The first I'd heard of it was on that afternoon in the hospice. And she might still have three weeks. No need to worry them just before bedtime. And when the phone rang and my brother told me the news, I just put the phone down, scooped my boy out of the bath and texted a neighbour while I read stories and sang lullabies as normal, even though my limbs were shaking and my mind was racing. When you're a single parent what else can you do? I went in to see my daughter, told her I had to go out.

'Where are you going?' she asked.

'I'm going to see Grandma in hospital,' I said, not wanting to lie, unable to tell the truth.

'Tell her I love her,' she said. 'And take her my card.'

'I will,' I said.

I took the Get-Well card that my daughter had made and went up to see Grandma, my mum, lying pale and calm on the hospice bed. I kissed her goodbye, went to the pub with family, texted you to meet me and found refuge in your arms for a while on the sofa. But you couldn't stay the night, not with the children there. So I said goodbye to you in the hall again and went to bed.

The clock went on ticking and life went on regardless.

Though it is the anniversary of my mum's death tomorrow, I feel like I already lived it this Thursday as I watched my little boy narrating the Christmas play (last year, on the day she died, he was a shepherd) and as we heaved our way through the school Christmas Fair. By the time the children were in bed, I was in tears again and there was no you to text for a hug this time. I longed for you, as I always do, but more so in this time of extra grief and remembrance. My mum's death was sad, but it didn't destroy me because I had you by my side. And because, though she went too soon, she still went along with the order of things. Parents should die before children. We will all be orphaned eventually. I was just orphaned a little sooner than my peers, and my children lost their lovely Grandma way younger than they should.

But the clock went on ticking and life went on regardless.

Until you died. At the wrong time. At who knows what time or why. Your heart just stopped, like a clock whose battery had run out, just like that with no warning. It was out of order. There was no goodbye. There was nothing calm or peaceful about the way I found you. There has been little calm or peace since. And I wanted everything to stop.

But the clock goes on ticking. Twelve months since she died. Nine months since you died. I have been grieving for a year, different kinds of grief, cumulative losses. I miss you both. But life goes on regardless.

Things not to say: 'Happy Christmas'

I'M NOT SENDING Christmas cards this year. Call me Scrooge, but I just don't feel like celebrating. I don't begrudge other people their happy Christmas (or maybe I do) but I don't want to think about it and I don't want to talk about it and I just want it to be over as soon as possible. I don't have any festive cheer to spare. It took all my energy to put up a Christmas tree for the children. I've booked the panto and the Christmas train and sometime between now and the twenty-fifth, I will buy the children some presents. But that's it. That's enough. I have turned off the radio and I'm staying away from the parties. I don't need to be constantly reminded that Christmas is a time for sharing love and that half of the people I love most in the world are missing. Frankly, Mariah Carey has it covered: all I want for Christmas is you. And Santa can't bring me what I want. So it's 'Bah Humbug' from me, I'm afraid.

I suppose I could do what other people seem to be doing and donate to a charity instead of sending cards, but I donate to charities all year long. Charity is for life, not just for Christmas, surely? I'm already saving a few trees. Isn't that enough? Why do I need to offset my sadness? Can't I just be selfish this year? Sometimes sadness is appropriate. We can't all make lemonade every time we get lemons. It's exhausting squeezing every drop of positivity from a negative situation when you're already broken.

Don't worry, it goes both ways. I don't want any Christmas cards either. I mean, I don't mind if other people have to follow the custom, if writing cards gives them some joy, if it just wouldn't be Christmas for them if they didn't send cards. But please don't send one on my account. Please don't think that sending me a snowy scene with the words 'Happy Christmas' and 'Happy New Year' is going to improve my lot during this festive period. Putting it bluntly, it's not.

I appreciate people thinking about me but love is for all of the year, not just for Christmas too. The friends who care about me have been here for me during what has been the worst year of my life. Some of them have sent me love on a daily or weekly basis. They have checked in on how I am regularly. Some of them have driven across the country to see me. A lot of good friends have read my blog, religiously or sporadically. They know how I am. They have sat me with while I've cried week after week after week. They know that I will not be happy just because it's Christmas. The word happy is just jarring. It's not appropriate for someone who is grieving.

This Christmas won't be a happy one. I'm not being negative, that's just the way it is. Sure, it will have some happy moments. I have two gorgeous children who are excited and there will be joy in seeing them open their presents and all that malarkey. And, yes, I'm grateful that I have them and that I'm not homeless and that I don't live in Syria. I have a lot of things to be grateful for. I can make lemonade when I need to. But I will mostly be sad and mostly thinking about the people who are missing. That's just the way it is. My life is half-empty, not half-full.

Of course I don't mind people thinking of me this Christmas. But if people want to send me a card, let it be a card acknowledging that this year will be hard. Let it be a card wishing me some peace or sending me some strength. And please, friends, keep sending me love. Make plans to hang out with me, knowing that there will probably be tears. But don't wish me a Happy Christmas. Christmas will be tough. As for 2017, with any luck it can't be as bad as 2016, but I hear bereaved people and counsellors routinely saying that the second year following the loss of a partner is worse than the first so I'm not counting my chickens – and the last time I said things couldn't get worse, you died. I'm not risking saying it again. Probably the second year following the death of a partner is worse, at least in part because friends forget that things don't get better just because the year on the calendar has changed. When the person you love is missing, they just keep being missing. So please, friends, forgive me for the lack of cards and for the Grinch-like behaviour and keep sending the love.

You didn't send me a card last year. You sent me a New Year's card instead. It was a beautiful scene of bluebells and trees. You acknowledged that life had been tough for me for years and that things could only get better. You were a big part of my future plans for life improvement.

'May all your dreams come true in 2016,' you wrote.

So much for that.

Bah Humbug.

Where do you start

'Where do you start? How do you separate the present
  from the past?
How do you deal with all the things you thought would
  last? That didn't last.
With bits of memories scattered here and there
I look around and don't know where to start.'

I'm not ready for another relationship. At least I don't
think I am. Mind you, I'm not sure what ready would
look like, anymore. At the beginning of this journey, I
imagined I might be ready when I had stopped loving
you. But I understand now, that that is never going
to happen. I was in love with you when you died
and you've not done anything since then to make me
change my mind so my feelings for you will always stay
the same. Which is kind of comforting to me but, I
imagine, rather disconcerting to any future partner. It's
a weird complication that I could have done without.
I was hardly straightforward before you came into my
life and died. I'm even more complicated now.

My other thought was that I might be ready when I'd
stopped grieving. But what does that even mean? When
someone you're in love with dies suddenly, in horrendous
circumstances, do you ever stop grieving? I am going to
be sad about losing you forever. Perhaps grieving has
nothing to do with being ready for a new love.

So I look to mourning traditions and am none the
wiser. In the Muslim tradition, widows must stay away
from potential suitors for a period of four months and

ten days. I'm long past that marker. On the other hand, in Victorian England, a widow wore mourning clothes for two years. But did that stop her from signing up to OK Cupid? I don't know. Anyway, I'm not a widow or a Victorian or Muslim. We were only together for eight months, and only the last four or five were official. In some ways it makes sense that I might be 'ready' sooner than someone who has been married for years. In other ways, not. I ask my bereavement counsellor how long it might take for things to improve and she tells me that, statistically speaking, the average time to regain equilibrium following a major loss is two years, eight months and four days. As I've had two major bereavements in the space of a year and lost three partners in three years (only one of them to death), I'm guessing I might need longer. It seems reasonable to round it up to five just to be on the safe side.

Besides, there's this blog to write. I thought I might be ready to meet someone new when I'd finished writing my blog. But when do you finish writing a blog – about someone you still love, who you're still grieving for? How long is appropriate? I'm committed now to recording this process, and I get messages all the time from people telling me not to stop. I can't let those people down. But how could I have a new relationship while I'm still writing about you? And what if I turn this into a book? That's going to take another year at least. Maybe two or three with editing and publication. Could someone please send me the manual for how to move forward?

The obvious solution is to never have another relationship, or at least not until the five years have passed and the book is out. I've considered that possibility and it makes sense. I've known great love. Maybe it's enough. On the other hand, I also know that love is the only thing of value in this life and that life can be snatched from our grasp at any moment. Still, people live good lives as single people all the time, so why shouldn't I? I know I don't need a man to complete me. I know I should love myself and I do. I have a great career, wonderful female friends, fabulous children and meaningful ways to spend my time. And yet, and yet... I am lonely. And I miss men. There, I said it. I feel like I'm betraying some feminist cause to say that a life lived entirely in sisterhood is lacking something for me. I miss male company, I miss male conversation and on a very primitive level, I miss being close to a male body. Of course I miss your conversation and your company and your body specifically, but you're not here anymore and though you are eternally in my heart, a metaphysical love is not enough for me. And as a self-employed, single mother, I live almost entirely in the company of women and children. I rarely speak to a man at all.

There are a few men in writing groups that I run, but I'm in a different role there and boundaries must be maintained. Then there are your friends. I see them occasionally. If I bump into one, in the park say, recently I've found myself hankering for hugs, hanging about waiting for them to offer, sometimes just asking outright. And in my mindfulness class, the other day I found myself staring at my neighbour's hands, instead of focusing my attention on my own feet. I'm not interested in him and the idea of being physically intimate with another man is horrifying at the moment. And yet I just want to be close to maleness. On

Saturday night it escalated to new heights. I went to a cabaret night that my friend was involved in. There was a man on stage doing a comedy juggling act in which he and his partner stripped down to their underpants. His physique was similar to yours and I found myself looking for him at the interval, as if I might seriously go up to him and say, 'Hi, I liked your act. Your belly reminds me of my deceased partner's. Can I hug you?' Sad times indeed.

So, I reactivated my Tinder account again, and updated my profile – making it clear that I am not ready for a relationship, that I just want male company. And, so far, it's been great. I've connected with an ex-vicar/ writer who is up for platonic debates about existential matters, and a seemingly nice man who's happy to be friends. He's offered me his ear and his shoulder, he's up for dog walks and, get this, he even likes playing Scrabble. Which is where the trouble starts.

Surely, nothing could be safer, tamer than a game of online Scrabble with a man – and yet I'd barely opened up the app, placed a few tiles, exchanged a few words of competitive banter and I was crying. I felt like I was cheating on you. Scrabble was our game. How can I contemplate playing Scrabble with someone new? We courted each other over Scrabble boards, with Scrabble banter. And yet, I find myself feeling happy, in amongst the tears. Because I love playing Scrabble and Scrabble isn't just our game, it's my game too. I played it every Friday night with my Grandma for years. I can't abandon all the parts of myself that remind me of you, can I?

'Which books are yours?
Which tapes and dreams belong to you and which are
    mine?
Our lives are tangled like the branches of a vine that
    intertwine
So many habits that we'll have to break
And yesterdays we'll have to take apart'

I sat on my own at the cabaret. Being out was tough
enough. A few people that I knew asked me if I'd
like to sit with them, but I declined. I couldn't cope
with speaking to people. It was the anniversary of my
mother's death and I was feeling bleak. I was in my
grief bubble, sitting inside a snow globe, watching the
world through a distorted lens. I smiled occasionally at
jokes, found some enjoyment in staring at the stage. It
was okay. Until the end, when they removed a curtain
from the back portion of the room and I saw the
maroon, velour bench where we had last sat together,
the week before you died. I could have, maybe should
have turned away, but I couldn't do that. I went and
sat down on that bench and suddenly you were there,
sitting next to me, just on the other side of unbreakable
glass. And I couldn't move. It was like I'd wandered into
the wrong show and I'd been hypnotised by Derren
Brown, my behind glued to the seat. And the panic
started rising because suddenly I was all at sea again
and I didn't know how I could get myself home. And
I was crying again, not wracking sobs, not conscious
tears, but the kind of tears that fall unbidden, seeping,
like blood from open wounds.

'One day there'll be a song or something in the air again
To catch me by surprise and you'll be there again
A moment in what might have been.'

Eventually I pulled myself from my seat and fell towards the door. I saw a friend of yours, didn't stop to talk, just hugged him, tears streaming and walked out. Then the sobs started and I managed to phone a friend and I was saying those words again: 'I just can't believe he's gone.' And then, again, 'I feel like I'll never be able to go out without crying.' What am I supposed to do with myself when I can't even go out for an evening without crying? Maybe I'll be ready for dating when I stop crying, I thought. Will I ever stop crying?

'Where do you start? Do you allow yourself a little time
    to cry?
Or do you close your eyes and kiss it all goodbye? I guess
    you try'

The next night was the Scrabble night, with the banter and the tears and the guilt and the niceness and the confusion. Am I ready, even, for playing Scrabble with a man? I was thinking about it and wondering how it is possible to even start to try to move forward as I made my way to bed. I turned on the radio just long enough to set the alarm. This song was playing, nostalgic, plaintive. I sat on the edge of the bed and listened to the end, waited to find out who the artist was (Barbra Streisand), Googled it ('Where Do You Start?') and listened again. It seemed like it was for me. It encapsulated my weekend and my feelings.

'And though I don't know where and don't know when
I'll find myself in love again
I promise there will always be a little place no one will see
A tiny part within my heart, that stays in love with you.'

I move forward and turn back, each forward movement a wrench away from the past. But you are with me every step of the way and I know you wouldn't begrudge me a game of Scrabble in my heartache. As for the tiny place in my heart, it's pretty huge and there for everyone to see. And anyone who wants to love future me is going to have to understand that. It's probably the best prophylactic there is.

The alchemy of love

I NEVER DISCUSSED the science or philosophy of alchemy with you, and I don't need to. I already know that the very word 'alchemy' would have made your heart sing and if you could play it on a Triple Word Score, all the better. Alchemy encapsulates the realms of physics and metaphysics and, at its simplest level, metallurgy. It epitomises for me the man you were: a giant who had his feet firmly planted in the ground of reality, and his head so far into the clouds that he could touch the stars. Historically, alchemists sought to transmute base metals into gold, to cure disease and to discover a way to prolong life but, metaphorically speaking, alchemy is, according to Merriam Webster, 'a power or process of transforming something common into something special'. Alchemy is akin to magic, and there was always something of the wizard about you. It was there from the first day we spent together, transforming old iron into the poker that looked like Ginny Weasley's wand. 'Magical thinking,' you said, with a nod to my ex, the rationalist. There was magic in the air from the moment we connected. When we first went for a walk together at Redmires, you took photos and I wrote you a poem: 'the perfect way to remember a magical day,' you said. And it really was.

In February, we walked further afield, along the river to Pateley Bridge and stopped off in the workshops of some makers, admiring the titanium jewellery. And then, in the autumn, I walked that path again, this time with the silver decanted into a plastic bag. Your family had found it in the junk shop that was your house and kindly agreed to let me take it to the jeweller. It was like something from a fairy tale, walking along the river with thirty pieces of silver, hoping that she could make a permanent reminder of our love.

We emptied the bag onto the counter and looked through the pile of common objects. Something about this mish-mash of the precious with the mundane was so very you. We found the innards of mobile phones, bottle tops and crucifixes, such an odd assortment, but all of it silver, all of it usable. You knew what you were doing when you stored it for some future date that never arrived, although in the end it did arrive, just not the way you planned it. I cried, of course, as I told her again about you and about our story and she promised to make me something, perhaps in time for Christmas.

Today the parcel arrived. I am nervous as I open the box, scared that I might not like it. I'd given the jeweller some ideas but left it to her to create something that she thought fitting. I gasp like a child opening a magic lid when I peep inside. It is perfect. From those old scraps of metal she has made something beautiful, special, magical. I put it on and it fits like Cinderella's slipper. It is a treasure trove of clouds and hearts, stars and rivets, intersected by the bark of trees. It is the perfect reminder of our time together, a way to keep you always with me.

As I sit here now, facing Christmas without you, I am surrounded by mementos of our time together. The photo from our first magical day out is blown up as a canvas and sitting in pride of place on my wall, the poker rests by the log-burning stove, the Stardust print that you gave me for my birthday is framed and sitting on my desk – and there is a little corner of my shelves which houses your bat in his tin, the collage that you made last new year and the photo that you first sent when you were hoping to capture my heart. And now, on my finger, this ring, a sign of our love. It is not a wedding ring. Death did us part. I can no longer give myself to you, or share my life with you, but with all that I am, I honour you and in all that I go on to do, I will remember you.

I am grateful, Blacksmith, for all the things that you gave me, the physical and the intangible, all the things that you left me with. You weren't able to prolong your own life or cure your disease but, nevertheless you were an alchemist: every day with you was a day out of the ordinary. You transformed the common into something special. I sit here and know that I am also transformed, by your love and by this grief that has ripped through my life like a tornado. I will never be the same because of you. But I'm so glad to have known the alchemy of your love.

Last Christmas I gave you my heart

WELL, NOT REALLY. I gave you my heart in stages, piece by piece, week by week, taking it slowly, figuring it out, working through the inevitable doubts, wanting to be sure. By the time you died, the puzzle was complete: my heart and your heart welded together. Giving someone your heart is a risky business. What becomes of it when they die? It seems that there are bits that are still living, bits that are gone to the grave, bits lost forever, bits that will stay always together. There are bits that I am still looking for.

Last year was not a happy Christmas. My mother died on the tenth of December, so the festive season was shrouded in sadness. The run up to Christmas was spent choosing coffins and flowers instead of presents. I sent funeral invites instead of Christmas cards. I read eulogies instead of singing carols. On the twenty-third, instead of riding with Grandma on the Christmas train, I travelled behind her coffin in a funeral cortege and said goodbye to my mum for the last time.

My memories of you though are threaded through that Christmas, brightening the darkness like the lights you strung around the artificial tree that we'd brought to my house after her death. We were just back from an evening of shopping in Meadowhall; I had to buy presents for the children even though my mum had just died and, as usual, you were alongside me. You were assembling the Christmas tree while I went through my mum's address book, writing letters to old friends, inviting them to her funeral. I remember looking up and smiling at you. You smiled back. We had these moments often, where it seemed we were wondering what strange domestic idyll we had wandered into. Like the time when you sat by my side threading my needle while I sewed my daughter a mermaid costume, or that last perfect Saturday when we danced around each other in my kitchen, concocting recipes from my allergy-friendly cookbook. We were completely content in each other's company, whatever we were doing. It's not a feeling I've had very often. I can't remember why you told me I was special as I was writing or what I said as you were arranging fake fern fronds around the metal stand, but I remember your response.

'Even if I wasn't completely besotted with you, I would still think you were special,' you said. And then you looked away. 'Anyhoo,' you said, with mock embarrassment, returning to your task, both of us radiating with the warmth of it all.

We had to find you something to wear for my mum's funeral. Your old suit was too big as you'd lost so much weight. I bought you an extra-large shirt and an extra-large jacket but they were still too small. You were XXL and worth your weight in gold. (They lay you in your coffin in your suit anyway. I thought at the time that it must have been baggy but I don't suppose it mattered.)

At the funeral, you hung around in the background with my friends. You still hadn't been introduced to my children and so you watched from the back as I gave the eulogy, stayed away from the family until it was your turn to walk along the funeral line. I remember my relief when it was my turn to shake your hand. I introduced you to my brother.

'This is Paul. He's been looking after me.'

My brother thanked you and told you to keep looking after me. And you did, for as long as you were able.

On Christmas Day, after the children had gone to their dad's and you were full of your family's Christmas dinner, you arrived at my door with a huge printer's tray, unwrapped, slung over your shoulder. I chastised you for the lack of wrapping paper and the lack of a card, though the present was perfect. You made up for it at New Year. And on my birthday. You were a man who listened to feedback, took things on board. I made you a tub of flapjack and bought you a notebook for your ideas along with two shirts that fit. (The shirts sit in my drawer now. I've thought about making something from them. It's a thing people do. But somehow I can't bring myself to cut into fabric that you once wore. I have so little of you left. I like to keep the shape of you in your clothes).

Later we watched the first half of *It's a Wonderful Life* in each other's arms. What a film to watch. What a wonderful man you were. What a difference you made to me.

Last Christmas, I gave you my heart. Less than three months later you died. You took part of my heart with you when you left. But at least you didn't give it away. At least I know that I gave it to someone really special. You kept my heart safe. I believe you would always have kept it safe.

You gave me your heart too and, though you died, I still keep yours safe, tucked up with what is left of mine. I write to keep you alive. And though the spectre of Christmases past hangs over this year too, the memory of your love helps to keep me alive as well.

2016: Worst year ever

I SUSPECT WE are going to see this headline a lot on social media over the next few days. Maybe we'll see it for months and years to come too. With any luck, 2016 will go down in history as the year when things hit an all-time low before they started to improve. Along with the majority of my peers, I will, mostly, be glad to see the back of 2016 and I even feel some tendrils of hope reaching out towards 2017. But I'm wary these days. I'm not sure I want to risk hoping anymore. In my personal life, 2014 was a bad year as the year that my children's father and I separated. I thought 2015 would be better but 2015 was worse, including as it did, the heart-breaking break-up of a new relationship and the death of my mother. Again I thought 2016 had to be an improvement. How wrong I was. The heartbreak of 2016 was on a scale that I didn't even know existed. As my daughter learned this week when the doctor added a noxious red antibiotic to the disgusting yellow one that she thought was the most horrendous thing she had ever tasted, there is always something worse.

Over this last year I have found myself eligible to be part of the clubs that no one wants to join – the online communities of the widowed and violently bereaved. For people who, this year, have felt like the ground has been torn from under their feet and that their very hearts have been ripped from their bodies, it can be galling to hear the constant refrain on social media about how bad this year has been. For people who have lost their soulmates, the fathers of their children, their income and their vision for the future, 2016 hasn't just been a bad year, it's been catastrophic. I picture a graph and a curve dipping down towards the baseline during 2016. A lot of people I know in the real world have been down there on that baseline. Understandably they have felt very low about the social and political climate, about rising poverty, about the refugee crisis, about Brexit and Trump and all the celebrities who have died this year. It has felt like our history and our culture is being eroded. It is really sad and scary. And yet, we, in the widowed community, find ourselves wanting to say, 'you think you feel bad. You should try feeling what I'm feeling.' If the baseline of that graph is ground level, some of us feel that we have spent this year in the underworld, trapped in a pothole or on the seabed, reaching for air, struggling to find some kind of foothold, trying to survive.

This year I have personally endured the kind of pain that I didn't know existed. For the first time in my life I have genuinely felt that I wasn't sure that I could go on, not just for one day, or a few days, but relentlessly day after day after day. I have cried so hard, so many times, that I couldn't breathe, that I felt I was going to die. At times the pain has been physically debilitating; there have been occasions when I've been unable to stand or walk. I still feel unsteady if try to go out in an evening. Having watched both parents die of terminal cancer and having held my new-born baby limp and breathless in my arms while I dialled 999, having been through my parents' divorce and experienced my own relationship breakdowns, having been through courtroom battles against my stepmother, having suffered from anxiety and depression and chronic illness and having cared for my son in his own chronic illness, I thought that I knew about pain. It turns out I didn't have a clue. The pain of losing is a partner is so much worse than anything I'd experienced before. The pain is indescribable and yet I have tried and tried to describe it. I don't know why. I'm a writer, it's what I do. For some reason, I want people to understand. But I know that no one can really understand unless they've been through it. And I don't wish this pain on anyone.

Without question, 2016 has been the worst year of my life, not because of Brexit or Trump, not because of Bowie, or Victoria Wood or George Michael. The thing that makes this the worst year ever for me didn't even make the news. 2016 is the worst year ever because you died. On a global scale it is insignificant but my world was altered forever when you left it.

And yet, as I approach the end of the year, as I climb slowly upwards out of darkest days of my grief, I am reaching a position where I can breathe more easily and where the vista is expanding so that I can see beyond my own pain and start to see things from the perspective of others again. I can recognise that my view this year has been, of necessity, solipsistic. When you're struggling to stay alive, you naturally turn inward. But I can see now that I am not the only person for whom this year has been agony. I am not the only person who has lost a partner; I've come to know lots of others who have too. And we're not the only people in pain. Around the world, people are struggling and suffering. 2016 has been really truly bad for a lot of people. It will be good to see the back of it.

As I approach New Year's Eve, I think about where I

was last year. At midnight, I was in your arms on the top of a hill warming myself by the bonfire that you'd built and watching the fireworks explode over Sheffield. For the rest of the bank holiday, we were cocooned at my house. We watched the second half of *It's a Wonderful Life* and made New Year collages, envisioning how we wanted the year to be. It is an annual tradition for me and you embraced it with gusto. I look back at my collage now, as I do at the end of every year. At the top is a quote cut out from a magazine. It reads, 'Those who don't jump will never fly.' I jumped into your arms and together we flew. It is true. It is also true that sometimes, when you jump, you land face down in a ditch and that it's a heck of a job to get out of that ditch. At the centre of my collage is another quote attributed to the Buddha: 'No one saves us but ourselves. No one can and no one may. We ourselves must walk the path.' This is also true. No one else can feel the pain that I have felt, and my path is mine to walk alone. What a journey this year has been.

And yet, when I look back on 2016, it hasn't all been bad. I have written more this year than I have written in any other year of my life and WRITING is the word that I have placed, in capitals, at the centre of my new year's collage every year for as far back as I can remember. For the first time, this year, writing has truly been at the centre of my life where it belongs. And I have learned a lot. As 2016 began, I was experiencing true love with you, and I feel confident now that I will never be mistaken again about what love is, as I have been so many times in the past. And this year, I haven't been afraid to speak out. I have stopped worrying about what other people think. I don't think

I will ever be silenced again. In 2016, I also stopped pretending that I was superwoman and I learned to ask for help. And it has been overwhelming, the way people have responded to my requests. I have walked alone in my pain but there have been people willing to walk alongside me and to those people I will be forever grateful. I have lost a few friends but gained a lot more. It has been a year of extraordinary pain but also of extraordinary compassion. And that gives me hope for the future. (It's not a trade. I wouldn't swap your life for my writing, or my learning or my spiritual growth. It's just the way it is).

In some ways I don't want to leave 2016 behind. 2016 was an awful year but it was the last year that you were alive. As the clock strikes midnight on Saturday, I will be walking alone into a year that you never lived in. Sometimes I'm not sure that I want to go there. But I look back at the collage that you made and know that I must go on without you. Yes, the world is a sorry mess but I will keep on keeping on, I will look for the bright side, even in the darkness and I will continue to explore. And I will love, until my heart stops beating. Because while-ever there is love, there is hope. Yes, there is always something worse but there is always the possibility of something better too. In spite of everything, it is still a wonderful life.

A rock and a hard place

I'VE ALWAYS SEEN New Year's Eve as a time for reflection. I've never been a party animal, preferring to muse on the year gone by and on my plans for the future. I like to sit, listening to music and making a collage, picking out inspirational images and photos. But today I just can't do it.

Partly it's the memory of making collages with you last year. I still have your collage and mine. I still have your glue. I just don't have you.

I thought Christmas would be the hard part. I thought I would be okay on my own tonight. But I fell in a grief ditch around the twenty-eighth, after I'd triumphed at Christmas and given my daughter a fantastic birthday, after I'd felt so proud for getting through it all. I'd even written my positive New Year blog a few days early. And then something happened, a couple of posts on social media, an aborted trip to the seaside and suddenly I was ambushed by grief again. Grief tripped me up and threw me down a deep hole and I've been struggling to get out ever since. I should have learned by now not to rest on my laurels. Grief goes on and on and on. Grief likes to pounce when I'm not paying attention.

I've been reflecting today on why New Year is so hard in grief and realise that it's the reflecting that is the problem. If I look back at the year that I'm leaving, I see mostly darkness. It was, as I have already said, the worst year of my life. But if I look to the future, I see an emptiness that I have to fill with something new.

Sometimes emptiness is exciting. Sometimes it's good to turn over a new leaf, to start a new chapter. But sometimes the blank page is frightening. I have griever's block. I don't know what to do with my future.

Sitting here, on this day, perched between the old year and the new, I feel stuck between a rock and a hard place. To look back or to look forwards is equally terrifying. So I'm back in the moment again, noticing my feet on the floor, clinging to my keyboard while the children watch another episode of whatever they're watching on Netflix, feeling the breath coming into and leaving my body, watching thoughts like clouds, knowing that I just need to get through it, that it will pass.

Tomorrow, your death will be last year's news. And maybe that's what I fear the most, the idea that you and I are moving further apart and the idea that somehow I should close the door on grief and embrace a new chapter. But grief goes on and on, with no respect for dates. And love goes on and on too. I will carry both over into the new year. For now I will sit, like patience on a monument, not smiling at grief but breathing and praying for it to be over soon.

Tonight, I build myself a fire in my log burning stove, and remember the fire that you built on the moors at Redmires at midnight last year. It was a defining moment for me, to have a man strong enough to carry logs and an axe up a mountain but gentle enough to make a collage. You were a rock to hold onto when I floundered and a soft place to land when I fell. You'll be a hard act to follow. Whatever the years ahead hold for me, I will love you and miss you and remember you for the rest of my days.

I don't write every day anymore

IT HAS BEEN almost two weeks since I last completed a blog. The significance is not lost on me. Perhaps it is the inevitable course of this horrible journey; the writing will naturally subside along with the tears. I don't cry every day anymore and I don't feel the need to write with the same urgency that I once did. There was so much to say back at the beginning, so many emotions to process: shock, disbelief, anger, guilt, fear, denial, nostalgia, love, remorse and, of course, sadness: a deep persistent sadness that lies beneath the surface like a dark pool. I've expressed myself in so many different ways on so many different days. There are no stages to this grief; emotions change as quickly as clouds shifting in the sky. It is a never-ending cycle. Grief is an inescapable part of my reality now.

Perhaps this is the holy grail of acceptance that I've been waiting for, but it's not the way I imagined it. Nothing is fixed, the situation is not better, everything is not okay. What broke is still broken, what is missing is still missed. I am not back to normal. I have changed and I have grown through the experience but time has brought neither the wisdom that it happened for a reason, nor the understanding that this was somehow for the best. The sun shines more than it did but there is no silver lining to this cloud. I am just learning to live with the dark pool of grief beneath the surface, learning the impossible art of walking on water, not falling quite so often, learning to swim when I do. I accept now that it will never go away.

And, yes, I accept that, though there was no reason, it did happen and that there is no going back. The facts are simple in the end: I fell in love with you and you died. It was a short, beautiful, brutal story with a beginning, a middle and an end. It can't be the whole story of my life. I can't just write about you for the rest of my days. There aren't enough words to keep you alive. There are only so many ways to say I love you.

And so, I must move forward. Part of the reason that I've written less over the last two weeks is that, spurred on by the new year, I've been investing time in trying to build something new. I've been putting scaffolding in place, laying foundations. I've been spending my days with coloured pens and paper, trying to map out a future. I've been consulting with the experts about the best way to build on top of dark waters, about how to live with absence.

I have, very tentatively, started dabbling with dating again. Oh the horror, the horror! I have faced again the awfulness of trawling through online profiles and making stilted conversation with men who don't know how to use full stops; the indignation of being deleted by randoms who are not getting where they wanted quickly enough; the dispiriting meetings with people who are not you. I have cried a lot in the process, have gone back to disbelief again: I shouldn't have to do this when I have only just found a man who really loves me, a man I really love.

I have also taken on some new work projects, and I have had to let some others go. As a self-employed professional whose life was blown to pieces, I have lost a lot of income and I need to start earning properly again, but I have also had to accept that some things are beyond my capabilities still. The big writing centre that I would like to establish will have to wait. There is only so much I can do whilst walking carefully over dark waters. Instead I'm thinking of buying a house by the sea.

The truth is, I spent the first week of January trying to run before I could walk and fell quite spectacularly. My foundations are still shaky. The darkness and depth of the grief pool has almost swallowed me several times and, even though the darkness is so familiar, I still fear, each time that I might drown. Grief is still snakes and ladders. I go backwards as often as I move forwards.

So I am back to taking baby steps, committing to self-care. I am swimming, doing yoga, trying to get more sleep. My herbalist says she would like to me to follow an 'old lady routine', but I am not an old lady yet and I still have things that I want to do with this life. That is progress, at least. I find that I want to live again. Instead of wanting to die, I now find myself panicking that my life will be over before I've had chance to rebuild and to live again. But I can't rush it. I must move slowly and gently now.

As part of my self-care routine, I went back to my mindfulness class this week and absorbed the words on the paper that were handed to me:

There will be no moving forward till we accept where we are with grace and compassion.
We may not like it.
We may want to be anywhere but here.
We have to believe that where we find ourselves is the best

place we can be, in order that we might learn what is needed and then place our attention and our feet in the direction that is right for us to tread.

(Fiona Watson, mindfulness teacher)

I don't believe that where I am is the best place for me. I do not like it. I wish I were anywhere but here. But I do accept it now. I am not the person that I was before you died. I must start again gently from where I am now.

The food of love

'PEOPLE ALWAYS WANTED to feed Paul,' says your mum. This information makes me smile because it leads me to conclude that this is how you got by. Even as a grown man, you'd rock up to people's houses unannounced and find yourself eating plates of toast, or cake, or staying for dinner. You loved food but you didn't know how to make it, though some of your concoctions were legendary: garlic sandwiches, cider vinegar potions. I don't really even know what you ate most of the time. I know you occasionally cooked fish and roast dinners for your friend but generally I assume you got by on a diet of tinned food. I know that you liked to mix things up, adding spices and garlic to tins of beans and soup and that it didn't always turn out the way you intended. And I know that you loved cheese.

'Do you like cheese?' I once asked you by Messenger.

'I am at least 40% cheese,' you replied. 'And must have it at every opportunity.'

You made me laugh.

At the beginning of our relationship, things proceeded in the manner to which you were evidently accustomed. I'd bake flapjack in anticipation of your arrival and you'd arrive hungry and eat your way through a plate of it with obvious gusto. If it was evening, I'd cook you sweet potato curry. You didn't like going out to eat. It wasn't really your style and you didn't like spending money. And nor did you like me to pay for you but, on the other hand, I really didn't like having to cook on my days off childcare. As a feminist it irked me to always be the one doing the cooking. It was another conundrum. 'I'm not cooking for you every time you come round,' I said. So, you started picking up a meal for one in the supermarket with mock seriousness, even though I protested that I didn't really mean that I would never cook for you; you took feedback on board and you were not going to have me resenting you.

One day, in January, you decided to show me that you could be the new man you felt I needed you to be. You determined to cook me dinner. You arrived, Ainsley Harriot cookbook in hand, with a bag of shopping and set about chopping in my kitchen while I went to a doctor's appointment. I returned to the smell of burning and you, dripping with sweat and visibly shaken in a way I'd never seen you, pans all over the kitchen and a pile of orange slop deposited onto two plates. It tasted okay, just slightly singed. I said it added to the depth of the flavour. It took you a full hour to calm down. It took another hour to clean the kitchen. You never cooked for me again. But I loved you all the more for trying.

Remembering with a smile

THEY SAID THE time would come when I would remember you with smiles instead of tears, with a heart buoyed by gratitude instead of weighed by sadness. I didn't believe them. They said a lot of things, most of them stupid. They said our time together was a gift to cherish, that there were lessons to be learned. They said that you had left me in a better place. They said that I would meet someone new, find happiness again. None of it made sense.

I've been turning corners for a while now, zigging and zagging backwards and forwards but today I turned a corner, literally. I'm in Bridlington investigating the possibility of buying a holiday property, and as I was looking for my B&B, I found myself standing in front of a cafe. It made me catch my breath as I was flung by a wave not of pain but of remembrance, into a cold December night, parking up on this street while the wind whipped across our faces and the sign on the pub swung and clanked like a gallows. And we dived inside to get warm, eating fish and chips under bright lights as night descended.

I didn't even know that I'd been to Bridlington before. I thought this was my first trip, at least since the one in the cine film, the one where I'm batting my grandma's cheeks with pudgy hands. I knew that we'd stayed nearby at Bempton but I didn't recall that we'd been here. But today I remembered: how we'd been to the lighthouse at Flamborough and how we'd nearly walked down to the beach, but that it was so cold and we'd already walked on the beach once that day at Thornwick Bay (with the rocks and the seal and the beautiful portrait of me in a funny hat) and how the sign was shining like a beacon on the head, beckoning us in: Fish and Chips. And how, by the time we'd finished looking at the sea and contemplating the steepness of the cliff path, the door was locked, chairs piled on tables and how our hearts sank because now we needed fish and chips like our lives depended on it. And how we'd got back into your van and driven through the rain in search of sustenance until we found ourselves here in Bridlington.

I didn't go in. I'd already eaten my fish and chips on the beach. But I looked through the window to see if I could see you still sitting there on the red leather seats. And I smiled and blew you a kiss. There were no tears and I felt only joy at the memory of the time we shared.

Today I took a portrait of myself in the funny hat that you loved and I made it my profile picture on Tinder. In this photo I look like a ghost, lost in the sea spray, a mirage of a girl I used to be, the girl I find, like Cummings, by the sea. And I said to the guy I was talking to that, hey, this is me. I'm the woman my friend calls Grief Girl. I write about death and wear funky hats. I'm not everyone's cup of tea. But I'm happy being me. And I feel you smiling down like some kind of giant guardian angel, hear your voice in my ear telling me which guys to steer clear of, which ones to give the time of day. Your death will never be okay, but maybe there's a gift in there somewhere.

Today has been a good day. Today I feel blessed. How I'll feel tomorrow is anybody's guess.

Treading water

THESE DAYS I feel like I am waiting, suspended between the past and the future, treading water, like a surfer hoping to catch a wave that never comes. Sometimes, I gear myself up, see something heading towards me, feel myself temporarily buoyed up, lifted on a positive tide. But it is always one of those waves that holds more promise than it can deliver, that subsides before it peaks, that leaves me stranded still, out at sea. Waiting.

At other times I feel myself to be trapped, looking out at the world through a window, wondering when I will be allowed back out there to join the throng of the living and the loving and the thriving. Instead, I stay inside, held hostage by grief. Surviving.

It is only six weeks now until the anniversary of your death and I feel it like an uneasy stillness in the air, like a darkening of the sky, like a tsunami building. I am afraid of the destruction it might bring, the memories it will dredge from the ocean floor, the way it will fling me backwards once again. And yet some part of me is counting still, counting down now, naively hoping that once the year is up, I can pack up my suitcase and leave the wreckage behind on Grief Island, start afresh.

A year is such a short time, they say, and they are right of course. If I live until I'm ninety, a year is but a drop of water in the ocean. But when the waves still come thick and fast and can't be ridden; when you have no one to love or to love you; when you find work hard and socialising harder, a year can feel like an eternity. When it is broken down into days to get through, hours to keep breathing, minutes to stay alive, a year can feel as vast as the whole ocean. Sometimes there is no shore in sight.

I dabble with dating, hoping someone might send a boat to rescue me but I flounder in the water, unsure where I want to go, not sure I even want to leave the sea. I try to watch a film but the sight of a lifeless body leaves me reeling, cast back in time, shipwrecked again. I push the boat out and go to a party, find myself washed onto a foreign shore, observing people like they are natives in a distant land. Though I listen, I do not understand what they say.

Things will get better, I'm sure. Time will keep healing, I have no doubt. There will be happiness probably, one day, and even love. But it is so hard to live like this, suspended between the past and future, tossed about on the waves with no anchor, treading water.

Stumpcross Caverns and the Coldstones Cut

W E SPENT FEBRUARY half-term on a three day
break together near Knaresborough. As soon as
we saw the sign, we made up a song with the words:
Stumpcross Caverns and the Coldstones Cut. You
invented a kind of jazz riff to go with it, tapped out
the rhythm on the dashboard. We kept muddling up
the words, had to practise several times to get it right,
had to debate the best tune to go with it. But there
was no debate about what we needed to do. We had
to go there.

But, before we did, we walked along the riverside
hand in hand talking. We were always talking. I try to
remember now what we talked about along that river
and during that time, that precious three days together
in North Yorkshire. It was exactly a month before you
died. It would have been utterly unthinkable to us
then that you might be about to die. It is still utterly
unthinkable to imagine that you did.

I remember talking about sailing. We were on the
other side of the river then. We were trying to walk
a circular route. I was trying to take you to an art
gallery that I'd been to with my young husband over
twenty years earlier, but it was gone, replaced by some
kind of chain pub. Wherever we went, the sailing kept
coming back. You'd read books about sailing for years
and worked on boats in your youth but you'd never
really learned to sail properly. 'What are you waiting

for Blacksmith?' I said. 'You're fifty-three. If you want to sail round the world, get yourself some lessons.' And then I said that I'd be sad if you left me to sail round the world but that I wanted you to fulfil your dreams. I only ever wanted the best for you and you for me. With you I learned that that's what love is. Sometimes, you would say, 'I just want to possess you,' and yet you let me be myself, would have set me free if you thought it was for the best. For the record, it wasn't for the best. I wanted to be possessed.

You stopped to take photos of doors and I walked on ahead. We had this joke that if we needed space we would set up elaborate signals to each other. We never needed space, weren't together enough to tire of each other, but it kept us entertained. I did the yogic tree pose from my position down the road and you replied by doing a blacksmith arabesque by the doors. (How it made me smile and cry to see a photo of you in that pose from years ago on the memorial Facebook page after your death.) Then we spotted a tiny path leading back down to the river and ducked under the leaves back to the van.

It was a week of mostly walking (and talking and Scrabble and swimming and reading and writing and making love – the perfect break). The day before, we'd clambered up Brimham Rocks and gone through the charade of trying to shift the giant rocks with our bare hands. (Somewhere there should be photographic evidence of you playing the caveman, pretending to topple the rocks down the hillside. But I've searched your phones and I cannot find them).

We stopped in a jeweller's workshop. You chatted to the jeweller about rivets and working with titanium and I was proud to be with you, enjoying your interest in the craft she was engaged in. I asked you if you'd ever tried to make jewellery – you were a metalworker, after all – and you said that you had plans to make me something. 'I've been saving silver in a coffee pot for years,' you said. It made me laugh and I wrote it down in my notebook. Only you could have silver stored in a coffee pot.

We ate lunch in a cafe in Pateley Bridge and then we headed to the Cut. We missed out the Caverns. I prefer to be up high, not down below. It was bitterly cold and windy as we assailed the hillside next to the quarry, striding towards the massive limestone sculpture carved into the landscape. We chased each other round the maze like children and stood, wrapped in each other's arms, staring at the view, like sailors on the deck of ship. We didn't stay long. We hurried back down the hill and holed ourselves up in a cosy cafe. I got out my notebook and wrote the following poem while we drank tea and you leafed through a magazine. Perfectly content, alongside each other.

I read the poem at the funeral but I had to change the last line. I couldn't bear to stand up there and break the already broken hearts of the congregation with my own heartbreak. I had to give them some hope, even though I had lost mine. And so I changed it to 'through love, we live again.' It is true, we do. And we love even though death can tear us apart.

The stones are cold, sober and grey,
sand in the wind, whipping around a spiral
sculpture, cut from the cliff,
a giant conch swirling up the hillside,
ice cream on a cone
but made of stone.

I am not alone.
You are my buffer against the breeze,
forging a path through the maze,
smiles frozen, eyes ablaze.
I put my hand in your glove,
remember honeymoon days of youthful love
as we race time around the bend.

You and I are steadfast friends.
On the banks of the Nidd, in Pateley Bridge,
artists trade silver and glass for cold hard cash.
We tread the well-worn river's path,
laugh our way through the bleakness.

You smell of metal and sweat and sweetness.
We marvel at doors we won't walk through
and you glimmer like a hint of February spring
bringing sunshine to everything,
daffodils in the snow.

And down we go, slipping through the snicket
arched with leaves. We are thick as thieves
stealing a moment as precious as titanium
as a light fans into a flame.

With you I start to live again.

Birthday Blues

IT IS MY birthday this week. It's okay, I'll be amongst friends. I have a strategy. That's how life is approached these days. It's a case of looking ahead for hazards, taking pre-emptive action where possible, thinking of the least worst option for how to get through it all, choosing the safest route. It's not always the quickest route, nor the shortest route. It's not even the most scenic route. It's just the one that seems like it might have the least potholes and the smallest chance of landmines, the one where I'm least likely to be ambushed.

Big dates are obvious danger zones although every day is an anniversary of a better day last year (until next month when the best year was swapped for the worst year overnight). Every day is filled with your absence. This time last year we were away at a holiday cottage having the best three days of our life together. It was half-term and I'd planned the perfect strategy, no pre-emptive action required. Last year was all about maximising the opportunities ahead: three blissful days in a holiday cottage in North Yorkshire with you, returning on the Tuesday (my birthday) for a pancake party with my kids and friends and then back to North Yorkshire for three days on my own with the kids. It was a wonderful week, the best birthday for a very long time. You were by my side all day long. On my birthday, we woke up in each other's arms in the cottage near Brimham Rocks. You gave me wrapped presents, bought from shops. Only someone who knew you well would understand the significance. Usually your presents came from the eBay stock in the storage unit of your house. But I had standards and you were rising to the challenge. One of the things you gave me was a limited-edition print called Stardust. You said it reminded you of the journey of our love. Or something like that. How I wish I was paying more attention, but we had to pack up and drive home ready to fetch the children and to host my pancake party.

We spent the day together, although you were in the background again, pretending we were just friends for the sake of my children. You coped admirably with the onslaught of mothers and young children, eventually seeking refuge in the making of pancakes. It was okay. We'd just had three beautiful days together. It was lovely just to see you there in the throng of people celebrating my special day.

This year you will be missing all day long. Soon you will have been missing all year long too.

You are missing every day when I wake in the morning and missing when I go to bed at night. You are missing every time I go out and every time I come home. You are missing even in the places you have never been and in the spaces in between.

Tonight I went to a friend's house to a clothes buying party. I weighed it up, as I weigh everything, thought it was safe, no pre-emptive action required. It was all women so not a place that you would have been, I was amongst friends who know and understand and there was an external focus – always good to have. And yet, it turned out you were still missing. You were missing as the host joked with the guests about the habits of husbands and the seductive positioning of zips, missing as I tried on the clothes, knowing that there is no one to appreciate them but me. You were missing as people tilted their heads and asked me how I was doing now, wondering if things were improving. You were missing as I walked home crying to an empty house, knowing that everyone else is going home to a shared bed. (Eleven months and still I am walking home crying.)

I remember the last time I went to one of these parties six months ago. The host didn't know then. She asked me something about my circumstances, looked at me aghast as I explained that you had died, that I had found your body, that my mum had died too. I remember her words: 'how are you still standing?' It made me wonder myself, made me feel ridiculous to be sitting there looking at clothes when you were dead. I left early and walked home crying that night too.

It wasn't so bad tonight. The truth is I have come a long way. Things are improving, thanks for asking. I had a nice time and was doing well, all things considered, and then a friend mentioned my birthday. She'd been wondering what I was doing, said that she was remembering last year. And my lip started to tremble and the tears started again because suddenly I could see you, like it was yesterday, flipping pancakes in the kitchen at my old house, as if you thought you had a lifetime left to live, not just twenty-nine more days.

Sometimes I can anticipate the triggers for grief but often it is like this and, when I think I am safe, I am ambushed again by memories – memories that are as alive as you are dead. I saw all of my memories of this time last year, times I have written about, as I walked home: the synchronised swimming in the pool at the holiday cottage, the walks by the river, the talk about the ring that you were going to make (that the jeweller made instead), the beautiful print that you gave me for my birthday, the conversation in the van about how you wished we'd been married and had children, the happiness at being together now with our future ahead of us. And that trip up to the Coldstones Cut and the poem that I wrote: a poem that is so full of life, that I read aloud at your funeral as we mourned your death. And that last line that cuts now like a cold stone through my heart: with you I learned to live again. You missed a lot more birthdays than you were there for. I only spent one birthday with you. But I will miss you still on this one. And I will do my best to hold onto the gifts that you gave me as I take a new path into the future, learning to live again without you.

It's that time of year

IT'S THAT TIME of year again. The shops are awash with red, the streets suddenly lined with hearts and flowers and teddy bears. Love is in the air. Love is on air. Love is everywhere. Valentine's Day is looming and there is no avoiding it.

Truth be told, I've always found Valentine's Day a bit grim. I'm not sure I've ever had a really good one. When I've been single, it has seemed that every man is out in the street carrying bunches of flowers and balloons that aren't for me – and when I've been in a relationship, the flowers and balloons that I have received have always seemed wrong. Who can be attracted to a man who has just presented you with a teddy holding a felt heart, or to someone whose best effort is a ready meal for two from M&S? (Not me, that's who, in case you're wondering.) And let's face it, nobody really wants to go out on Valentine's Day – too expensive, too cheesy – but if you stay home watching TV what does that say about the state of affairs? In my experience, it's usually a day of pressure and expectation, commercialism and disappointment. One could almost be grateful not have to deal with it, except…

When the one you loved died not so long ago, Valentine's Day just becomes another obstacle to navigate (along with Christmas, New Year, his birthday, your birthday, your anniversaries – first kiss, first date, last kiss, last date – the list is endless). However much you might believe that love continues after death and that signs from beyond the grave do occur (and I do), when the odds of your partner sending a celestial greetings card are as remote as the possibility of him walking through the door with a bunch of flowers, Valentine's Day, like most days, sucks. It is a day of missing, of remembering.

Last Valentine's Day I didn't give you anything. I bought you a card from a shop in Knaresborough but I never wrote on it. I found it the other day in a pile of papers, a plain white card with a drawing of lilac crystals and the words, 'You're a gem' on the front. The words were right. You were, a most precious gem, a real diamond in the rough. But something about the colour and the crispness of the white card was wrong. Instead I just sent you a text in amongst a string of other messages: 'Happy Valentine's Day by the way'. You sent me a message too but, for some reason, I didn't see it. I found it on the Saturday after your death as I lay crying on my bed, re-reading all of your messages – a little red heart that opened up as I scrolled past it, the words 'I love you' popping up like a message from the grave to soothe my aching heart. That Valentine's evening, we went to the cinema. I booked us a couple's seat. It was just cheesy enough. We sat wrapped up in each other, wrapped up the movie. Perfect.

This year, for Valentine's Day, I give you a park bench: sturdy and solid and a place to rest, just as you were. It will be by the edge of the water next to the old grinding workshop, a deep pool whose water still powers the wheel, just as your love still powers the cogs of my life, keeping me moving, living, loving, creating even in your absence.

I give you a park bench, a place of calm as you were.

Strong and stable with a view of trees and clouds, and an inscription of the words you spoke to me in that park, a few weeks before your death: 'Stop: feel the sun.' It will be a place for tired folk to take a moment to rest and reflect on the beauty of nature, the fragility of life.

I give you a bench, like a pause in the vast breadth of time. It is small in the scheme of things. It has edges, a beginning and an end. Over time it will weather, no doubt and the words will fade. Nothing lasts forever. Though we never got married, I give you this bench as a sign of my love. In all that I go on to do, I will remember you. You will be with me every step of the way.

This year, I'll buy my own flowers and eat my meal for one, loving myself as you once loved me. You were a gem, Blacksmith Paul. Happy Valentine's Day, my love.

Signs

I BOUGHT A 'Best of the Nineties' CD the other week from a service station. I was on a long journey and I'd forgotten the CDs. The truth is, I forget a lot of things. I was bad enough before you died; I'm hopeless now. My mind is just never on the practicalities of life. I'm away with the fairies, head in the clouds, a walking cliché of a hapless artist. I'm even worse at the moment because I'm chatting to men on dating sites in between appointments, distracting myself with thoughts of some kind of future love. Crazy, I know, that I could even think of having another relationship, but there it is. It turns out the human spirit is amazing in its capacity to rebuild and to hope in spite of everything. It turns out I can hold the past and the future in my heart at the same time, though sometimes I forget to focus on the present.

Last week, I left my wallet (unusually full of cash) on the bus. Luckily I got it back with the notes still inside it. I'm annoying like that. I always get things back. In some ways I'm the unluckiest person I know, but in other ways I am lucky. I hear my mum's voice telling me that I need to learn to be responsible, but I know I'm a lost cause. I will never learn to be responsible and I will never learn my lesson. Instead I learn only that the world is mostly filled with lovely, trustworthy people. Yesterday I took my friend to the cafe on the corner for a cup of coffee (because I'd forgotten to buy coffee so there was none in my house) and, as we left, we waved goodbye to the cafe owner but I forgot to pay. (I went to pay him today, of course, because what goes around comes around and I like to add to the statistics of the lovely trustworthy people in the world.) Today, I took the dog to the groomers on the way to work and forgot to pick her up on the way home. But I had a good reason for that.

Today I was just leaving my writing group, checking my emails as I walked and thinking about you and how you used to hate the way people do that, heads down staring at screens instead of looking around them at the wonder of the world, when an email appeared in my inbox telling me that your bench had been fitted yesterday. Yesterday. On Valentine's Day! I'd known that it must be on its way soon but they'd said that they would give me two weeks' notice when it was going to be fitted so I was surprised, and pleased. How appropriate that it should have been secured to the ground right then, when I had only just written a blog about giving you a bench for Valentine's Day, making full use of artistic licence as I'd ordered the bench at the beginning of December with no idea when it would arrive. How utterly perfect that it should have been done just then. And how unutterably sad to see your life reduced to a bench.

I've been practising mindfulness recently, learning to name my emotions, to watch them pass like clouds, rather than diving headfirst into them, digging around for answers. I've found it immeasurably helpful over the last twelve months to watch that cloud of grief come and go, knowing that there is nothing to be done about it, knowing that there is no intervention that I can launch to change things. But sometimes, like today, my emotions move so quickly that I can't catch them. It's like I've walked into a time-lapse photography sequence with the clouds whizzing across the sky so fast that they merge into one mass and I can't make anything out. I think I catch a glimpse of joy and wonder but it is replaced so quickly with sadness and shock that I'm not sure what's what. There is a dash of hope in there for sure but it is eclipsed by doubt; and yet there is love, always love. I was smiling and crying too, shaking so much that I had to sit down.

On the one hand, how perfect and how lovely that you or the universe seemed to have conspired to put your bench there just then, as if my present for you was also a present for me, a reassurance, again, that there is more going on than I can understand, that there is some kind of mystical order even in chaos, that love abounds even when it seems all hope is lost. On the other hand, the bench is like the end of something. It has taken nearly a year to get it organised and there are only three weeks to go until the anniversary of your death. 'Bench' has been on my to-do list for a long time. When I tick it off, what is there left to do? It is the last memorial I have planned. Only my memories remain now, memories that I still try to capture, hoping to immortalise what we shared in words – even though memories, like clouds, can't quite be pinned down.

I went to look at the bench after work, before I picked the kids up from school, forgetting the dog in my excitement. Rushing and distracted, I managed to scrape my van on a parked car. I left a note, of course, because what goes around comes around and, though I don't care at all if someone bumps into my van, I am aware that some people love their cars as if they are children. I dashed to the bench with barely enough time to take it in, just a moment to check that the location is perfect (with its view of the water wheel and building) and that the inscription is right, complete with the punctuation that your mum and I laboured over:

In memory of Blacksmith, Paul Harding who loved
Sheffield's industry and landscape:
much loved, much missed, remembered always.

And I checked that your words were there too: '*Stop: feel the Sun*' and the dates *1963-2016*. Full stop. But I couldn't stop and feel the sun. I was in too much of a rush and it was raining. Still, I paused for a moment and felt the smooth wood under my hand, looked up at the clouds and told you I love you again. And then I ran.

Back in the van, I was listening to the CD when the 4 Non Blondes started playing 'What's Up?' – and I was cast back, as I often am, to that day in the autumn, the autumn of the year before you died (how strange it feels to say that now) when we danced by the marquee in town so full of hope and love. When we danced again at the poetry evening and my friend's mum said it was a good sign.

It was a good sign too when your bench was fitted on Valentine's Day. A sign of what, I don't know – but it made me feel good, like somehow, someone or something is still holding me in spite of everything. At the moment, I have a feeling of well-being, like something is falling into place. On Valentine's Day my friend brought me flowers with the message: 'For loves lost and loves to come.' The truth is, I don't know what's to come. None of us can know. My thoughts, like this blog, are a muddle of the past and the future and the present, my emotions merging like those sped-up clouds. I don't really know what's going on. But I know this much: I will never learn my lesson and, when the time comes, I will love again. Because, though I don't know what's going on, I know that at the end of the day, nothing else matters. It's all about how much love we can give and receive in the time that we have. And I know that there is still an abundance of goodness in the world even in the darkest of times.

The condition of my heart / Signs

THIS IS THE scene. A writing workshop in an art space in Sheffield. A dozen or so writers brought together in a room to write their way through the gloom of a winter afternoon. And I am at the helm, as usual, conjuring ways to stir the creative juices, to fire the imaginations of the assembled group.

I have grabbed a box full of random objects in the morning, whilst cooking breakfast and feeding the dog, cajoling children out of pyjamas and into clothes, whilst talking to suitors on Tinder and bereaved people on Facebook. This is how I live and work these days. The boundary between my multiple identities has almost completely dissolved and I find myself switching hats so many times and so quickly within the space of a day or an hour, that I might as well be doing one of those juggling routines, where the man (does it always have to be a man?) is tossing bowler hats from head to foot and back again, like they are seats on a Ferris wheel. I am mother, friend, writer, teacher, coach, griever, comfort, potential date, all day long. I've come to like it this way though it means my mind is often scattered, though I am acting often on instinct, following my heart rather than my head, winging it. It is just a few days since my instinct led to me to write about your bench in a Valentine's blog for *The Huffington Post*, a couple of days since I learned that your bench is now in place, positioned by the water on Valentine's Day.

I lay the objects out on the table and ask my writers

to pick one that appeals to them. 'Don't think about it,' I say. I am always saying this. To my mind, the magic of writing happens when you don't think about it, when you let the object choose you, when you let the words flow and follow their lead, not trying to drag them after you like reluctant children on a country walk. Magic, like love, happens when you least expect it. Magic, like love, can be found in unlikely places.

I grab my mum's old charm bracelet. I haven't looked at it since I was a child but it brings back memories of sitting on her bed (the one with the wooden surround) rummaging in the old leather jewellery box, the smell of her perfume. And this is what I write:

So many stories hung on one intersecting chain. Too much for my brain to take in. The smell of metal taking me to too many places: silverware on the dining room table and tubs of polish, things that were once precious, buffed, taken care of, now tarnished, unwanted, boxed off and sent to who knows where.

And you, of course, and your coffee pot of silver, melted down now to make my ring, metal transformed by heat, like the iron rod in your forge, whisked from the fire and hammered into shape by your loving hands, striking while the iron was hot. Leave it too long and metal, like a heart, can turn cold, fixed and unmalleable. Love, like heat transforms.

My eye is drawn to a battered heart, hanging on the chain, so crushed that it is barely recognisable as the symbol of love and hope that it once was. This heart has been through the mill, wrung out and strung out, pushed through rollers, stamped on, tossed out to sea, returning to me like a message in a bottle on an empty beach. This heart is like my heart, I think.

And then I spy another heart, shiny and intact, on my mother's bracelet. This one is nestled on a bench, like the one I bought for you. This heart looks brand new, gleaming like joy; a message from the past, from her to me to you. A symbol of love and magic in an unexpected place.

If I jingle the bracelet, it tinkles like bells, like a promise of something good, presents at Christmas. I do believe in fairies, I do.

My heart may be battered but love is powerful magic – and our love, you said, was good and right and true. Love, like life, renews. And sometimes, when the fog clears again, I know for sure that life and death are an intersecting chain, that there is no end to love.

The last great day

THE LAST REALLY great day we had was twelve days before you died. It was Saturday again but this Saturday you had jobs to do, the first of which involved erecting a giant ostrich outside of the Psychology building at Sheffield University. You were done early and came to meet me and the dog in the park. It is one of those snapshot moments again: the sight of you running towards me, the reciprocal smiles, the open arms, the warm embrace on a cold day, the way we held each other, pulled apart, linked hands and moved on together in one motion, already deep in conversation.

On that day we walked the dog along the Porter Brook towards Shepherd's Wheel. I was talking about work and about a house that I was considering buying and you squeezed my hand suddenly and paused right there on the path. 'Stop: feel the sun,' you said. And you spread your arms wide and raised your face to the sun right there in the middle of the path with no care for who saw. It is a lasting image that I remember now. I try to make time to look up from my grief. There is always something beautiful to see when you look up. You taught me that.

I saw a friend of yours the other day. Sometimes I think your friends find it hard to imagine us together. The big, scruffy blacksmith who they saw at home in industrial workshops seems incongruous maybe with this – how do they see me – posh, arty type? They never saw us together. 'What did you and Paul do?' he said. I want to tell him that we made love morning, noon and night, the way new lovers do. That it really was love we made. That we talked and talked and talked. That we walked the hills and lay down on bracken, gazing at clouds shifting above us. That we hugged a lifetime's hugs, in hallways, on steps, in parks and kitchens. That we danced and cooked and sang and played, like life was a game and we were winning. That we shared music and ideas. That we sat together on sofas and benches and across the table, debating the rules of Scrabble. That we read poems and recited Shakespeare standing on kitchen chairs and compared our artistic tastes in galleries across town. That we browsed bookshops and craft stalls in search of hidden treasure. That we raced to fill the gaps in crosswords and conversation but could sit peacefully together. That we loved words but didn't need them. That we tossed those words between us like the ping pong balls across the table at the Abbeydale Picture House, equally matched, always. That we opened our hearts and cried tears of sadness and joy together, that we shared our dreams. (How it hurts now to be the keeper of your dreams.) That we schemed and planned and how we laughed. They can all understand, I'm sure, how we laughed.

That day was no different. After the walk we made love at lunchtime and hung out in my kitchen cooking. I made sweet potato brownies for the first time while you investigated the delights of turmeric tonic. (An interest in nutrition was another surprising thing we shared. You were looking after your health. You wanted to live. 'I want, I want, I want,' you said, like you needed to squeeze every last drop of pleasure out of your time on earth.)

My brother called round with his partner and children. I wanted to introduce you to my family. I watched you sitting across from each other chatting and saw the future – barbecues, bonfires, you constructing braziers in his garden, a world of harmonious family Sundays to come. The world that I had never known. He knew, like I did, that finally I had found a good one.

You went back then to take down the ostrich. I stood on the plinth and nearly broke it. You chided me. We laughed. I watched you and Ed prostrate yourselves beneath the ostrich's feet, watched you doing ninja moves with his kids. You wheeled the beast back into the building and we hugged again and I watched you hug Ed's crying child and saw my own sweet son in your arms and, at that moment, I knew. I really knew.

I went to have tea with my friend and you went to the gym. (You were keeping healthy, losing weight. You wanted so much to live.) We were reunited with you at the Free Radicals gig; you were working as their roadie, as you had been back when I'd seen you years before. We made a gooseberry of my friend, kissing and cuddling in public. I'm so glad now that we did. You drew pictures on the tablecloth – a tree and an owl, I think. And you won her over, teasing her gently. I saw an old boss from a previous job. She told me how her partner had died of a brain tumour. 'Spend time with your loved ones while they are alive,' she said, like a harbinger of doom.

I tried to dance but I was tired and grieving still for my mum, so you drove me home, stayed for a quick cup of tea and then went back to help the band dismantle the equipment. It was a day of putting things together and taking them apart. That day, for me, it all came together. I didn't know that it would fall apart.

I met my friend in the cafe on the Monday to write, updated her as I did each week. 'I'm going to introduce him to the kids,' I said. 'I just can't see any more how it can ever go wrong.'

The (not so final) countdown

I AM COUNTING again. But instead of counting the days, weeks, months since you died, now I count the days until the anniversary of the day that you died. Instead of counting firsts, I am now getting ready to count the lasts: the last good day together, the last party, the last walk, the last night, the last time I saw your face, the last time we spoke. And I am remembering this period last year when you didn't seem quite well. When maybe something could have been done. It is only fourteen days now until the anniversary and the anticipation hangs in the air. The feeling of dread is back when I wake up in the morning and my dreams are anxious. I already know from other big dates that the anticipation is worse than the actual day. The sky is darkening as it approaches.

I'm not exactly sure what I think will happen when the day arrives. I'm not even sure which date to be afraid of. Your death certificate says the thirteenth but you were missing for three days. It is crazy to be afraid of the thirteenth of March. I keep hearing those words from Julius Caesar in my mind: 'beware the ides of March'. But you died on the tenth of March and it is only a date, surely, like any other. Nothing will be monumentally changed by the knowledge that it will have been a year. You will still be dead and I will still be alive, it's just that the distance between us will have grown incrementally again.

Maybe it's the memories that I fear. They are already seeping back in. Those really seriously horrible traumatic memories that I generally try very hard not to remember. They are coming out of the darkness where they are buried, ready to attack. I am prepared for them; though, in truth, I'm still not sure how to arm myself against the kind of monsters that can't be seen.

Other emotions will be there too. Sadness of course, at what we lost and what you lost and at the fact that you just continue to get further and further away. And maybe some relief, even pride, as I reflect that somehow I have lived through the worst 365 days of my life. It feels like a miracle that I am still here to tell the tale, that I can even, with hindsight, tell new arrivals into this world of loss how I did it.

There is uncertainty too, and I find myself wishing again that I knew the hour and the moment of your death like some people do. There is a time, on the birthdays of my children, when I remember the exact moment that they were born, the moment when I first held them in my arms, when their birthdays truly begin. And I have that same knowledge of the time when my mother drew her last breath. But with you, it is all a mystery. I knew nothing when you died and felt nothing (I should surely have felt something). And no one knows when it was. I wish that I knew when it was.

I found myself wondering about the last hours of your life again this week as I walked the coastal path from Ravenscar to Robin Hood's Bay, missing the feel of your hand in mine, missing your side of the conversation. You'd have thought that by now, I'd have gone over the events from every possible angle and tortured myself enough, but no, it turns out there are still things that I haven't considered.

I go over the details again in my mind. I have your phone now so I know that the last message you sent from it was at 8.30pm, about an eBay purchase that you weren't well enough to collect. I know that your last words were spoken to a stranger. He was the only person who knew how ill you were feeling, so ill that you wrote that you didn't think you'd be better tomorrow. I also know that when I messaged you at ten, you didn't reply. My detective skills tell me that you probably died some time in that ninety minutes.

On the cliff path, I found myself talking to the sky again, saying, 'why didn't you phone me? Why didn't you call an ambulance?' even though I know the answer. You weren't the kind of man who wanted to bother people with his problems, nor the kind who would go to the doctor unless you were forced. You'd been for the first time in years a month or two earlier, to get your ears syringed – but only because your deafness was annoying me so much. In the end, you couldn't be bothered to wait for a week for them to do it and, instead, you fashioned some makeshift tool (from what, I'll never know) and did the job yourself. (Your mum and I have both wondered if you did yourself some damage, but we'll never know that either). I've been over all this before. Why rehash it again now? Then, suddenly, out on the cliff path, I had another thought. What if I had messaged you at eight thirty once the children were in bed, instead of waiting until ten? What was I even doing for that ninety minutes that was more important than making sure you were still alive? If I'd messaged earlier, you might have replied and I might have been able to persuade you to go to the doctors. Or maybe I'd have called you an ambulance myself. Instead, when I messaged you at ten, there was no reply. Probably, you were already dead. I was too late.

I've already apologised, to your dead body and to your mum, and I've thought it through before. I can't take responsibility for whatever happened. It wasn't my fault. If an ambulance had been called they might have been too late as well. And even if you'd been to the doctor's weeks before, complaining of what: a cough, fatigue, memory loss, a headache? What would they have done? I know there is nothing. Even now, we don't even know really how you died. Suspected heart disease is a nebulous cause of death. There is probably nothing that anyone could have done. But still, it haunts me. It will, most likely, always haunt me, especially at this time of year.

I'm aware, as well, that there is some part of me that hopes for some kind of closure when a year has passed, even though I know that this is naïve and stupid. I've heard people say that the second year of grief is worse than the first following the loss of a partner (though I think I am different and have less to rebuild because of the brevity of our relationship), and my bereavement counsellor has warned me that the time after the first anniversary can be difficult. Maybe it is the writer in me that is expecting closure, still hoping to form a neat narrative of events. I've thought sometimes that I will stop writing my blog after a year, and that the year following your death would be an appropriate period to base a memoir on. I'm nearly at that milestone. I have a book.

But as I said at the very beginning of my writing, soon after your death, I didn't want the plot for another novel and I didn't want a memoir of loss. I wanted a living love that lasted. Maybe I will stop my blog and maybe I won't. Either way, I will probably start writing a memoir of the first year of grief. I know that, as a writer, I can tie the story up neatly at the end of a year with a message of love and hope and some kind of clear trajectory of healing; but as a human, I don't imagine I can tie it up so completely. The end of a year of grief is not the last page for grief itself. Life is not literature and I know that, whatever the date, there will be loose ends of love and grief that will go on and on with no respect for dates.

At the end of the day, the anniversary of your death is just another date. It changes nothing.

Somewhere over the rainbow

I WAS STANDING in the hut that you called your music studio. Usually, you came to my house on a Saturday, but you'd been working on your new studio for weeks and I asked you if you'd like me to come and see it before we went out for the day.

You were exuberant on the days when you'd been building, sending me little updates by Messenger, lots of smiley faces: you were always so happy when you were making. I don't really remember how you built it, not being one for details, but you had been hammering pieces of wood and reshaping doors. I think you'd even put the roof on it, fashioning something akin to an animal pen, but soundproofed with carpet tiles and housing synthesisers instead of pigs. I was amazed to see it, so impressed that you could create something so solid with your own bare hands; all I can create are flimsy words from flighty thoughts, pinning sensations with fingertips that dance intuitively across the keys.

When I arrived you had a heater blasting in anticipation of my presence and the synthesisers and microphones were set up ready; I'd asked you to play me something, intrigued to see in action what I'd only heard recorded. When I got there, I was irritable, though. I was tired and grieving for my mum and, in spite of the heater, I was feeling the cold, the kind of cold that feels bone deep in spite of hats and gloves and fleeces. There was snow on the ground out in the Peak District and it was a grey day. I would really rather have been at home. 'Will it take long?' I asked, rather churlishly. 'Three hours,' you said, with a straight face. 'Didn't you get the programme?' You made me laugh, took me out of myself for a moment, as only you could.

And then you played, although I'm not sure played is even the right word. You described it as 'twiddling some knobs'. You didn't have much faith in your ability with music but you loved it, really loved it. And as I watched you stroking pads and tweaking dials, there seemed to be something intuitive in your movements and there was beauty in the sounds that filled the air that day. The dance of fingertips on keyboards, feeling their way into something intangible.

Afterwards, you handed me the microphone. 'Sing to me, please,' you said. Maybe you were auditioning me for this band that you wanted to create. You had me down as lead singer even though I had less confidence in my singing than you had in your music. I sang to you anyway; 'Somewhere Over the Rainbow', because it's the only song I feel I sing well, having crooned it almost every night to my children for the last eight years. I perfected it in the wee small hours while I rocked infants in my arms, imagining I was Judy Garland in Kansas, with ruby slippers on my feet. When I'd finished singing, you locked up and we went out into the snow for a walk. There was something wrong with you that day, something really wrong. I knew it intuitively but I couldn't put my finger on what it was. The day was clouded in unease.

I think of you now every night as I smooth my little boy's curls with my hand, lying next to him on the bed, holding onto him too tightly, lonely for your touch. I sing those words and understand why they play it at funerals. I wonder if, one day, I will wake up where these clouds are far behind me. And I wonder if there's a place that one day I will find you again. One thing is for sure. I'm not in Kansas anymore. And there is no way home.

Spring is in the air

THERE HAVE BEEN some lovely springy days recently. The sun is pushing between clouds and there's a lightening of the sky. Bulbs that were hidden are peeping out of the soil, breaking through to feel the early spring warmth in the air.

Your snowdrops are blooming too. I walk past them every time I pass the front door. They sit in a pot that I took from your garden after your death, shovelling earth with my bare hands, panic rising; I needed to grasp any part of you that I could before your home was completely emptied, your belongings sold off or chucked in a skip in the weeks following your death. I can conjure it in my mind like it was yesterday: old shoes and clothes (that you were wearing just the other day), bloody mattress, broken tyres, iron rods all jumbled up. It felt like you were being torn apart in front of my eyes. I wandered through your home and the surrounding land, like a trespasser combing a bomb site, looking for remnants of treasure, no idea what to hold onto and what to let go, no idea what my rights were. I was not your wife, or your widow and I was not family, but your heart belonged to me and your heart, the only thing I really wanted, was gone.

I was there with my friend that day, just wanting to sit once more on the veranda where we were first drank tea, our boots side by side on the railings, the promise of love hanging in the air, our future spread out like the vista of the wide expanse of moorland in front of us. I wanted to show someone where you lived. She was talking about her boyfriend and, for a moment, I was okay, comparing notes – and then I remember the moment when the world cracked open again, and I lost the plot because the boyfriend I was comparing to hers was dead. And I walked away from her crying and started digging up the ground with my hands because suddenly I needed snowdrops like the ones your brother had dug up for your mum and I needed them now, in case they too were stolen from me. It was a moment when I realised that everything had changed, that I couldn't relate anymore to normal people with their normal experiences of life.

I'm glad I took the snowdrops now. They are a little symbol of the cycle of life, of regrowth and rebirth and they hold, somehow, a little memory of you in each fragile bud. They sit next to the moon-gazing hare that I took from my mum's garden at the last minute, before the new owners moved in. My mum's friend told me that a moon-gazing hare is a symbol of growth and new beginnings, so I brought it to my new house in the hope that it might bring me some luck. But the wind blew it over and smashed it; now it is a one-eared hare, which doesn't feel quite so auspicious.

I took the photo of the snowdrops a couple of weeks ago, thinking that it would make a nice metaphor for grief. I thought I would write an uplifting piece in the run up to the anniversary of your death in which I was a snowdrop, buried grief-deep through the winter but pushing through the darkness into the light, ready to create a new future. It would be a convenient comparison. A year of grief is enough for anyone. Seriously, a year of this kind of grief is too *much* for anyone. I can't live in the underworld forever. I want so much to live again, to love again, to touch someone that breathes. A metaphysical love is not enough for me. Eight months of love is not enough for me. I want something more. And yet...

As usual, grief does not do my bidding, and for the last week or so I have felt like I am back at the beginning again. 'Grief is snakes and ladders,' I wrote a while back, only it's snakes and ladders without a winner or an end point and, even when you've made it through three hundred and fifty-five days of grief and you think the end is in sight, you can land on a snake and feel like you've gone right back to square one. 'I don't cry every day anymore,' I wrote, back in October, and I didn't. But now I am crying every day again, I feel all at sea again, waves crashing, storm raging, tossed about like I don't know which way is up and which way is down, like I can't separate the past and the present from the future. I feel I'm part of some mythological drama where the gods and the devils are fighting for my soul, like I'm being dragged to the underworld and pulled back into the light over and over again while some kind of orchestral crescendo builds and cymbals crash and I'm not sure where I'm going to land. It is horrible to be flung about like this and the logical part of my brain asks why this is necessary. I know what happened. Why re-live every moment? But grief is not logical and I can't control it so I must go with it and know that, as it has before, it will pass and there will be calm again soon.

And as I sit here, clearing out my old office in town, trying to let go of the past, I realise that there is a huge difference between the grief that is raging now and the grief that I felt at the beginning; I know now that I will survive. I know now that, for as long as I'm alive, I can survive anything. I am not at square one after all. I can see ladders scattered about and I know how to climb them, if I just keep rolling the dice and moving forwards. Regardless of how I feel now, I know that new life will come, and I know that the metaphor I started out with still serves. I am as fragile as a snowdrop, fighting through the frost and the cold, reaching for the light, peeping out of the darkness, and I am a moon gazing hare with one ear – irreparably broken but still here, still hoping that something better is around the corner.

The last time ever I saw your face

I DON'T REMEMBER the first time that I saw your face. I wish I did. I wrote a poem about it. It was the first thing I wrote after you died. All I could think about was all the years that we could have been together and weren't, all the chances that we'd missed. That, and how impossible it was that you could be dead, and how impossible it was for me to imagine a world in which I could carry on without you.

I remember the last time that I saw your face, though I didn't know it. No one told me it would be the last time. This year has been the longest and most painful year of my life and yet, in some ways it feels like it was yesterday. The truth is that it was yesterday, just yesterday in 2016, not 2017.

My memories of the last week of your life are plagued with shadows. I was about to introduce you properly to the children that week. You wanted them to come to your bonfire so that you could show me what fun you were with kids, what a great stepdad you might become. I had been ready to do it, but suddenly I couldn't. Something happened on that last Saturday to make me question things. I was feeling sad that day. The prospect of my first Mother's Day without my mum was a cloud over the day and I was tired, so tired. And you were not yourself. You'd had what seemed to be a chest infection for weeks and you had dark bags under your eyes. You were forgetting things, not in the way that you usually forgot things (you were always scatty), but in a way that seemed pathological, that now seems like it was a warning. It was the day we went walking in Longshaw after I'd sung to you in your studio. It seemed like you didn't know what you were doing from one moment to the next. It was so bad that I asked you what was wrong with your brain. 'There's nothing wrong with my brain!' you said. Sitting on your knee later, I pointed out the droopy eyes and you laughed it off as a sign of my critical nature. 'What fault of yours can I pick on?' you asked and made me laugh too. I loved that you would give as good as you got. We agreed that I was tired, grieving, paranoid. After all, I had a father who died from brain tumours, a recent ex-boyfriend with a brain injury, a child with a rare disease. I was hyper-vigilant. Still, I wasn't sure I was ready to introduce you just yet. 'There's no rush,' you said.

Mother's Day arrived, and my mind was flooded with memories. I was not feeling great. My last boyfriend had left on Mother's Day 2015 and my mum had only recently died. Besides which, being a single parent of young children on Mother's Day sucks at the best of times, as you struggle on cooking and tidying and trying to keep people happy, all the time seething because this is your day and someone should be looking after you for a change. But no one is.

We said goodbye in the morning as we always did, just before the children came back from their dad's. You'd gone to buy your mum some flowers and taken them to her. (It was to be the last time that she would see your face too.) I wasn't expecting to see you until Tuesday. I never saw you on a Sunday.

Later on that evening, the children and I were coming back from a play centre when we noticed that the neighbours were having a bonfire. We watched for a while, throwing sticks into the fire over the fence, and I told the children that my friend Paul was having a bonfire and that they were invited. They squealed with excitement and then my daughter asked me if we would let off the paper lanterns that you'd left at our house. And suddenly I found myself asking if they wanted to do it right now, with you, if you were free. I sent you a text and asked you if you wanted to come and meet them and set off the lanterns, all the while wondering what I was doing and you said, 'be there in ten.'

The rest of it feels like the stuff of mythology. You came straight round and made offerings to the Greek gods my daughter was obsessed with, burning rosemary in a circle of pebbles. And then we wrote on the paper lanterns. We wrote on one for my deceased parents and the other one you sent to the gods. You and she were in clear accord that Hephaestus, the blacksmith god, was the best. You wrote a message to him, though I didn't look what it said; then you lit the papers, my children held the lanterns, and we waited patiently for them to balloon with the heat. We stood and watched them together, floating off into the night sky, like we were a little family waiting to be born.

'I really like Paul,' my daughter said when you were out of earshot. 'Can he stay?' I said he could and I left the two of you watching *The Witches* while I put the little one to bed. Afterwards, you said goodnight to her and then there was just us two. I held you tightly in the hall, swaying in your arms, still feeling the glow from watching you with them and the lanterns. 'I love you,' I said. And 'I love you too,' came your reply. We kissed goodnight and then you left with that move that was uniquely yours: the twist on the ball of a foot, one foot on the step, one on the ground, graceful like a dancer, hand raised and your voice tossed into the darkness saying 'goodnight'.

And there we were, just at the beginning of a lifetime together, not knowing that we were at the end. I didn't know that it was the last time I would see your face. You didn't know it was the last time you would see mine. The next day I phoned you in tears, in a panic, saying I wasn't sure I could do it, it was all too big, what if it all went wrong again. You calmed me down, said I was grieving for my mum, said it would take longer before I could trust again after what had happened last time when I had introduced someone to the children. You said that we had all the time in the world, that there was no rush. You told me to rest, to go to bed early on Tuesday instead of staying up all night with you, to go and see my friend on Saturday and have a week off from you; I'd spent every spare moment with you from the day we met. You told me to take some time, said you weren't going anywhere. Though neither of us knew it, it turned out that you were.

The mother-in-law I never had

YOUR MUM IS dying. She lies now in a bed at the hospice, propped up on clean white pillows, while friends and family sit by her bedside as her organs gradually fail. Somehow her broken heart still pumps the blood around her body, but we know that soon it will slow to a halt and that she will be gone.

I have been to this hospice many times and it, like your mum, has started to feel like home. My own mum was only in here for twenty-four hours, but I have been eligible to come here for bereavement counselling for the last year, and for the last few weeks I have also been visiting the mother-in-law I never had, preparing gradually to say goodbye. Though I am so sad to lose her, it is a blessing, this time, to have chance to say goodbye. Unlike you and my own mother she is taking her time, putting her things in order, going slowly.

In fact she is going too slowly for the hospice's liking; so slowly, in fact, that they have recently talked of having to move her to residential care. Death, like grief, has no rulebook and though she is dying just as fast as she can, she is not dying fast enough. They need her bed for the people who are more committed to dying quickly. Though I am outraged that the hospice could move her, I reflect that those people are probably people like my own other mother, who was so committed to living that she refused palliative care until the last week. She spent what we didn't know would be her final days waiting for a hospice bed, while unfamiliar district nurses pumped her with drugs and all of us wondered what on earth was going on. It was not a good ending. Moving your mum will, of course, kill her but there are other people who need care too. It is not a lifestyle conundrum but an end of life conundrum. Though I don't like to swear in a piece about your mum, the narrative once more is fucked.

Your mum is dying so slowly because, for once in her tragically hard life, she is receiving the care she deserves. In fact, though it's not saying much considering the year she has had, I've never seen her look so well. When I visit her she smiles and asks me about the children. She hands me some of your old Meccano for my son and a pile of Flower Fairy books for my daughter. She is still thinking about others. She tells me about the new dishes on the menu that she is going to try, as if she is staying in the Savoy Hotel. For the first time she experiences a jacuzzi and a hand massage, and though it leaves her exhausted she is thoroughly delighted with the last-chance spa that she has found herself in. I am humbled by her gratitude, and vow never to take for granted my own health or the inheritance that allows me the luxury of self-care.

A year ago we'd never met and yet, when the palliative care consultant comes round to talk to her about her end of life choices, she asks me to stay as if I am part of her immediate family and I am honoured to play my part. 'I'm so glad we've had this chance to be friends,' she says, holding my hand. She asks me if I will come on the anniversary of your death, and I do. We don't ask each other how we are. It is still not okay. But we sit, quietly holding hands as we watch a film of babbling brooks and crashing waves and think of you.

Over the last year or so we have spent many hours like this. Week after week we drank chamomile tea and talked about where we thought you'd gone, the manner in which you might have died, whether we could see your shape in clouds and rainbows, how much you were missed. It was such a relief to talk to someone who knew that I was not okay, that this was not okay. Together, we filled in the jigsaw pieces of your past. She told me of your childhood and your family; I told her of our adventures and our love, of the happiness we shared for those last eight months of your life. We went on our own adventures together too, in search of ducks on a pond in the Peak District and in search of locations for a memorial bench. We watched clouds scud across the sky and held each other's hands as we walked and as we talked. We drove together clutching your ashes in a green plastic jar to say our goodbyes. Sometimes we cried and sometimes, in the early days, desperate for connection with someone who loved you as much as I did, I would phone her sobbing and she was always so kind, never competitive in her grief as some people can be. She invited me into your family and into her home, once even asking if I would come and sleep on her sofa because she didn't like to think of me being alone.

Your mum was the loveliest mother-in-law I never had, and I am so lucky to have had the chance to know her. She helps me to see that, even in the darkest of times, there are still things to live for. Though I know she must die now and leave me to join you, this year, she has helped me to stay alive.

Today I was your girlfriend again

TODAY WAS A weird day. It was your mum's funeral. I guess you already know that. I hope that you and she are already reunited somewhere, and that you were looking down on the crowd of people crying and smiling. Perhaps you cried and smiled too. And perhaps you saw me there. Perhaps you watched me take a deep breath as I walked up the steps and saw me looking around like a lost child wondering where her mum was, or where your mum was or where you were. It wasn't right to be going to your mum's funeral without you. You supported me when my mum died; I should have been there supporting you. Or maybe I felt you should have been there supporting me. I have come to love your mum and I will miss her greatly. It wasn't right to be going back to the place where I last said goodbye to your body, or my mum's body either. It wasn't right to be saying goodbye to her body. Today was all wrong. As I said, it was weird.

I didn't think that I would know anyone there apart from your family and I didn't but, of course, a lot of people knew who I was. After all, I gave the eulogy at your funeral and your mum's friends would have been there. They had watched me then, this strange being, this non-widow that no one knew, standing shaking at the pulpit telling them how wonderful you were, how safe you made me feel, how much I loved you. They had probably seen me hold it together until I'd finished speaking and had watched me crumple back into my pew weeping. They will have watched me as I stood by your coffin on the way out too, and seen how I kissed it and held onto it, wanting to jump on top of it, wanting to scream, wanting to drag you back to life. I remember afterwards, your mum told me that her friends had said they admired her dignity for not crying at your funeral. I guess they felt that I'd lost mine. They didn't know that I felt myself being held there by a magnetic force, that I'd lost the use of my limbs, that I didn't know where I was, that all I could see was that box and a lump of oak separating you from me. They will have watched as my friend strode down the aisle and pulled me to her, sobbing, as she steered me outside, away from you.

Today, as I stood outside the crematorium, the tears came even before the funeral cortege. A woman had just introduced herself to me. I can't tell you what her name was but she had a kind face. 'Can I sit with you?' I said having lost my social skills again, remembering the same moment at your funeral when I had suddenly grabbed the arm of my most motherly friend and asked her to stay by my side. She was kind. They were all so kind, like your mum. There was a lot of kindness in that room. It was a lovely service.

Still, it was a weird kind of day, a sad day. Sad to be saying more goodbyes, sad to lose another connection with you. The strangest thing though was that, just for today, I was your girlfriend again. Perhaps today, I was your girlfriend for the first time. I'm not sure anyone has ever introduced me as your girlfriend before. You certainly never had the chance. It was weird to be ushered around, being introduced to people: 'This is Paul's girlfriend,' they said. 'Oh, you're Paul's girlfriend, aren't you?' they said. It was nice to be your girlfriend again, just for a day. I wish you'd been there to see it. I hope you and your mum saw it. I hope you both know how much you are loved.

Clouds

THE NIGHT BEFORE you died, I sent you a poem. It was nothing unusual. After my panic about you meeting the children, we were back on track and there we were catching up by Messenger at the end of the day. 'Send me a poem Beverley Writer,' you'd say. I'd written the poem that day during my writing group. We'd been writing pieces inspired by Wallace Steven's poem 'Thirteen Ways of Looking at a Blackbird' and somehow I had gone via Paul Simon's 'Fifty Ways to Leave Your Lover' to Joni Mitchell and to my own poem about clouds. My poem reminded you of a photograph you'd recently taken whilst planting trees. You sent it to me and something about its beauty made me cry. We talked on messenger about doing something again with my writing and your photographs. We talked of coffee table books, fridge magnets, greetings cards. 'We must do something,' I said. 'We will,' you said. And then I lectured you. 'You're hugely talented,' I said, 'and hiding your light under a pile of other people's cast-off junk. Break free blacksmith.' I didn't mean you to take me literally.

I asked you again if you liked my poem and you

said you did. 'I love the poem, I love clouds and I love you,' you said. And that was the last time we spoke. Poignant, poetic, the end of a beautiful love story. And the beginning of grief and a life without you.

How do you survive that?

I T I S O V E R a year now since I found your body. The anniversary of your death passed on the tenth but there was a strange period in which, for me, it felt like it was still ahead. On the tenth of March last year I didn't know you were dead. At that time I didn't know what to think but I'm not sure that the idea that you might be dead had even crossed my mind or, if it had crossed my mind, it had been swiftly discarded as a possibility because that kind of thing doesn't really happen. Only sometimes it does. Sometimes, when you least expect it, when it's really the last thing on earth you could do with having to deal with, monumentally bad stuff happens. And when you died like that and I found your body, it was by far the worst thing that had ever happened to me. One minute I thought you were alive and then, at some point late that night, out in the Peak District in my pyjamas, I found you were dead. At that moment my world imploded. A few hours later I got up, got the kids to school and began an unexpected journey into a world of pain that I didn't know existed. Sure I had been though some dreadful things, and I had experienced a lot of grief, but nothing had prepared me for the life-changing trauma of your death. I didn't think I could survive it. But I did. Like lots of other people who have been through impossible heartbreak, I continue to survive.

I thought about this a lot recently when I attended the AGM of Widowed and Young. The organisation has been a lifeline to me and it seemed fitting to round off my year of grief with other people whose worlds have been torn apart. There is a strange solidarity and comfort that can be found from being in a room full of people who have known great tragedy. And as I stood in the hall of the hotel in Stratford last weekend, I looked around me and was overwhelmed by the thought that every one of the people in the room had lost a partner, that all of those people had had their worlds blown to pieces. Gradually, inevitably the stories came out. I found a girl (really, just a girl) crying in the toilets and offered her a hug. My heart broke for her. How could someone so young survive something like this? Then I spoke to a man who had lost his wife just after his baby girl had been born. She'd developed ovarian cancer while she was pregnant. 'That's so sad,' I said feebly and he nodded wearily. He had told this story before. And then there was my online friend, who had given birth to her only child the week after her partner had been killed in a bike accident. She was choosing funeral flowers when she should have been choosing baby clothes. 'How do you survive something like that?' I found myself thinking, kicking myself at the same time because I already know the answer. You survive because you have to.

As I sit here, just over a year on, I find myself reflecting not just on my enormous loss and sadness but at the resilience of the human spirit. Sure, my grief is still deep and I still cry a lot. I still wish that I could rewind time and bring Paul back. I wish I could undo this long year of pain. And I know that grief cannot be tied up neatly at the end of a year but will go on for as long as love goes on (forever). But I can also see how far I have come. I have moved house and started new ventures. I have let go of work that was weighing me down, and now only do work that I love. I have written more than ever before and made new friends. And I experience joy, like sunshine between clouds of sadness, on a regular basis. Slowly I am building a new life for myself.

Time heals, they say, and I guess it does. Slowly, gradually, new paths into the future are forged, though what I have learned is that there are no shortcuts. There are surely things you can do to make it more bearable but, in the end, you just have to live with it, feel it, work within it and hope one day to emerge. If you're lucky, maybe you get to emerge like a butterfly from a chrysalis, but it is perhaps more likely that you emerge like an amputee from a hospital in a war zone. Either way, you're never going to be quite the same again.

Just over twelve months on, I'm pleased to say that I do feel a kind of re-emergence taking place and a transformation too. In some ways I am probably a better person and in other ways not. I find myself softer but also harder, in many ways more able to empathise with others and yet also impatient with struggles that sometimes seem lesser than my own; there's nothing quite like losing the one you love to give you a clear sense of what matters. I'm able to look forwards again now in a way that I never thought would be possible. I'm even starting to get tired of writing about grief, and beginning to contemplate a return to writing fiction. My bereavement counsellor is getting ready to discharge me too. She thinks I'm doing okay. She's using my writing when she trains other bereavement counsellors, and says she's now getting clients coming through who are quoting my blog back to her. 'You're as good as you're going to be,' she said recently. I'm not sure whether to be proud of my achievement, or terrified that she's saying I'm going to feel like this for the rest of my life. Either way, I can see that there are other people who need her more than me. Unlike most bereaved people, I've been so lucky to have had fantastic, regular counselling from a trained professional free of charge. But my counsellor is like Mary Poppins, Nanny McPhee or Pete's dragon – she needs to fly away to help someone new whose world has been freshly decimated. Eventually, whether I am a butterfly or an amputee, I need to learn to survive on my own.

When I found you last March, you were already gone and I was already on my own, with a new journey beginning. It wasn't a journey that I chose and it isn't a journey that I would recommend to anyone. If you've been on this journey, I look into your eyes, hold your hand and salute you. And if you haven't, I hope it's a journey that you never have to make. There are surely better ways to achieve transformation and there are easier ways to break out of a chrysalis. And maybe, sometimes, it's okay to stay in a cocoon.

A blessing to the grieving hearts

I see you standing there trying to look normal,
see the grieving heart that you hold
like a rock or a marble,
a bleeding tree or a sodden sponge.
Don't hide it.
It tells me of your love.
It is beating still and it is keeping you alive.

Cradle it like a tender creature in the rock pool of
  your soul.
Feed it with memories and tell stories about where it
  has been,
the way it has been battered and torn, the beauty it
  has seen.
Sing it soothing songs at night-time when you can,
so that it can sleep in peace.

And, when it comes, this thing called grief
and threatens to overpower you with its force
I wish you a soft patch of grass to lie on
where the pain can wash over you like waves
and the sun can warm your shivering skin.

When you want to be cocooned in it,
I hope the past may be a soft blanket around you
hugging you close and keeping you safe.
And when you're ready to emerge,
let there be a hand reaching out to take yours,
saying, 'yes, you can go on'.

And one day, may the seeping colours of your love
make patterns on your wings,
and may your memories be the breeze that lifts you,
may you be able to carry your heart lightly in your
    breast
as you take flight again, transformed by grief
but fully alive.

Without love there would be no pain,
without pain, there would be no love,
without love there would be no life.
May you find a way to feel the pain,
to hold onto the love
and to keep living.

SPRING

I would do it again

I would do it again

'Each griever must ask the question, "Who am I, now that you're gone?" And the answer to that question often revises one's self-narrative. Grief is a story you tell yourself. It's a story of the death of someone you loved. It's a story of the life of someone you loved. It's a story of your life with them, and it's a story of your life without them.'

(Ron Marasco and Brian Shuff, *About Grief*)

A LITTLE WHILE ago I went to see *La La Land* at the cinema. It was a bit of a milestone for me as the first film that I managed to sit through in the past year that wasn't grief-related; in fact I really loved it. Essentially I'm a sucker for whimsy and romance, the classic dreamer, head in the clouds and all that jazz. I want always to believe in destiny and true love, even though my own life hasn't done much to encourage those beliefs. *La La Land* is a perfect dreamers' film. It reminded me of our magical love affair, of course, and also a bit of my first true love. He was an aspiring actor from California and I was an aspiring writer from Yorkshire. We had a fairy-tale meeting in Eastern Europe (dancing in the snow in Prague as opposed to the sunset in LA), a wonderful courtship (including drama and deportation) and we had a beautiful wedding after eighteen months. A few years later, we divorced. It was a harsh lesson to learn, at twenty-six, that happy ever afters are often just the stuff of Hollywood and not of real life.

For that reason, I quite liked the ending of *La La Land*, even though I still sat crying on the back row with my friend when it finished, not because the hero and heroine didn't end up together but because it reminded me of the unsatisfactory nature of my own love stories. 'What is it all supposed to mean?' I asked her. Like the couple in *La La Land*, you and I seemed destined to be together. I felt you were my soulmate and that it was written in the stars that we should collide. Our paths had criss-crossed so often throughout our lives that it was only a matter of time, or timing, before we would get the message and fall in love. And when we finally made it, I thought I'd made it too, to the end of some kind of convoluted romantic journey, to my own (slightly later than expected, slightly unconventional) happy ever after. And then suddenly you died and the narrative was shredded and I was bewildered again, wondering what to make of it all. 'The end just happened in the middle,' I wrote. The path into the future had disappeared overnight and I didn't see how I could go on. Essentially, I lost the plot.

As a graduate of English literature and a writer (predominantly of fiction), narrative is important to me and something that has preoccupied me a lot in my grief. I'm painfully aware that the narrative of my own life (put simply) is a complete mess and not something any publisher would be interested in; there's no clear narrative arc at all, certainly not from a romantic point of view. It might make a good collection of short stories, mostly tragic, but it's a hopeless romance novel. Every time someone looks like the hero of the piece and I invest in them, they vanish – and your particular vanishing act was truly spectacular. In a pitching workshop that I once attended, I was told that I needed to be able to encapsulate the plot of my novel in a one-line summary. At the beginning of my grief journey, this is how the story looked: 'Two lovers, destined to be together, miss their chance repeatedly, spend their lives apart having a pretty miserable time, finally unite and then, just when things are going great, he dies and her life is ruined'. Maybe it makes a good weepy but it's certainly not an easy story to write a sequel to and, left here without you, that is, essentially, what I have to do. My bereavement counsellor says that the work of bereavement is to find a new narrative and perhaps, in this respect, I'm lucky that I know a lot about making up stories. Perhaps that's why I have written so many thousands of words since you died, trying to find a way to write the story in such a way that it makes your narrative bearable (though it would take a genius to achieve that) and also leaves the way open for me to continue to write a better future for myself. When you died, my overwhelming feeling was that I just wanted to die with you but gradually, over the course of the last twelve months I've been forced to consider the possibility that your ending can't be the ending of my own story. If I'm going to go on to live a rich and fulfilling life (and how can I contemplate anything else when I have the privilege to still be here when you are not?) I can't afford to have my narrative be the one in which the love of my life appears and disappears in the space of a year during middle age. It's just too ridiculous. So, I must try to find a new way to frame things and, though I have raged against the people who talk of gifts and silver linings, I find myself looking for them anyway. Because who wants to read a narrative without hope?

And who can live a life in which there are no gifts?

So, I try to rework the narrative and I'm left with something like this: 'Just as they are both about to give up on hope and true love, two star-crossed lovers, battered by ill-fortune and plagued by self-doubt, find each other and repair each other's broken hearts, restoring their faith in love. Though he tragically dies, he dies happy in the knowledge that he is truly loved and accepted for who he is. And, though she is heartbroken at being left behind, she is left with the same knowledge: she has known what it is to love deeply and to be loved deeply in return. He has left her with the gift of knowing she is worthy of true love.' It still needs work, but it's an improvement, at least, on the first version.

Sometimes, I reflect that, overall, my own story is perhaps not a romance at all. When I got divorced, my mum, bless her, suggested that perhaps I was just 'one of those people who isn't meant to be in a relationship.' Cheers for that, Mum. I don't like to think she was right, but there are allegedly seven possible plots, and not all of them are 'boy meets girl'. Probably my narrative is more a voyage of self-discovery, of becoming. Mostly, in my life, the men along the way feel like they have been obstacles and distractions from my main work, of being my true self and being the writer that I was always meant to be. I remember once saying to a now well-known author that I felt I couldn't be a writer and have love. 'With the right person, you can,' she said wisely. You were the right person and I learned that I could. I learned that someone could love both the writer and the person that I am. In truth, the person and the writer are one and the same thing.

I don't know what the next chapter of my story will be as I've yet to write it. Maybe I will go on to find my fulfilment in my writing and you will remain the one true love of my life, but I don't think that's my story. I don't think my mum was right. I've learned a lot over the last few decades of living tragic short stories. I'd like the chance to apply my learning to a bigger and more sustainable project. Maybe I'm greedy but I'd like to have my writing and still have love. I can understand the widows who feel that the love they shared with their spouses is enough to sustain them, but I only had a few months. It's not enough for me. I don't know what the point would be of finally understanding what love is, if I'm never to have it again. It may be crazy but the romantic in me didn't die with you. If anything, it has been reborn.

In the van, I sing along to the soundtrack to *La La Land*, turning the volume up every time Emma Stone's audition number comes back round. 'Here's to the ones who dream,' she sings. 'Bring on the rebels, the ripples from pebbles, the painters and poets and plays.' She doesn't mention blacksmiths but I see you and our story in every word. It was a magical story completely devoid of pragmatism, a real romance. A story of madness and colour, a triumph of heart over head. Together we captured that feeling, 'a sky with no ceiling, a sunset inside a frame.' And whatever happens next, 'I'll always remember the flame' of our love. Like you, it lives on, in me.

'Here's to the ones who dream. Foolish as they may seem.
Here's to the hearts that break. Here's to the mess we make.'

And here's to you, Blacksmith Paul, the ultimate dreamer.

At the bonfire that we held after your funeral, I scrawled a message on a paper lantern. I still remember the words that I wrote: *'What an adventure we had! I wouldn't have missed it for the world.'* It's true. I wouldn't. And even though, during this last twelve months, my journey has been a nightmarish trip to the underworld, I am still so grateful for the love we shared. I know that if I had my time again, I wouldn't change a thing, apart from the ending (and perhaps I'd bring forward the beginning). The storyteller in me is able to write new endings and she will. She can conjure worlds in which we will have our time again, in some other lifetime or some parallel universe. Maybe there we will get to have a happy ever after. But in this universe, I will go on and, when the time is right and the person is right (and he will have to be right, now), I know I will risk my heart once more. Because I'm a foolish dreamer, like the aunt who jumped barefoot into the Seine.

'Smiling through it, she said, she'd do it again.'

The other side

At the end of life there was a door.
It's a cliché I know, but that's how it was
and you know me, I love a door,
can't resist the allure of hardwood and sturdy hinges,
will always want to know what's on the other side.
I am 'insatiably curious',
you said so yourself in the eulogy
(beautiful words, by the way. And, thank you.)
I went through that door before I realised
that I couldn't get back to the life I loved
on the other side.

It hurts to see how you have cried, my darling.
'May I call you darling?' I once said.
Hurting you was the last thing on earth I wanted to do
but it was the last thing on earth I did.
I never meant to cause you any sorrow,
never meant to cause you any pain.
Of course, Prince and Bowie are here with me
and we party like it's 1999 again
but I hate to see you lost down there
in the purple rain.

Yes, we still have feelings on the other side.

It broke my heart to leave you.
Did you feel me trying to reach you
as you cried on the coffin that you'd helped to choose?

It was a good one, by the way, and the flowers,
I can see why you picked them.
Lovely message too. So perfect.
You always were so perfect
for me.

It was agony to feel you on the other side
of that heavy door of wood,
unable to put my arms around you and tell you,
'It's okay. I understand. There was nothing you could
   have done.'
I couldn't get to you just as you couldn't have got to me.
I know you felt the jolt of my soul straining for yours –
I'm sorry that I scared you.
Thank you for the comfort of the things you sent me,
the things they slipped through that wooden door,
that I have taken with me,
although, in reality, I took it all.

I'm so pleased you see my messages.
It's as much of a mystery to me as it is to you,
how somehow both of us knew
that this was where we were going to end up.
We couldn't see the future and yet we laid a trail
that I see you following now
like a puzzle or a treasure hunt.
We loved that kind of stuff.

Yes, the words on the collage are for you,
and the words on the paper in the bathroom –
thanks for sharing them.

I'm so glad you found the ones I wrote about you
though there are other things I wish you hadn't found
and I really am sorry about the mess.
You know I was trying to clean up my act.
I thought I had more time.

I'm doing fine though, rest assured.
I miss you of course but I'm the lucky one, I know
because I can follow you everywhere you go.
I still touch your hair as you lay sleeping
and I watch you as you swim and walk.
I listen to you talk, so much of it about me.
I read your beautiful words
and hear your beautiful voice.
If I had a choice, I would hold you still
but some things are out of my control.
I am just a soul.

I can't hold your body but I'm by your side and in
    your heart.
It's that quantum superposition that I wrote about.
I can be in more than one place simultaneously,
both alive and dead at the same time;
Schrodinger didn't know quite what he was onto with
    that cat.
I am everywhere and with everyone
if they take the time to look.
I'm in the starry skies and in the dark blue sea.
I am part of you and still somewhat me.

Keep your eyes open, darling –
I will call you darling, if that's okay –
and please don't shut down your heart.
I know there is no bright side to look on
but walk on the sunny side of the street when you can
and follow the feathers and coins that I leave
like a path into the future –
I know you don't want to go there but you must.
Keep the collage, it's yours now and my words are
   yours too:
remember to explore,
keep on keeping on,
you were my inspiration, let me be yours
and most of all,
love.

P.P.S.
Sorry, again, about the mess.

Acknowledgements

This book is the product of some of the worst years of my life and I am eternally grateful to the people who kept me from going under, especially during those early days of extreme shock and grief. To the people who kept reaching out and who were there when I needed you, I will never forget your kindness. To the people who listened without judgement and who sat with me when I cried, the people who came in their droves to help me when I moved house and the people who showed their support by reading and responding to my blog. You are too many to name but I remember each and every one of you and want to thank you. You made me feel that life was still worth living.

Special thanks to long-term friends: Karina Brookes, Arabella Thomas, Natalie Hunt and Anni Swinburne and to the mums who have helped to share the burden of my losses and single parenthood over the years, especially Kesia Reeve, Jan Dalgleish, Bryony Shannon and Katie Shipley. Thank you particularly to all of my writing buddies, both in person and online, especially Stacey Sampson and Suzannah Evans. Also, much love and thanks to my Get Writing Wednesday class who, while I was ostensibly there to support them, were a vital part of my support network in the aftermath of Paul's death. Thanks also to the people who encouraged me to keep writing and to turn this into a book and to Jamie McGarry at Valley Press for making it a reality.

This book came out of a blog that began as part of Megan Devine's Writing Your Grief course and I'm grateful to Megan for setting me on this path. Writing was a natural reaction to grief for me but Megan's community made me feel that I wasn't alone. Thank you also to Ingrid Hanson who reached out to me in her own grief and encouraged me to write with Megan. I was also massively supported by the bereavement counselling service at St Luke's hospice, Sheffield, and am particularly grateful to my counsellor, Julia Twigg, who bore witness to both my sadness and my love.

Likewise, thanks to the community of Widowed and Young in whose online Facebook group I spent many lonely nights. Nothing is more healing in grief than being around other people who really understand what you're going through and, through grief, I have made new connections and great friends with others who have trodden this path. Thanks to those friends – Rosie Carnall, Sarah Hawley, Shuna Beckett – who understand better than most that the sadness never goes away.

Thank you also to Paul's friends at Shirle Hill who made me an adjunct to their community and to Paul's family who welcomed me into their midst, especially his mum, Pat, who will always have a place in my heart.

Finally, thank you to my own family and, most importantly, my children – Edie and Douglas – who make every day a precious gift to be cherished. Your wonder and beauty sustains me every day. And, of course, to Paul, the dear blacksmith, for his photographs and for the gift of his love.